SOURCE BOOK OF HEALTH INSURANCE DATA

1994

CONTENTS

FIGURES AND TABLES

CHAPTER 5

Figures

Tables

CHAPTER 6

PREFACE

The *Source Book of Health Insurance Data 1994* is the thirty-fourth consecutive edition of this report, published annually by the Health Insurance Association of America (HIAA) since 1960.

Compiled by HIAA's Department of Policy Development and Research, the *Source Book* is a comprehensive collection of statistical data on private health insurance in the United States. The 1994 edition provides current data on major forms of health insurance coverage with special emphasis on managed care programs, the insurance market, medical care costs, utilization of the nation's medical facilities, medical care providers, and the latest national morbidity and mortality trends.

This year, several of the historical data series have been expanded and revised. Premium and claims data tables now indicate health maintenance organization figures in addition to conventional insurance, and new tables appear on health care providers, health care facilities, health service organizations, inpatient and outpatient admissions and costs, and transplantation.

Data in the *Source Book* are compiled from HIAA surveys, reports of commercial insurance companies, government agencies, hospital and medical associations, and private research organizations.

HIAA trusts this edition of the *Source Book* will continue to serve as a valuable reference for writers, editors, researchers, educators, government officials, private industry leaders, hospital and medical professionals, associations, and other organizations that are interested or involved in the health care industry.

Edward Neuschler
Director, Department of Policy Development and Research

Chapter 1

THE ROLE AND HISTORY OF HEALTH INSURANCE

Health insurance eases the financial burden caused by adverse changes in personal health; it protects people against financial catastrophe and assures them access to the health care system.

Health insurance has a long and diverse history. The ancient Chinese probably had a form of sickness insurance based on the custom of paying the doctor while in good health and discontinuing payment during periods of illness. The benevolent societies of classical Greece (probably the earliest known insurers) served both the military and civilian populations; individuals contributed toward the cost of coverage. The Romans adopted this practice, increasing the coverage to include death benefits, as well as old age and disability payments.

These types of insurance coverage continued in Europe, evolving over the centuries. During the Middle Ages, the trade guilds provided assistance to their members during times of economic distress. Centuries later, we find (for example) the government of the Netherlands providing dismemberment insurance for soldiers in the mid-seventeenth century.

In 1850, The Accidental Death Association of London was the first company to offer coverage for medical expense for bodily injuries that did not result in death. In the United States at the end of that same year, the Franklin Health Assurance Company of Massachusetts offered the same type of coverage. Ten years later, The Travelers Insurance Company of Hartford began offering medical expense coverage that resembled present-day health insurance. By 1866, health insurance policies were being written by 60 other insurance companies.

At the beginning of the twentieth century, both accident insurance companies and life insurance companies were writing health insurance policies. The early policies were essentially loss-of-income policies and provided benefits for a limited number of diseases such as typhus, typhoid, scarlet fever, smallpox, diphtheria, and diabetes. But in 1911 Montgomery Ward and Company started providing weekly benefits for its sick or injured employees. Many consider this to have been the first group health insurance plan.

◆ The Beginnings of Modern Health Insurance

The birth of modern health insurance, however, came in 1929, when a group of school teachers contracted with Baylor Hospital in Dallas, Texas, to provide room, board, and specified ancillary services at a predetermined monthly cost. This arrangement is probably the earliest example of what came to be called Blue Cross plans.

The Blue Cross plans were attractive not only to consumers but to hospitals, which were seeking a mechanism to assure that patients would be able to pay for services rendered. For patients covered by Blue Cross, payment was made directly by the plan to the hospital, rather than to the patient (who would then pay the hospital). Coverage under the Blue Cross policies was typically for a hospital stay of a specified number of days or for particular hospital services. Blue Cross plans, then, were unlike the indemnity plans offered by private insurance carriers, which reimbursed (that is, "indemnified") the patient for a covered service up to a specified dollar limit, leaving it up to the hospital to collect the money from the patient.

Blue Shield plans, initiated by physicians, followed; these were based on similar concepts except that they offered coverage for physician services. The Blue Cross and Blue Shield plans traditionally set premiums by community rating: everybody in the community paid the same premium.

Starting in the 1930s and continuing into the war years, traditional insurance companies began to add health insurance coverage for hospital, surgical, and medical expenses to their accident and life insurance lines of business. During World War II group health insurance became an attractive benefit to workers at a time when wages were frozen. The trend was strengthened by the favorable tax treatment that fringe benefits received. Unlike money wages, benefits were not subject to income or Social Security taxes, so a dollar of health insurance was worth more than an after-tax dollar spent on medical services. Health insurance quickly became a benefit that was covered by the collective bargaining contracts of employee groups.

◆ Health Insurance in the Post-War Years

The position of health insurance as a permanent part of employee benefits was assured in the post-war era when the Supreme Court ruled that employee benefits, including health insurance, were a legitimate part of the labor-management bargaining process. The dynamic growth of health insurance was also spurred by a growing population and the prosperity of the 1950s.

Although early policies were often sufficiently broad to cover the expenses of common accidents and illness, they were inadequate to cover extended illnesses or long hospital stays. To correct this deficiency, in the early 1950s insurers began to offer major medical expense insurance that covered catastrophic cases. Soon thereafter, Blue Cross/Blue Shield followed the lead of the private insurers and offered similar plans. Typically the policyholder under major medical expense insurance paid a specified deductible amount after which the insured and the insurer shared the covered losses according to a specified ratio (coinsurance).

During the 1950s, health insurance protection expanded rapidly, and by the middle of the decade 77 million people had hospital expense insurance in either the indemnity form or under a major medical plan. This was followed by a new high-benefit major medical plan, which established "out-of-pocket" cutoff points beyond which the insurance company paid 100 percent of covered expenses. (These plans, whose expanded coverage was a response to advances in medical technology, were the models for plans still in use today.) Thus, while from its beginnings health care reimbursement emphasized hospital expenses, pressures mounted for increased coverage.

Among the pressures was the fact that health insurance policies now occupied a niche in the financial plans of the majority of Americans. Advances in surgical techniques and technology (along with higher costs) also spurred demand for increased coverage; by the 1950s nearly 60 million people had surgical expense insurance. In addition, a growing realization that physician care is critical to good health encouraged 21 million people to purchase insurance coverage for physicians' medical fees. Consequently, during the 1950s and 1960s most health insurance policies sold by insurance companies contained the three basic coverages: hospital care, surgical fees, and related physicians' services.

◆ Medicare and Medicaid

During the next 20 years, private health insurance would not only continue to cover an increasing number of people, but the government would enter the arena as a major insurer. The federal government's programs (Medicare, for people over the age of 65, and Medicaid, for some of the low-income population) became effective in 1966.

For the portion of the working population covered by Social Security, Medicare provided compulsory hospitalization insurance (Part A) as well as voluntary supplementary medical insurance (Part B) to help pay for physicians' services, medical services, and supplies not covered by the hospitalization plan.

But there were still gaps in Medicare coverage. To fill these gaps, nearly 23 million or 70 percent of today's Medicare enrollees supplement their Medicare benefits with private insurance (usually known as MedSup or Medigap policies).

Medicaid, designed to share the cost of medical care for low-income people, became effective under Title 19 of the Social Security Act. It allowed states to add health coverage, with federal matching funds, to their public assistance programs for low-income groups, families with dependent children, the aged, and the disabled. Because eligibility is based not only on low income but upon other criteria, a decreasing proportion of the population living below the poverty line has been covered by Medicaid, falling to an estimated 40 percent.

◆ Insurance in the 1970s and 1980s

Insurance underwent dynamic change in the 1970s and 1980s. Anticipating the requirements of the public, insurance companies began offering more comprehensive coverages and increased benefit levels that ranged from $50,000 to several million dollars under comprehensive major medical expense policies. And changes in coverage were accompanied by changes in risk assessment and in the administration of benefits.

In the 1970s, private insurance companies were determining premiums through actuarial assessments of the risk associated with the insured group; premiums differed from group to group because the risk of groups varied. In other words, premiums for groups were based on their own medical claims experience, a practice that came to be known as "experience rating." It was only a short step from experience rating to self-insurance.

Self-insurance began when some big employers realized that the aggregate medical experience and expenses of their large workforce would vary little from year to year (except for inflation in medical prices). Given this predictability, it was feasible for these large companies to self-insure: rather than pay insurers a premium to bear the risk, the employer simply assumed the risk by budgeting a certain amount to pay claims. In addition, the firm could retain control over funds until the time a medical bill needed to be paid.

Two other factors related to government regulations spurred self-insurance. In virtually all states, insurance companies had to pay a premium tax of several percentage points, the cost of which was passed on to customers. Self-insured firms could avoid this cost. In addition, states began mandating that insurance policies cover certain specified benefits and the services of particular provider groups. But the Employee Retirement Income Security Act of 1974 (ERISA) prohibited states from applying these mandates to self-insured plans. Thus employers could avoid paying the extra costs of these mandated benefits (now numbering about 900 when aggregated across all states) by self-insuring.

Self-insurance grew rapidly in the mid-to-late 1970s. But, while self-insurance became a dominant form of group coverage, employers still often turned to insurers to administer their plans: these contractual arrangements are known as administrative services only (ASO). In 1992, the various kinds of plans in which the employer group assumes all or a substantial portion of the risk account for 60 percent of total commercial health insurance business, with ASO arrangements accounting for 45 percent and minimum premium plans and stop-loss plans accounting for another 15 percent.

Once self-insurance became an option, community rating was no longer a viable way of determining premiums for groups that were large enough to self-insure; clearly, it became cheaper for any group of below-average risk to leave the "community" and to self-insure. ("Community rated" premiums necessarily reflect the risk of the total community, which inludes higher risk groups or individuals.) As a consequence, not just private insurance carriers but also Blue Cross/Blue Shield plans turned to experience rating as the predominant method of premium rating for the types of groups that have the option of self-insuring.

It should be noted that some very large accounts that stayed in federally qualified health maintenance organizations (HMOs) continued to practice community rating. These HMOs were themselves a comparatively new phenomenon, a response to the dramatic escalation in health care costs. They were soon followed by preferred provider organizations (PPOs) and other hybrid arrangements. These new delivery systems (now called managed care) offered the potential to control costs by organizing providers into coherent networks and by integrating the financing and delivery of medical care. (Managed care plans coordinate a broad range of patient services, and monitor care to assure that it is appropriate and delivered in the most efficient and inexpensive way.)

◆ Recent Trends

In 1992, the Bureau of the Census reported that public and private health insurance protected 217 million Americans, but 37 million persons—many employed by firms that do not offer coverage, many below the poverty line— were still without health insurance coverage. Of those without health insurance, 10 million were children. Many of these people without coverage were poor but still did not qualify for Medicaid.

Commercial insurance companies, Blue Cross/Blue Shield plans, self-funded employer plans, and prepayment plans (such as HMOs) cover 90 percent of the

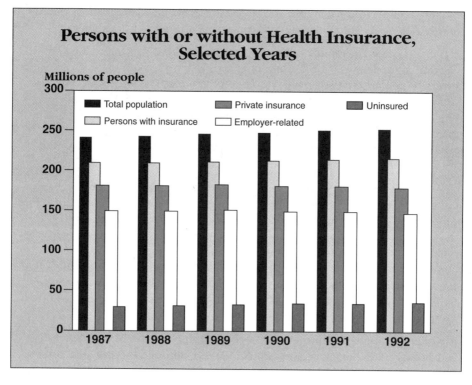

Persons with or without Health Insurance, Selected Years

Figure 1.1

SOURCE: Bureau of the Census.

people who purchase private coverage. During 1992, these private programs paid more than $246 billion for health care claims (Table 2.6A).

In 1992, Americans spent $820 billion ($443 billion in private funds and $377 billion in public funds) for medical and health care services, research, and construction of medical facilities. Private insurance companies spent over $252 billion on personal health care, an $18 billion increase over the previous year.

Rising health care costs continue to be the most pressing problem of the health care system in the United States. By 1992, for example, Americans were spending $67 billion on physicians' services through private insurance. Per capita figures are even more alarming. While 1972 per capita expenditures for health care were $387, by 1992 the figure had increased to $3,098. During the same 20-year period, health expenditures grew from 7.7 percent of the gross domestic product (GDP) to 13.6 percent. By the end of this decade, the Health Care Financing Administration (HCFA) of the U.S. Department of Health and Human Services (HHS) projects the per capita at $5,712 and the National Healthcare Expenditures (NHE) at $1,616 trillion dollars, approximately 16.4 percent of the gross national product (GNP).

Three factors continue to inflate health care costs. Increases in coverage have raised levels of expectation and demand; incentives for providers and consumers have encouraged high levels of utilization, discouraged cost consciousness, and created tolerance for inefficiency and only marginally useful care; and new technologies have often brought improvements in quality at substantial increases in the cost of treating an episode of illness.

The major responses to cost escalation have been the greater use of managed care, a new focus on prevention, and more intense monitoring of claims and service. For example, insurers, public and private, recognized early on that hospital services are an important factor in determining a large proportion of physician expenses; thus it became imperative to start monitoring the use and costs of hospital services.

◆ Managed Care Today

At the beginning of 1994, over 100 million persons were enrolled in HMOs, PPOs, exclusive provider organizations, and point-of-service plans. (Data for 1993 indicated that 51 percent of people covered by employer-sponsored health plans are enrolled in managed care plans.) And managed care companies now are developing specialty networks for mental health, vision, dental, chiropractic, podiatric, and physical therapy care. Sophisticated managed care principles also are being applied to other fields, such as long-term care, as well as to medical bills associated with auto liability and workers' compensation claims. The growth of managed care can be expected to continue as new permutations on existing models (and new applications) develop.

◆ Promoting Good Health

Drug and alcohol abuse, smoking, failure to use seatbelts, unsafe sex, and sharing contaminated needles are all behaviors that account for more than one fourth of the billions of dollars that Americans spend on health care each year. It is estimated that a total of $188 billion of the dollars spent on health care in this country is attributable to unhealthy life styles.

The American Medical Association (AMA) estimates that from 25 to 40 percent of patients occupying general hospital beds are there for treatment of ailments that are the result of alcoholism. Drug abuse, rising steadily, costs the health care system billions of dollars for care, treatment, and rehabilitation.

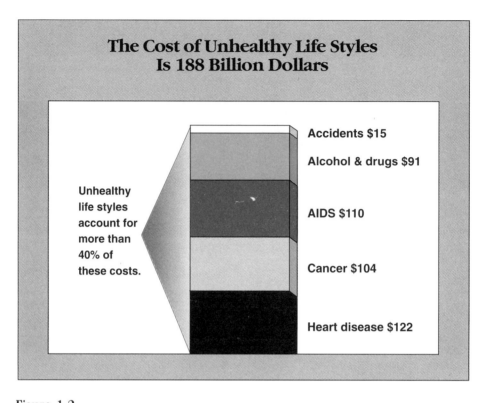

**The Cost of Unhealthy Life Styles
Is 188 Billion Dollars**

Accidents $15

Alcohol & drugs $91

Unhealthy
life styles
account for
more than
40% of
these costs.

AIDS $110

Cancer $104

Heart disease $122

Figure 1.2

SOURCES: American Health Association, Centers for Disease Control, American Medical Association.

Other factors, such as the failure to get routine medical checkups that might detect early signs of cancer and other treatable illnesses, also contribute to this problem.

Commercial health insurance companies, realizing that healthy life styles and early detection can save millions of dollars, began to focus on health promotion in the early 1980s, with growth in such programs continuing into the 1990s.

According to a 1994 survey of all major health insurance companies (conducted by the Center for Corporate Public Involvement), a high percentage of these companies continued to offer health promotion programs in 1993.

Insurers have long offered rate advantages for non-smokers and individuals who maintain a healthy weight; many companies also include medical screening benefits as an intergral part of their policies. Several others now have programs such

Health Promotion Programs Offered by Major Health Insurers, by Percentage of Companies, 1993

Smoking cessation 98
Stress management 97
Exercise/fitness programs 91
Alcohol/drug abuse 87
Periodic health exam 85
Hypertension screening 91
AIDS education 82
Cancer risk reduction 71
Nutrition 48
Prenatal maternity 49

Figure 1.3

as *Healthy Beginnings*, offered by a major commercial insurance company as a part of a benefit package available to employers; the program helps identify women at risk of delivering premature or low birth-weight babies.

The Center on Addiction and Substance Abuse (CASA) at Columbia University reports that the use and abuse of cigarettes, alcohol, pills, and drugs is a major

Preventable Medical Conditions and Cost of Treatment

Condition	Magnitude	Cost per patient
Heart disease	7 million affected 500,000 deaths/year 284,000 bypass procedures/year	$30,000.00 (bypass surgery)
Cancer	1 million new cases/year 510,000 deaths/year	$29,000.00 (lung cancer treatment)
Stroke	600,000 strokes/year 150,000 deaths/year	$22,000.00
Injuries	2.3 million hospitalized/year 142,500 deaths/year 177,000 persons with spinal cord injuries	$570,000.00 (lifetime, quadriplegia)
HIV infection	1–1.5 million infected 147,525 AIDS cases (01/1990)	$75,000.00 (lifetime treatment)
Alcoholism	18.5 million persons abuse alcohol 105,000 alcohol deaths/year	$250,000.00 (liver transplant)
Drug abuse	Regular users: 1.3 million persons use cocaine; 900,000, IV drugs; 500,000, heroin; drug-exposed babies: 375,000	$63,000.00 (5 years)
Low birth-weight baby (LBWB)	260,000 LBWB born/year 23,000 deaths/year	$50,000.00 (intensive care)

Figure 1.4

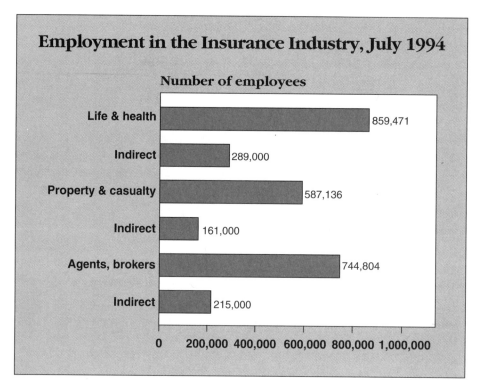

Figure 1.5

NOTE: In addition to the 2,191,411 direct employees in the industry there are 665,000 indirect employees, bringing the total industry employment figure up to 2,856,411.
SOURCE: Alliance of American Insurers.

cause of many diseases that eventually result in hospitalization for which Medicare pays.

Nearly one out of every four dollars Medicare spends on inpatient hospital care and one out of every five medicare hospital admissions, is attributable to substance abuse. In 1994, CASA estimates that substance abuse will cost the Medicare program an estimated $20 billion in inpatient hospital costs alone.

◆ Employment in the Health Insurance Industry

Nationwide, nearly 900,000 agents, brokers, and service personnel employed in the health insurance industry added nearly $30 billion to the nation's payrolls in 1992.

Employment in Health Care Services 1990–1993

Health care services	1990	1991	1992	1993
Health services	9,147,200	9,500,900	9,856,300	10,239,400
Medical doctors' offices/clinics	1,342,100	1,407,100	1,470,000	1,547,900
Dentists' offices/clinics	516,500	528,900	535,600	562,000
Nursing/personal care facilities	1,415,600	1,494,800	1,539,900	1,614,500
Home health care services	290,900	345,700	401,000	473,100
Hospitals	4,869,200	4,963,900	5,098,000	5,184,600

Figure 1.6

SOURCE: U.S. Industrial Outlook.

The insurance industry employs nearly 3 million people in the United States, with 23 states having direct employment of more than 25,000 persons. The top five states correspond to the five most populous states: California, New York, Illinois, Texas, and Pennsylvania. The states that have the most insurance employment relative to their total employment are Connecticut, Nebraska, Iowa, Massachusetts, and Illinois.

The majority of persons employed by the insurance industry, about 1.4 million, work directly for insurance carriers. A total of 744,804 persons work for insurance agencies, brokerage operations, for other service organizations such as rating bureaus, or are independent claims adjusters, appraisers, and loss control service providers.

◆ Employment in Health Services

Employment in health care rose at an average annual pace of 3.8 percent from 9.1 million in June 1990 to 10.2 million in June 1993.

The United States is the world leader in the development of new medical technologies. Breakthroughs in science help create new companies that manufacture and export medical products. In 1993 U.S. makers of medical and dental equipment and supplies exported $8.1 billion worth of goods, generating a trade surplus of $3.5 million.

Table 1.1

Key Health Insurance Statistics

Category	1987	1988	1989	1990	1991	1992	Percent change 1990-1991
Persons with and without health care coverage (millions)							
Total population	241.2	243.7	246.2	248.9	251.4	254.2	1.1
Persons with public and private coverage	210.2	211.0	212.8	214.2	216.0	216.8	0.4
Private health insurance	182.2	182.0	183.6	182.1	181.4	180.8	−0.3
Employer-related	149.7	150.9	151.6	150.2	150.1	148.2	−1.3
Persons without coverage	31.0	32.7	33.4	34.7	35.4	37.4	5.7
Private health insurance claims payments (billions)							
Total†	151.7	171.1	194.5	208.9	223.0	246.4	10.5
Insurance companies	72.5	83.0	89.4	92.5	97.6	104.8	7.3
Blue Cross-Blue Shield	44.5	48.2	50.7	55.9	60.0	63.1	5.2
Other plans†	56.5	62.8	79.8	93.4	112.0	132.1	17.9
Private health insurance payment by category of service (billions)							
Total	138.1	154.9	170.6	191.2	209.3	216.6	3.5
Hospital care	69.4	76.2	84.3	94.3	101.5	104.3	2.8
Physicians' services	42.6	49.1	53.9	60.7	66.8	66.9	0.2
Dentists' services	11.0	12.4	13.5	14.6	16.1	17.0	5.6
Other professional services‡	7.5	8.9	10.1	11.4	13.3	16.0	20.3
Home health care	0.3	0.3	0.4	0.5	0.7	0.7	0.0
Drugs and medical nondurables	5.5	6.5	6.9	7.9	9.0	9.7	7.8
Vision products and other medical durables	0.9	1.0	1.1	1.2	1.2	1.2	0.0
Nursing home care	0.4	0.5	0.5	0.6	0.6	0.7	0.0
Program administration and cost of private health insurance	17.1	20.4	26.5	30.9	35.1	35.5	1.3
National Health Expenditure (NHE) (billions)							
National Health Expenditure	494.2	546.1	604.3	675.0	751.8	819.9	9.1
Personal health care	439.3	482.8	530.9	591.5	660.2	727.1	8.6
All private funds	286.2	319.0	351.0	390.0	421.8	443.5	5.1
All public funds	208.0	227.1	253.3	285.1	330.0	376.5	14.1
NHE as percent of GNP	10.9	11.2	11.6	12.1	13.2	113.6	3.8
NHE as percent of GDP	10.9	11.1	11.5	12.1	13.1	13.6	3.8
Per capita national health expenditure, private and public	1,960.7	2,145.7	2,345.5	2,566.5	2,809.0	3,098.0	10.3
Private funds	1,133.9	1,253.1	1,362.8	1,477.7	1,575.0	1,675.0	4.0
Public funds	827.0	893.0	983.0	1,089.0	1,234.0	1,422.0	15.2

NOTE: Coverage and population numbers have been revised.
†Other plans include self-insured plans, self-administered plans, plans employing third-party administrators, and health maintenance organizations.
‡Other professional services include fees for chiropractors, podiatrists, psychologists, therapists, audiologists, optometrists, and portable x-ray suppliers.
SOURCES: U.S. Department of Commerce, Bureau of the Census, Current Population Survey, March of each year, Health Insurance Association of America, Annual Source Book Survey, U. S. Department of Health and Human Services, Health Care Financing Administration.

Chapter 2

THE PRIVATE HEALTH INSURANCE INDUSTRY

◆ Coverage

According to the Current Population Survey (CPS) issued by the Bureau of the Census, more than 216.8 million Americans, representing 85 percent of the civilian noninstitutionalized population, were protected by health care coverage by the end of 1992 (Table 1.1).

More than 180.8 million persons obtained their coverage from private health insurers, including commercial insurance companies, Blue Cross/Blue Shield plans, self-funded employer plans, and prepayment plans (such as HMOs).

The Health Insurance Association of America's (HIAA) 1993 survey of commercial insurance companies found that in 1992 over 80 million persons were insured under group policies, and 8.5 million persons carried individual or family policies (Table 2.5).

Most commercial health insurance companies provide two basic categories of coverage: medical expense insurance and disability income insurance. Medical expense insurance provides broad benefits that can cover virtually all expenses connected with hospital and medical care and related services. Disability income insurance provides periodic payments when the insured is unable to work as a result of sickness or injury.

Blue Cross/Blue Shield nonprofit membership plans serve state and regional areas and offer both individual and group health insurance coverage. The Blue Cross/Blue Shield Association coordinates the Blue Cross/Blue Shield plans of the nation.

Health care coverage also is obtainable from HMOs offering comprehensive health care services to their members for a fixed periodic payment. In such plans, the HMO is both insurer and provider; it is obligated to furnish needed care as specified in the subscriber's contract.

National enrollment in HMO membership continues to increase, increasing from 6 million people in 1976 to nearly 47 million members enrolled in a total of 546 HMOs in 1993, according to a recent report (Table 2.14).

Health Insurance (HI) Status of Americans, 1993

Insured, by Source of Coverage	Nonelderly		Elderly	
	Millions	Percentage	Millions	Percentage
Total population	220.8	100	30.9	100
With private HI	156.6	70.9	20.9	67.7
Employer coverage	138.0	62.5	10.1	32.6
Other private HI	18.8	8.5	10.8	35.0
With public HI	33.4	15.1	29.8	96.6
Medicare	4.0	1.8	29.7	96.2
Medicaid	25.6	11.6	2.9	9.4
CHAMPUS/VA	5.7	2.6	1.2	3.9
Uninsured	38.5	17.4	0.4	1.2

Figure 2.1

SOURCE: EBRI analysis of the March 1993 CPS.

Self-insurance also plays an important role in the private coverage system. In this arrangement, employers, not insurers, assume the risk, although insurers or third-party administrators (TPAs) may administer the plan.

Plans administered by employers, labor unions, fraternal societies, communities, and rural and consumer health cooperatives often make health insurance available to specific groups of people who are not covered under conventional plans.

In 1992, nearly 58 percent of persons with commercial insurance company group insurance were covered under ASO arrangements and minimum premium plans (MPPs). Under ASO arrangements, corporations and other organizations establish self-funded health plans and pay insurance carriers or private organizations a fee to process claims. Under MPPs, employers self-fund their plans yet insure against very large claims (Table 2.5a).

Nearly 57 million persons were covered in 1992 by self-insured plans, self-administered plans, and plans employing TPAs not associated with an insurance company. HMOs covered over 42 million persons.

◆Types of Private Health Insurance

Today's market makes available an endless variety of health insurance. Descriptions of the major types of health insurance follow.

◆ Hospital/Medical Insurance

Hospital expense coverage provides specific benefits for daily room and board and usual services and supplies during hospital confinements.

Room and board benefits usually take one of two forms: an indemnity plan will reimburse for the actual room-and-board charge, up to a specified maximum dollar amount per day for hospital confinement, while a service-type benefit pays the full cost of a semiprivate room-and-board charge.

Hospital/medical coverage may be extended in one of three ways: a health insurance policy usually sold in combination with a physician's or surgical expense policy that provides benefits for both surgical operations and doctor's in-hospital visits; a major medical policy that provides broad and substantial coverage for many types of medical expenses; or a combination of hospital-physician-surgical coverage plus a supplemental major medical policy.

Major Medical Expense Insurance

Major medical expense insurance has grown rapidly since it was introduced nationally by insurance companies in 1951. There are two types of major medical plans: one supplements basic hospital-physician-surgeon expense insurance programs and the other offers comprehensive protection that integrates basic coverage and extended health care benefits. Major medical coverage offers broad and substantial protection for large, unpredictable medical expenses. It covers a wide range of medical charges and has few internal limits and a high overall maximum benefit. The majority of major medical policies, whether written for individuals or under group plans, are subject to some form of deductible and coinsurance payments by the insured person.

Medicare Supplement Insurance

Medicare supplement insurance, referred to as Medigap or MedSup, is accident and sickness insurance that supplements the hospital, medical, or surgical expenses of persons covered by Medicare. Nearly 26 million persons have MedSup (Table 2.22).

Disability Income (DI) Insurance

DI insurance replaces part of income lost by an individual as the result of an accident, illness, or pregnancy. Generally, DI policies are divided into those that provide benefits for up to two years (short-term) and those that provide benefits for a longer period, usually for at least five years, to age 65, or for a lifetime (long-term).

When DI is provided as part of group insurance, the benefits are usually integrated with those derived from public programs such as Social Security. The total benefits from these sources generally is set at a level that does not exceed 60 percent of earnings.

Individual disability income policies usually pay a fixed dollar amount of coverage. This amount may be greater for those who are turned down by Social Security. Individual disability income policies take many forms and may be designed to fit the special needs of the individual policyowner.

Dental Expense Insurance

Dental expense insurance, generally available through insurance company group plans, prepayment plans, and dental service corporations, reimburses for expenses of dental service and supplies and encourages preventive care. The coverage normally provides for oral examinations (including X-rays and cleaning), fillings, extractions, inlays, bridgework, and dentures, as well as oral surgery, root canal therapy, and orthodontics. Plans normally include substantial consumer copayments, although the copayments may be lower for preventive services (Tables 5.13 and 5.14).

Long-Term Care Insurance

The market for insurance coverage that continues broad-ranged maintenance and health services to the chronically ill, disabled, or retarded began in earnest in 1985 when the number of companies selling this coverage doubled. The services covered by these policies may be provided on an inpatient or outpatient basis or entirely at home. It is estimated that by December 1992 almost 3 million people had purchased long-term care insurance from more than 135 commercial insurance companies.

Group Self-Insurance

The growth in the number of insurance plans for which the employer or union assumes all or part of the responsibility for paying claims continues; in 1993, this made the nation's employers among the principal bearers of the financial risks of illness and non-job-related injury.

Self-insured plans are usually either fully insured or MPPs. In a totally self-insured plan, the employer assumes all the risk for paying claims. Under an MPP, the employer pays up to a specified maximum; then an insurer pays, or shares in the payment of additional claims. The administration of a self-insured plan includes processing claims, making actuarial estimates of plan costs, and conducting utilization reviews. These responsibilities may be assumed by the employer, an insurance carrier, a TPA, or a combination of all three.

These plans, as with fully insured plans, typically cover medical expenses under basic coverage only, major medical coverage only, or basic plus major medical coverage. Commercial insurance and Blue Cross/Blue Shield plans offer basic plus major medical coverage.

Most self-insured plans are free-standing major medical plans and do not contain a basic hospital benefit that provides full and unlimited coverage for hospital-related charges. In most self-insured plans, covered services are subject to a deductible and coinsurance.

According to a 1992 report by Charles D. Spencer & Associates, TPAs paid $19 billion in claims in 1991. There was a significant shift from self-funding to full insurance in TPA-administered plans. Respondents indicated that 51 percent of the plans they administered were self-funded with stop-loss, 13 percent assumed total responsibility, and another 34 percent were fully insured. In 1990, 70 percent of the plans were self-funded with stop-loss, and 15 percent were totally self-funded and fully insured.

◆Employers Offering Health Insurance

Coverage differs from industry to industry. Among the employers that offer health insurance coverage are virtually all state and local governments. In the private sector, goods-producing firms are more likely to offer health benefits than are firms that sell services. Less likely to offer health insurance coverage are firms that employ significant proportions of low-wage workers, or have a large proportion of part-time workers, or that experience high employee turnover.

◆The Population without Health Care Coverage

While 83 percent of nonelderly Americans and 99 percent of elderly Americans (age 65 and older) were covered by either public or private health insurance in 1992 the number of uninsured increased between 1991 and 1992 to 37.4 million people according to the U. S. Bureau of the Census. The Employee Benefit Research Institute (EBRI) in the 1994 analysis of the March 1993 CPS estimated 38.9 million Americans were uninsured during that period.

The population without health insurance defies stereotype. EBRI reports that contrary to intuition, those who are uninsured are not predominately the unemployed. Among the 220.8 million nonelderly Americans who were unin-

The Population without Health Care Coverage, 1993
(Millions)

	Total population	Number insured	Number without coverage	Percent without coverage
Total population	251.7	212.8	38.9	15.4
Under age 65 population	220.8	182.3	38.5	17.4

Figure 2.2

SOURCE: U. S. Department of Commerce, Bureau of the Census, Current Population Reports, Series P-70, No.17 and Employee Benefit Research Institute, *Uninsured in the United States: an analysis of the 1992 Current Population Survey.*

sured in 1993, 53.4 percent were working adults, 26.3 percent were children, and 20.3 percent were nonworking adults. More than 60 percent of the uninsured were part of families of full-year, steadily employed workers in 1993, the majority of whom were employed full-time. (EBRI, *Americans without Health Insurance*, January 1994.) Recent studies indicate that uninsured persons span all income groups but are predominantly in low- and middle-income families.

Several factors are responsible for the growth in the uninsured population. These include the economic downturn in the early 1980s (and its effect on employment); the erosion of the Medicaid program's coverage of the poor; demographic changes; and, to a small extent, shifts of workers to industries less likely to offer health insurance. An additional factor is the increase in health care insurance costs, which has outpaced growth in incomes.

According to EBRI, 29 percent of the non-elderly uninsured had incomes of $30,000 or more, 19 percent had incomes of $20,000 to $30,000, and the remaining earned salaries under $20,000. (According to Health and Human Services, the federal poverty standard for a family of four in 1992 was $13,950.) Among American children, 15 percent under age 18 are uninsured (10 million), and two-thirds of these uninsured children are older than 6 years. Fully 75 percent of uninsured children belong to families whose family head is also uninsured.

A Continuing Problem

Large numbers of uninsured pose a major national problem. Growing evidence shows that uninsured persons have difficulty gaining access to the health care system; if and when they do, it is often too late or more costly to treat their health problems. The cost of this care is borne indirectly by providers and insurers through "unsponsored care" or cost-shifting. It has been estimated that

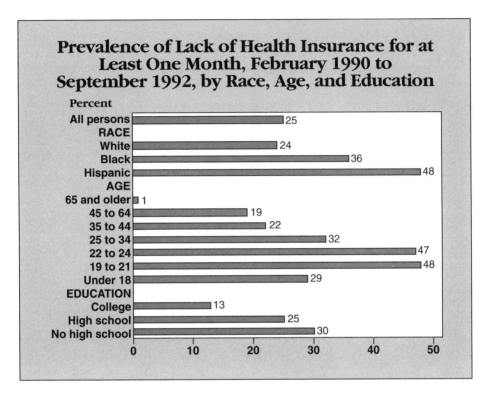

Prevalence of Lack of Health Insurance for at Least One Month, February 1990 to September 1992, by Race, Age, and Education

Figure 2.3

SOURCE: Bureau of the Census, 1994.

the uninsured population is responsible for as much as 72 percent of unsponsored care.

◆ Health Insurance Claims

In 1992, private health insurers in the United States paid a total of $246 billion for medical care and disability claims (Table 2.6), an 11 percent increase over 1991. Commercial insurance companies paid $105 billion of the total. This represents almost a 7 percent increase over the $98 billion paid in 1991.

Blue Cross/Blue Shield plans paid $63 billion in benefits in 1992. Self-insured and HMO plans paid $132 billion in paid claims for the same period.

Hospital, surgical, physician expense, and major medical insurance claims totaled $78.6 billion under group policies and $6.5 billion under individual poli-

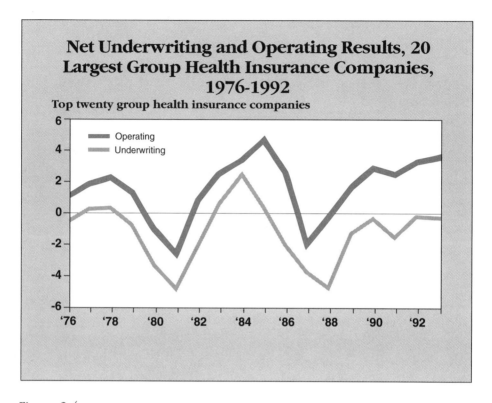

Net Underwriting and Operating Results, 20 Largest Group Health Insurance Companies, 1976-1992

Top twenty group health insurance companies

Figure 2.4

NOTE: In 1992, group health insurers experienced another year of profitability, with a net operating gain of 3.54 percent.

cies in 1992, an overall increase of 6 percent over 1991 (Tables 2.7 and 2.9). Dental claim payments totaled $7.1 billion in 1992.

Medicare supplement coverage disbursed over $4 billion to claimants. Loss of income claims (including both short-term and long-term disability) in the amount of $5.2 billion were paid by insurance companies in 1992.

Many group insurance buyers began to turn to ASO and MPP instead of traditional insured plans in the late 1970s. By 1992, nearly $60 billion (63 percent of the total group claims payments of the $95.2 billion paid by insurance companies) came from these plans.

A recent survey that examined the 20 leading writers of health insurance found an underwriting loss of 0.31 percent for group insurance; this represents a slight improvement but is nevertheless a continuation of the downward trend that began in 1986 (HIAA, *Operating Results from the Leading Writers of Group and Individual Insurance: 1993*). Individual health insurance showed a 1.30 percent underwriting loss, somewhat better than the 3.73 percent loss reported for 1992. (Of the premiums written by commercial insurers in the United States, the companies surveyed account for 60 percent of the total group health insurance premiums and 76 percent of the total individual health insurance premiums.)

The dollar totals noted in this chapter refer to incurred claims. Premium figures reported are on an earned basis for the calendar year to reflect a true picture of premiums for the year. Additions to claim reserves for persons already disabled are extracted from current year premiums but not reflected in the claims payments. These claim reserves will be used to make future disability income payments under the contracts.

◆ Health Insurance Premiums

In 1992, health insurance premium income for private insurance companies, self-insured plans, HMOs, and Blue Cross/Blue Shield plans was $281.3 billion (Table 2.10). Private insurance companies earned $125 billion in premiums in 1992: 88 percent of these premium dollars were for group insurance coverage (Table 2.12). Americans spent nearly 7 percent of disposable personal income (personal income minus personal taxes) in 1992 for health insurance premiums.

Group and Individual Premiums

Increasing health care cost is the most important factor driving up the price of group health insurance premiums.

In 1992, insurance companies earned $110.4 billion in group premiums and $14.6 billion in individual and family policy premiums. During this year, 59 percent of the group premiums derived from self-insured arrangements (Table 2.12). (For this analysis, premiums for self-insured plans [ASO and MPP] are defined as the sum of claims paid plus the insurer's administrative fee.)

A recent KPMG survey of 1,953 large, mid-sized, and small employers from the public and private sectors found that in 1993 the average monthly premium for coverage in a conventional plan was $175 for an individual and $439 for a family.

For group/staff HMO coverage, the monthly premium for an individual was $157 and $415 for a family. For PPOs, the monthly premium was $176 for an individual and $435 for a family; for point-of-service plans, the monthly cost was $184 for an individual and $482 for a family. However, average premium levels may not be good indicators of the relative efficiency of different plan

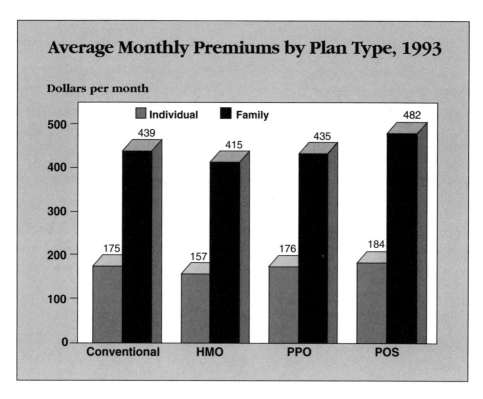

Average Monthly Premiums by Plan Type, 1993

Dollars per month

Figure 2.5

SOURCE: KPMG, Survey of 1953 Firms, 1993.

types because premium levels may well be affected by such variables as scope and level of benefits and the amount of patient cost-sharing.

According to HIAA's 1992 survey of employers, nearly 25 percent of individuals covered by employer-sponsored health insurance are members of an HMO; the combination of 17 percent in PPOs and 5 percent in point-of-service plans represents a total PPO market share of 22 percent, a 29 percent increase over 1991.

The survey also reported that the majority of employers interviewed was satisfied with all aspects of the health plans offered to employees. More than 92 percent were planning to continue with their current health plan.

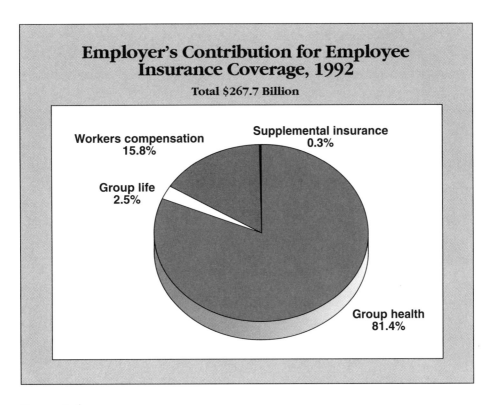

Employer's Contribution for Employee Insurance Coverage, 1992

Total $267.7 Billion

Figure 2.6

SOURCE: U. S. Department of Commerce, Survey of Business, August 1993.

Premiums Paid by Employers

Between 1970 and 1980, the amount of insurance premiums paid by American employers for their employee group insurance policies increased by 352 percent. During the mid-1980s, premium increases were between 6 and 8 percent annually; by 1990 premium increases were in double digits again. In 1992, according to the U.S. Department of Commerce, group health insurance amounted to 81 percent of all insurance costs paid by employers in private industry; group life insurance acccounted for 2.5 percent, and workers compensation insurance 16 percent.

According to the U.S. Department of Commerce, employers contributed $218 billion for group health insurance to benefit their employees in 1992. In one survey (conducted by Deloitte & Touche) New England employers attributed rising health care costs first to the advent of new medical technologies and second to cost-shifting (originating in Medicare and Medicaid and in the problem

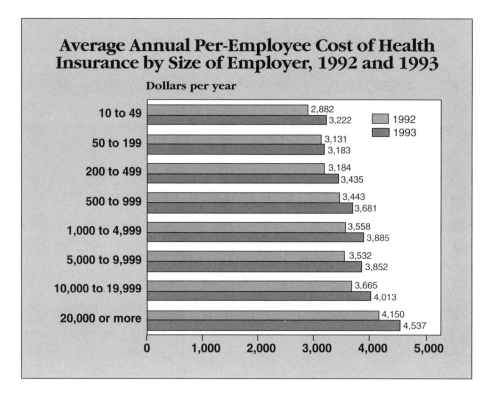

Average Annual Per-Employee Cost of Health Insurance by Size of Employer, 1992 and 1993

Dollars per year

Size	1992	1993
10 to 49	2,882	3,222
50 to 199	3,131	3,183
200 to 499	3,184	3,435
500 to 999	3,443	3,681
1,000 to 4,999	3,558	3,885
5,000 to 9,999	3,532	3,852
10,000 to 19,999	3,665	4,013
20,000 or more	4,150	4,537

Figure 2.7

SOURCE: Foster Higgins, 1994.

of the uninsured). Other reasons cited were overutilization of the system by employees, unnecessary procedures performed by providers, inefficient hospitals, and the cost of AIDS and other diseases.

◆ The Evolution of Managed Care

During the past five to ten years, the health care system has evolved at a pace that few expected, largely in response to the ever-rising cost of care: the most visible change has been the explosion of managed care, of which HMOs and PPOs are the best-known examples.

Although managed care is still evolving in response to changes in medical practice and the needs of consumers and payers, it can be defined as a system that integrates the financing and delivery of appropriate health care services to covered individuals. Managed care plans have the following common elements:

- Arrangements with selected providers to furnish a comprehensive set of health care services to members;
- Explicit standards for the selection of health care providers;
- Formal programs for ongoing quality assurance and utilization review; and
- Significant financial incentives for members to use providers and procedures covered by the plan.

Managed care plans employ a variety of techniques to assure quality and appropriateness of care, including utilization review, case management, and the use of primary care physicians as coordinators and managers of care. A variety of managed care models exist today; health care reform and changing markets are expected to lead to yet other forms.

◆ The History of Managed Care

Managed care began in the 1930s when the first prepaid group practices were established. The founders of this early type of managed care saw it as a way to improve quality and continuity of care and as a vehicle to provide preventive health care services. The early prepaid group practices are one example of what are now known as health maintenance organizations, or HMOs.

Health Maintenance Organizations (HMOs)

Since the 1930s, the HMO delivery system has taken many forms. Yet all provide a defined, comprehensive set of health services to a voluntarily enrolled population within a specified geographic service area; and providers typically are reimbursed on a capitated basis or through another "at risk" arrangement.

There are a number of models. In the group model HMO, of which Kaiser Permanente is perhaps the best-known example, a physician medical group contracts with the entity that is financially responsible for covering enrollees. In the staff model, physicians are employees of the HMO.

Although there was some growth in HMOs from the 1930s through the 1960s, particularly on the West Coast, interest in this alternative delivery system was sparked by the unanticipated rapid increases in health care costs that the country experienced in the late 1960s and 1970s. HMOs seemed to solve the cost problem by economizing on services, particularly by reducing hospitalization rates.

In 1973, Congress enacted legislation to promote HMOs. The HMO Act, P.L. 93-222, authorized federal funds to establish and develop HMOs over a period of five years. The act required most employers to offer an HMO option to employees where federally qualified HMOs were available. To meet the qualifica-

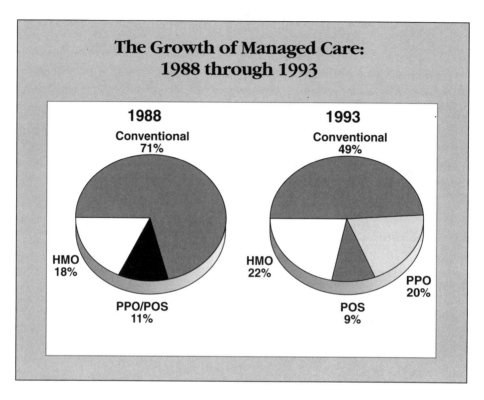

Figure 2.8

SOURCE: KPMG Peat Marwick Survey 1993.

tion tests, HMOs had to provide a prescribed range of basic health services and to offer the subscriber the opportunity to purchase optional health services.

In response to the favorable cost record of HMOs, Medicare and Medicaid also turned to HMOs with the hope that they could help bring the costs of these federal programs under control. Total HMO enrollment of Medicare beneficiaries, including risk contracts, cost contracts, and PPOs, was approximately 2.1 million people: this represents approximately 7 percent of all Medicare beneficiaries and about one-third of the total market for HMOs in the under-65 population.

By January 1992, the majority of HMOs were using cost control measures. Home health care was used by 97.1 percent of all HMOs, preventive health by 90.2 percent, and preferred provider negotiations by 83.6 percent. The most significant increase was in the percentage of HMOs offering "self-care" patient education programs. The use of these programs increased from 46.9 percent in

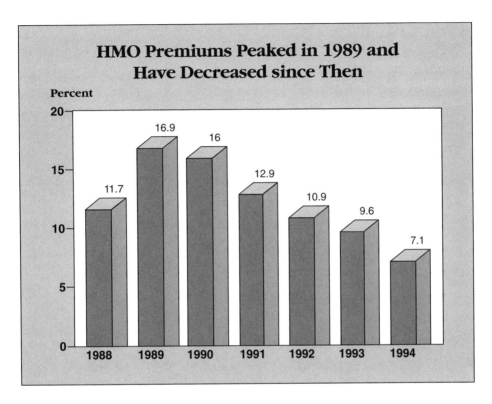

HMO Premiums Peaked in 1989 and Have Decreased since Then

Figure 2.9

SOURCE: Group Health Association of America, 1993.

1991 to 72.4 percent by January 1992. Other cost control measures were risk management programs, durable medical equipment monitoring, retrospective review of admissions, discharge planning, and the usual inpatient and outpatient utilization review.

The greatest increase in statewide penetration rates between 1992 and 1993 were in Arizona (43%), North Carolina (40%), and Connecticut (32%) (Table 2.17). According to the Group Health Association of America (GHAA), HMO penetration rates are no longer necessarily highest in states where there is a long history of support from employers and where HMOs have been in operation for a long time, but in states where employers and employees are enrolling in new managed care plans with enthusiasm.

Types of HMOs

Staff Model In a staff model HMO, the physicians practice solely as employees and are usually paid a salary.

Group Model In this model, the HMO pays a physician group a negotiated, per capita rate, which the group in turn distributes among individual physicians.

Network Model This kind of HMO contracts with two or more independent (single- or multispecialty) group practices to provide services and pays a fixed monthly fee per enrollee. The group decides how fees will be distributed to individual physicians.

Independent Practice Association (IPA) In this model, the managed care plan contracts with individual physicians in independent practice or with associations of independent physicians to provide services to the plan members at a negotiated rate per capita, or a flat retainer, or a negotiated fee-for-service rate. Physicians maintain their own offices and see patients on a fee-for-service basis while contracting with one or more plans.

Preferred Provider Organizations (PPOs)

Another prominent example of managed care is the PPO. Developed during the 1980s, the PPO offers more flexibility than the HMO, giving consumers greater freedom in choosing providers, but, as with the HMO, it tries to achieve savings by directing patients to providers who are committed to cost-effective delivery of care.

PPOs are financing and delivery systems that combine features of standard fee-for-service indemnity plans and HMOs. Typically organized by insurers but sometimes by providers or others, PPOs have contracts with networks or panels of providers who agree to provide medical services and to be paid according to a negotiated fee schedule. Individuals who are enrolled in the PPO typically experience a financial penalty if they choose to get care from a non-affiliated provider, but that option is available. Ideally, providers are chosen for their efficiency, and the system monitors its own activities to assure that care is efficiently provided.

According to a survey by the AMCRA Foundation, Inc., by October 1993 there were 895 operating PPOs, covering over 50 million eligible employees in the United States (Table 2.19). SMG Marketing found that coverage provided by PPOs varies according to the type of ownership. For example, 87.5 percent of the PPOs owned and operated by HMOs offer mental health coverage. Of independent investor-owned PPOs, 68.3 percent offer workers' compensation coverage, followed by 43.8 percent of the hospital alliance PPOs. Of the HMOs with PPOs, 87 percent offered mental health coverage and 63 percent offered wellness programs, respectively (Table 2.20).

Exclusive Provider Organizations (EPOs)

The EPO represents the extreme of the PPO. Services rendered by nonaffiliated providers are not reimbursed, so people belonging to an EPO must receive their care from affiliated providers or pay the entire cost themselves ("out-of-pocket"). Providers typically are reimbursed on a fee-for-service basis according to a negotiated discount or fee schedule.

Point-of-Service Plans (POS)

POS plans, sometimes called HMO-PPO hybrids or open-ended HMOs, combine characteristics of both HMOs and PPOs. POS plans utilize a network of selected contracted, participating providers. Employees select a primary care physician, who controls referrals for medical specialists. If an employee receives care from a plan provider, the employee pays little or nothing out-of-pocket as in an HMO and does not file claims. Care provided by out-of-plan providers will be reimbursed, but employees must pay significantly higher copayments and deductibles. The basis of provider reimbursement may be fee-for-service or capitation; however, there are usually financial incentives for providers to avoid over-utilization.

As cost-containment pressures continue, and as these alternative delivery systems try to increase their market share, each tries to make its system more attractive. Often that means borrowing features from others. It is likely that this hybridization will continue, and it may become increasingly difficult to characterize a particular managed care delivery system as adhering to any particular model.

Current Trends

HMO growth regained its momentum in 1993. There were 546 HMOs at the end of 1993 with a total enrollment of 46.7 million persons. HMOs thus enroll nearly 18 percent of the population, with twelve states having more than 20 percent of their populations in HMOs (Table 2.14). Massachusetts, with almost 39 percent, has the highest HMO enrollment in both relative and absolute terms. Alaska, West Virginia, and Wyoming were the only states in which HMOs did not operate in 1993 (Table 2.14).

Large HMOs (more than 100,000 members) grew at a rapid pace by the end of 1993. Although there are now 85 HMOs in the United States with more than 100,000 members, 83 percent of all HMOs have fewer than 100,000 enrollees.

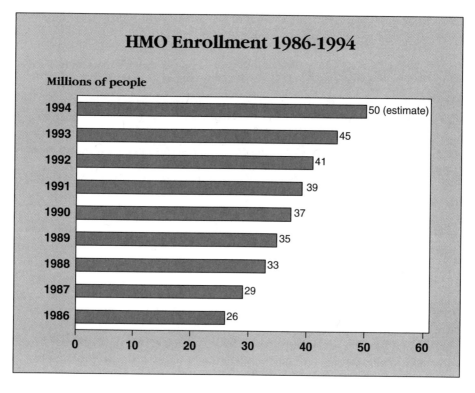

HMO Enrollment 1986-1994

Millions of people

1994	50 (estimate)
1993	45
1992	41
1991	39
1990	37
1989	35
1988	33
1987	29
1986	26

Figure 2.10

SOURCE: GHAA, December 1993. (1993 and 1994 are estimated)

PPOs also have become increasingly popular as replacement products for fee-for-service operations or as alternatives to more restrictive HMOs.

The inclusion of workers' compensation coverage, coupled with group health insurance in managed care settings, has enabled PPOs to provide "24 hour coverage" for some clients.

Hospital-based PPOs often serve chiefly to expand the number of providers and invade the self-insured market and small payer groups.

Differences in the number of PPOs (and employees covered) result from varying definitions of this type of organization in several ongoing surveys conducted during the past year.

The market shares of the various kinds of managed care plans vary by firm size and region; as firm size increases, employees are more likely to be enrolled in managed-care plans. Conventional plans with utilization management contin-

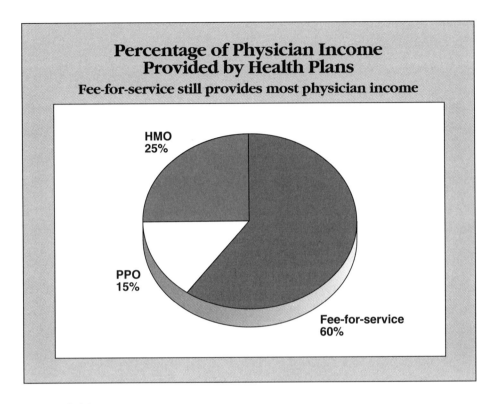

Percentage of Physician Income Provided by Health Plans

Fee-for-service still provides most physician income

- HMO 25%
- PPO 15%
- Fee-for-service 60%

Figure 2.11

SOURCE: Medical Economics Magazine.

ued to have the largest market share among private sector managed care plans, occupying 53 percent of the employer-based market. PPOs and HMOs followed with approximately equal shares of the market, 20 and 19 percent, respectively, and POS plans continued to grow, with 3 percent of the market.

Managed Mental Health Plans

The expansion of managed mental health care is the result of the increased cost and utilization of mental health treatment; the rate of cost increases in this area has been higher than that of other medical costs during the past decade. Currently, more than 73 percent of employers have Employee Assistance Programs (EAPs) as utilization management programs for mental health cases, or case management for mental health, alcohol, and drug abuse cases.

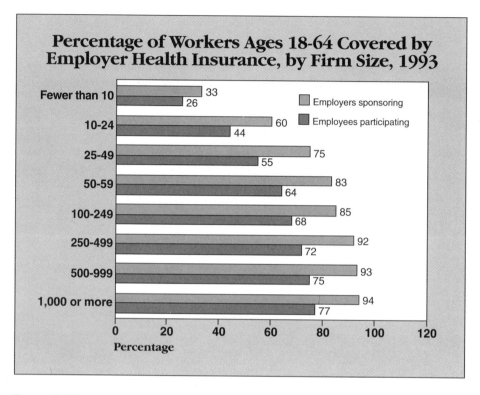

Percentage of Workers Ages 18-64 Covered by Employer Health Insurance, by Firm Size, 1993

Figure 2.12

SOURCE: EBRI analysis of the April 1993 CPS.

Outlook for the Future

The rapid growth of managed care reflects the recognition by major employers and insurers that ways must be found to reduce costs while assuring that patients get appropriate care. Insurers increasingly see that unmanaged fee-for-service indemnity plans do not have mechanisms to contain costs. As a consequence, many insurers have made major commitments to develop and sustain comprehensive managed care systems.

National managed care firms (defined as firms operating HMOs in two or more states, including commercial insurance companies that meet this criteria), along with Blue Cross/Blue Shield plans, will continue to account for nearly two-thirds of all HMOs and represent an overwhelming majority of Americans enrolled in managed care plans.

Table 2.1

Persons Covered by Insurance, by Age and by Type of Coverage, 1991 (Thousands)

Type of coverage	Total	Percentage	Age 0–64	Percentage	Age 65 or older	Percentage
Total population	248,886	100.0	218,793	100.0	30,093	100.0
Total insured	214,167	86.1	184,351	84.3	29,816	99.1
Private only	153,202	61.6	152,284	69.6	918	3.1
Public only	32,031	12.9	22,781	10.4	9,250	30.7
Medicare only	7,781	3.1	1,048	0.5	6,733	22.4
Medicaid only	16,743	6.7	16,723	7.6	20	0.1
CHAMPUS only	3,577	1.4	3,535	1.3	44	0.1
Medicare and Medicaid	3,019	1.2	1,035	0.5	1,985	6.6
Medicare and CHAMPUS	510	0.2	103	0.0	4,087	1.4
Medicaid and CHAMPUS	312	0.1	312	0.1	0	0.0
Medicare, Medicaid, and CHAMPUS	89	0.0	28	0.0	61	0.2
Private and Public	28,933	11.6	9,285	4.2	19,648	65.3
Private and Medicare	19,543	7.9	1,027	0.5	18,516	61.5
Private and Medicaid	3,316	1.3	3,314	1.5	2	0.0
Private and CHAMPUS	4,650	1.9	4,613	2.1	37	0.1
Private, Medicaid, and Medicare	640	0.3	148	0.1	492	1.6
Private, Medicaid, and CHAMPUS	106	0.0	106	0.0	0	0.0
Private, Medicare, and CHAMPUS	644	0.3	65	0.0	578	1.9
Private, Medicare, Medicaid, and CHAMPUS	34	0.0	11	0.0	23	0.1
Total uninsured	34,719	13.9	34,443	15.7	276	0.9
Privately insured	156,770	73.2	136,051	73.8	2,036	68.3
Insured by Medicare	27,841	13.0	2,949	1.6	28,534	95.7
Insured by Medicaid	20,774	9.7	18,251	9.9	2,564	8.6
Insured by CHAMPUS	8,567	4.0	7,374	4.0	1,133	3.8

NOTE: 1988 revisions to the CPS questions affected comprehensiveness of information on insurance coverage for children, young adults, and retirees. The Health Care Financing Administration's analysis of the 1991 CPS resulted in a larger number of covered persons than is reported by the U.S. Bureau of the Census, 1991 CPS.

NOTE: CHAMPUS includes other programs covering current and former military personnel and their dependents.

NOTE: Numbers may not add to totals due to rounding.

SOURCE: U. S. Department of Commerce, Bureau of the Census, CPS, 1991, as analyzed by U. S. Department of Health and Human Services, Health Care Financing Administration.

Table 2.2

Insurance Coverage in Major Metropolitan Areas of the United States (Nonelderly Population) (Millions)

Metropolitan Area	Nonelderly population	Total private	Total employer coverage	Other private	Total public	Medicaid	Without health insurance
Northeast	29.1	21.4	19.0	2.4	4.0	3.4	4.4
New York City, Long Island, NY; Northern New Jersey	15.3	10.7	9.4	1.3	2.3	1.9	2.7
Philadelphia, PA; Wilmington, DE; Trenton, NJ	5.0	3.8	3.4	0.4	0.7	0.6	0.7
Boston, Salem, MA; Lawrence, NH	3.7	5.9	2.6	0.3	0.4	0.3	0.5
Pittsburgh, Deaver Valley, PA	2.0	1.6	1.4	0.2	0.2	0.2	0.2
Buffalo, Niagara Falls, NY	1.1	0.9	0.8	0.1	0.1	0.1	0.1
Providence, Pawtucket, RI	1.0	0.8	0.7	0.1	0.1	0.1	0.1
Hartford, New Britain, Middletown, CT	0.9	0.7	0.7	NA	0.1	0.1	0.1
Midwest	25.9	19.6	17.8	1.8	3.6	3.0	3.3
Chicago, IL; Gary, IN; Lake City, WI	7.5	5.5	5.0	0.6	1.1	0.9	1.1
Detroit, Ann Arbor, MI	4.0	3.1	2.8	0.3	0.6	0.5	0.4
Cleveland, Akron, Lorainne, OH	2.4	1.8	1.6	0.1	0.4	0.3	0.3
Minneapolis, St. Paul, MN	2.2	1.7	1.5	0.2	0.4	0.3	0.2
St. Louis, MO	2.0	1.7	1.5	0.2	0.2	0.1	0.2
Cincinnati, Hamilton, OH	1.8	1.4	1.3	0.1	0.2	0.2	0.2
Milwaukee, Racine, WI	1.8	1.4	1.3	0.1	0.2	0.2	0.2
Kansas City, MO	1.6	1.1	1.0	0.1	0.2	0.1	0.3
Columbus, OH	1.3	1.0	0.9	0.1	0.2	0.1	0.1
Indianapolis, IN	1.2	1.0	0.9	0.1	0.2	0.2	0.1
South	25.0	16.8	14.8	2.0	3.6	2.7	5.4
Dallas, Ft. Worth, TX	3.9	2.6	2.3	0.3	0.6	0.4	0.9
Washington, DC	3.7	2.7	2.4	0.3	0.5	0.3	0.7
Houston, Galveston, Brazonia, TX	3.6	2.4	2.1	0.3	0.4	0.3	0.9
Atlanta, GA	2.9	2.0	1.8	0.2	0.4	0.3	0.6
Miami, Fort Lauderdale, FL	2.8	1.6	1.3	0.3	0.5	0.4	0.8
Baltimore, MD	2.0	1.6	1.4	0.1	0.3	0.2	0.2
Tampa, St. Petersburg, Clearwater, FL	1.7	1.1	1.0	0.1	0.2	0.2	0.4
Charlotte, NC; Gastonia, SC	1.2	1.0	0.9	0.1	0.2	0.1	0.1
New Orleans, LA	1.2	0.6	0.5	0.1	0.3	0.2	0.4
Norfolk, Virginia Beach, VA	1.0	0.7	0.6	0.1	0.2	0.1	0.2
San Antonio, TX	1.0	0.5	0.4	NA	0.2	0.2	0.3
West	30.8	20.8	18.1	2.8	4.5	3.7	6.5
Los Angeles, Anaheim, Riverside, CA	14.0	8.5	7.5	1.1	2.2	1.9	3.7
San Francisco, Oakland, San Jose, CA	5.6	4.1	3.5	0.6	0.7	0.6	1.0
Seattle, Tacoma, WA	2.4	2.0	1.7	0.3	0.3	0.2	0.3
San Diego, CA	2.1	1.2	1.1	0.2	0.5	0.4	0.5
Phoenix, AZ	2.1	1.4	1.3	0.1	0.3	0.2	0.4
Denver, Boulder, CO	1.8	1.4	1.2	0.2	0.2	0.2	0.2
Portland, OR; Vancouver, WA	1.5	1.2	1.0	0.1	0.2	0.1	0.2
Sacramento, CA	1.3	0.9	0.8	0.1	0.2	0.2	0.2

NOTE: Numbers do not add to totals due to rounding.

NA: Not available.

SOURCE: Employee Benefit Research Institute, January 1994 Analysis of the March 1993 CPS.

Table 2.3

Persons Age 18–64 with or without Health Insurance, by Gender and Age (Millions)

Gender and Age	Total persons	Total private	Employer coverage	Total public	Medicaid	No health insurance
Total persons	154.5	113.1	98.1	17.7	11.2	28.7
Age 18–20	9.7	6.2	4.7	1.6	1.3	2.4
Age 21–24	14.2	8.3	5.8	1.7	1.4	4.6
Age 25–29	19.2	12.8	11.4	2.2	1.9	4.6
Age 30–44	61.8	47.0	42.6	5.7	4.0	10.4
Age 45–54	28.4	22.6	20.1	2.8	1.3	4.0
Age 55–64	21.2	16.4	13.6	3.7	1.2	2.7
Men	76.0	55.2	48.1	7.0	3.4	16.0
Age 18–20	4.8	3.1	2.4	0.5	0.4	1.3
Age 21–24	7.1	4.0	2.7	0.4	0.3	2.7
Age 25–29	9.6	6.3	5.6	0.6	0.5	2.8
Age 30–44	30.6	22.8	20.6	2.2	1.3	6.0
Age 45–64	13.8	11.0	9.8	1.4	0.5	2.0
Age 55–64	10.2	8.0	6.9	1.8	0.4	1.2
Women	78.7	57.9	50.0	10.7	7.7	12.7
Age 18–20	4.9	3.1	2.3	1.0	0.9	1.1
Age 21–24	7.2	4.2	3.1	1.3	1.2	1.9
Age 25–29	9.7	6.5	5.8	1.6	1.4	1.8
Age 30–44	31.2	24.2	21.9	3.5	2.7	4.3
Age 45–54	14.6	11.6	10.3	1.5	0.8	2.0
Age 55–64	11.0	8.4	6.7	1.9	0.8	1.5

NOTE: Numbers do not add to totals due to rounding.
SOURCE: Employee Benefit Research Institute analysis of March 1993 CPS.

Table 2.4

Uninsured Persons by Census Region, 1980, 1988, 1991, 1992 (Millions)

Census Region	1980	1988	1991	1992
Total U. S.	30.2	32.7	35.4	37.4
New England	1.3	0.9	1.2	1.3
Middle Atlantic	4.1	3.5	4.2	4.6
East North Central	4.2	3.9	4.2	5.0
West North Central	1.9	1.6	1.8	2.0
South Atlantic	5.5	5.6	6.8	7.6
East South Central	2.2	2.3	2.4	2.5
West South Central	4.4	5.3	5.4	6.1
Mountain	1.9	2.1	2.1	2.1
Pacific	4.8	5.9	6.8	7.2
Percent of total population				
Total U. S.	13.7	13.4	14.1	14.7
New England	10.4	7.0	9.0	11.8
Middle Atlantic	11.3	9.4	11.0	14.2
East North Central	10.2	9.4	9.9	13.1
West North Central	11.6	9.0	10.1	13.0
South Atlantic	15.0	13.5	15.7	20.0
East South Central	15.7	15.5	15.7	18.5
West South Cental	19.1	20.1	20.3	25.5
Mountain	17.7	16.1	15.1	17.6
Pacific	15.3	15.9	17.3	20.2

NOTE: Numbers do not add to totals due to rounding.

SOURCE: U. S. Department of Commerce, Bureau of the Census, CPS, 1992 (analyzed by the U. S. Department of Health and Human Services, Health Care Financing Administration).

Table 2.5

Number of Persons with Private Insurance, by Type of Insurer (Millions)

| End of year | All insurers* | Total insurance companies | | Individual/ family | Blue Cross/ Blue Shield | Self-insured and HMOs |
		Total persons	Group			
1940	12.0	3.7	2.5	1.2	6.0	2.3
1945	32.0	10.5	7.8	2.7	18.9	2.7
1950	76.6	37.0	22.3	17.3	38.8	4.4
1955	101.4	53.5	38.6	19.9	50.7	6.5
1960	122.5	69.2	54.4	22.2	58.1	6.0
1961	125.8	70.4	56.1	22.4	58.7	7.1
1962	129.4	72.2	58.1	23.1	60.1	6.9
1963	133.5	74.5	61.5	23.5	61.0	7.2
1964	136.3	75.8	63.1	34.0	62.1	6.8
1965	138.7	77.6	65.4	24.4	63.3	7.0
1966	142.4	80.4	67.8	24.9	54.3	6.6
1967	146.4	82.6	71.5	24.6	67.2	7.1
1968	151.9	85.7	74.1	25.3	70.1	7.3
1969	155.0	88.8	77.9	25.9	82.7	7.7
1970	158.8	89.7	80.5	26.7	85.1	8.1
1971	161.8	91.5	80.6	27.8	76.5	8.5
1972	164.1	93.7	81.5	29.1	78.2	8.1
1973	168.5	94.5	83.6	27.5	81.3	9.6
1974	173.1	97.0	85.4	28.8	83.8	11.1
1975	178.2	99.5	87.2	30.1	86.4	13.1
1976	176.9	97.0	86.8	27.0	86.6	14.9
1977	179.9	100.4	89.2	28.7	86.0	18.1
1978	185.7	106.0	92.5	36.1	85.8	21.5
1979	185.7	104.1	94.1	34.4	86.1	25.5
1980	187.4	105.5	97.4	33.8	86.7	33.2
1981	186.2	105.9	103.0	25.3	85.8	40.3
1982	188.3	109.6	103.9	29.4	82.0	48.2
1983	186.6	105.9	104.6	22.2	79.6	53.6
1984	184.4	103.1	103.0	20.4	79.4	54.4 **
1985	181.3	100.4	99.5	21.2	78.7	55.1 **
1986	180.9	98.2	106.6	12.1	78.0	64.9 **
1987	179.7	96.7	106.1	10.4	76.9	66.9 **
1988	182.3	92.6	100.5	10.7	74.0	71.3 **
1989	182.5	88.9	98.7	10.0	72.5	78.6 **
1990	181.7	83.1	88.7	10.2	70.9	86.2 **
1991	181.0	78.0	83.3	9.9	68.1	93.5 **
1992	180.1	75.0	80.3	8.5	67.5	98.6 **

*The data in this column refer to the net total of persons protected, i.e., duplication among persons protected by more than one kind of insuring organization or more than one insurance company policy providing the same type of coverage has been eliminated. Excludes Hospital Indemnity coverage included in prior years. 1992 Hospital Indemnity count was 8.2 billion for group and 5.4 billion for individual policies.
**For 1984 and later, estimates of persons covered by 'other plans' have been developed by HIAA in the absence of other available data.
NOTE: The category entitled Self-insured and HMOs includes persons covered under ASO arrangements and MPPs. Some data were revised from previous editions. Data for 1978 and later have been adjusted downward because of new data on average family size. For 1975 and later, data include the number of persons covered in Puerto Rico and U. S. territories and possessions.
NOTE: Data for 1987 and 1988 reflect revised HIAA survey form. Data for 1989 and 1990 reflect a change in methodology.
NOTE: Data split is available for years 1990, 1991, and 1992 only.
SOURCES: Health Insurance Association of America, Group Health Association of America, Inc., Blue Cross and Blue Shield Association.

Table 2.5a

Distribution of Persons with Private Insurance, by Type of Insurer (Millions)

Type of insurer	1990	1991	1992
All Insurers	181.7	181.0	180.1
Insurance companies (net)	83.1	78.0	75.0
Group	88.7	83.3	80.3
Fully insured	40.9	36.2	33.8
ASO	30.8	35.3	34.1
MPP	16.9	11.8	12.4
Individual	10.2	9.9	8.5
Blue Cross/Blue Shield	70.9	68.1	67.5
Self-insured	49.7	54.8	56.5
HMO	36.5	38.7	42.1
Blue Cross/Blue Shield	4.6	4.7	5.9
Insurance companies	5.4	6.0	6.3
Other	26.5	28.0	29.9

SOURCE: Health Insurance Association of America, Annual Survey of Health Insurance Companies.

Table 2.6

Private Health Insurance Claims Payments, by Type of Insurer (Billions)

Year	Total	Insurance companies	Self-insured and HMOs	Blue Cross/ Blue Shield
1950	$ 1.3	$ 0.8	$ NA	$ 0.6
1955	3.1	1.8	NA	1.4
1960	5.7	3.0	NA	2.6
1965	9.6	5.2	NA	4.5
1970	17.2	9.1	NA	8.1
1975	32.1	16.5	NA	16.9
1980	76.3	37.0	16.2	25.5
1981	85.9	41.6	18.9	29.2
1982	97.1	49.2	21.6	32.2
1983	104.1	51.7	24.1	34.4
1984	107.5	56.0	26.1	34.7
1985	117.6	60.0	32.5	37.5
1986	128.5	64.3	36.8	40.6
1987	151.7	72.5	56.5	44.5
1988	171.1	83.0	62.8	48.2
1989	194.5	89.4	79.8	50.7
1990	208.9	92.5	93.4	55.9
1991	223.0	97.6	112.0	60.0
1992	246.4	104.8	132.1	63.1

NOTE: Totals do not add due to duplication between insurance companies and self-insured and HMO plans.
NA: Not available.
SOURCE: Health Insurance Association of America, Annual Survey of Health Insurance Companies, Blue Cross/Blue Shield Association, and Group Health Association of America, Inc.

Table 2.6a

Private Health Insurance Claims Payments, by Type of Coverage (Billions)

Type of Insurer	1990	1991	1992
All insurers	$208.9	$223.0	$246.4
Insurance companies (net)	92.5	97.6	104.8
Group	84.4	88.8	95.2
Fully insured	34.8	34.7	35.7
ASO	34.3	40.9	45.5
MPP	15.2	13.2	14.0
Individual	8.2	8.8	9.6
Blue Cross/Blue Shield	55.9	60.0	63.1
Self-insured	56.7	65.0	74.5
HMO	36.5	47.0	57.6
Blue Cross/Blue Shield	4.6	5.7	8.2
Insurance companies	5.4	7.2	8.5
Other	26.5	34.1	40.9

SOURCE: Health Insurance Association of America, Annual Survey of Health Insurance Companies.

Table 2.7

Group Health Claims Payments of Insurance Companies, by Type of Coverage (Billions)

Year	Total group	Hospital/ medical	Dental	Medicare supplement	Loss of income
1950	$ 0.4	$ NA	$NA	$NA	$NA
1955	1.3	NA	NA	NA	NA
1960	2.4	1.8	NA	NA	0.8
1965	4.0	3.3	NA	NA	1.0
1970	7.5	6.0	0.1	NA	1.8
1975	14.2	11.6	0.6	NA	2.7
1980	33.0	25.8	2.8	0.1	4.3
1981	37.7	30.0	3.5	0.2	4.2
1982	44.2	35.9	4.0	0.1	4.1
1983	46.9	38.6	4.4	0.1	3.9
1984	50.3	41.1	4.9	0.4	3.9
1985	53.7	43.9	5.3	0.5	4.0
1986	58.9	48.1	5.3	1.5	4.0
1987	66.5	54.6	5.9	1.5	4.6
1988	76.4	63.3	6.3	2.2	4.6
1989	82.2	68.6	6.5	2.1	5.0
1990*	84.4	69.9	6.4	3.1	5.0
1991	88.8	73.5	6.4	3.7	5.2
1992	95.2	78.6	7.1	4.3	5.2

*1990 revised.
NA: Not available.
SOURCE: Health Insurance Association of America, Annual Survey of Insurance Companies.

Table 2.8

Group Health Claims Payments of Insurance Companies, by Type of Risk (Billions)

Year	Total group	Fully insured		Administrative services only		Minimum premium plan	
		Hospital/ medical	Loss of income	Hospital/ medical	Loss of income	Hospital/ medical	Loss of income
1950	$ 0.4	$ NA	$NA	$ NA	$NA	$ NA	$NA
1955	1.3	NA	NA	NA	NA	NA	NA
1960	2.4	1.9	NA	NA	NA	NA	NA
1965	4.0	3.3	NA	NA	NA	NA	NA
1970	7.5	6.0	NA	NA	NA	NA	NA
1975	14.2	11.6	NA	NA	NA	NA	NA
1980	33.0	21.7	3.8	2.2	0.2	5.6	0.4
1981	37.7	19.8	3.2	3.6	0.3	10.2	0.7
1982	44.2	21.7	3.0	5.4	0.4	13.0	0.8
1983	46.9	22.8	2.9	5.7	0.2	14.5	0.7
1984	50.3	20.6	2.7	9.7	0.4	16.1	0.8
1985	53.7	21.5	2.8	11.8	0.5	16.3	0.8
1986	58.9	23.1	2.7	14.1	0.7	17.7	0.6
1987	66.5	27.8	3.0	17.8	0.9	16.4	0.7
1988	76.4	32.5	3.1	22.0	0.9	17.4	0.5
1989	82.2	31.3	3.5	28.3	1.0	17.7	0.4
1990*	84.4	31.4	3.5	33.1	1.2	14.9	0.3
1991	88.8	31.0	3.7	39.7	1.1	12.9	0.4
1992	95.2	32.0	3.6	44.3	1.2	13.7	0.4

*1990 revised.

NA: Not available.

SOURCE: Health Insurance Association of America, Annual Survey of Health Insurance Companies.

Table 2.9

Individual Health Insurance Claims Payments of Insurance Companies, by Type of Coverage (Billions)

Year	Total individual	Hospital/ medical	Loss of income
1978	$3.5	$2.5	$1.0
1979	3.7	2.6	1.1
1980	4.0	3.0	1.0
1981	4.0	3.0	1.0
1982	5.0	3.6	1.4
1983	4.8	3.8	1.0
1984	5.7	4.4	1.3
1985	6.3	4.7	1.6
1986	5.4	3.8	1.6
1987	5.9	4.1	1.8
1988	6.5	4.7	1.8
1989	7.2	5.0	2.2
1990	8.2	5.8	2.4
1991	8.8	6.5	2.3
1992	9.6	6.5	3.1

SOURCE: Health Insurance Association of America, Annual Survey of Health Insurance Companies.

Table 2.10

Health Insurance Premiums of Insurance Companies, Self-Insured, HMOs, and Blue Cross/Blue Shield Plans (Billions)

Year	Net total all insurers*	Insurance companies	Self-insured and HMOs	Blue Cross/ Blue Shield
1950	$ 2.0	$ 1.3	$ NA	$ 0.7
1955	4.3	2.7	NA	1.5
1960	7.5	4.7	NA	2.8
1965	12.1	7.4	NA	4.8
1970	20.0	11.5	NA	8.4
1975	37.0	20.8	NA	17.6
1980	84.7	43.7	17.3	26.3
1981	95.1	49.0	20.0	30.4
1982	109.5	58.3	22.9	34.3
1983	119.9	63.2	25.6	37.6
1984	127.6	70.4	28.6	40.0
1985	139.5	75.2	36.7	41.5
1986	143.4	75.5	40.6	43.5
1987	167.1	84.1	59.8	46.3
1988	189.9	98.2	71.1	51.2
1989	215.6	108.0	89.1	56.0
1990**	235.8	112.9	103.9	62.6
1991	256.2	116.4	123.4	67.1
1992	281.3	125.0	143.9	70.9

*Does not add to sum of types because of duplication among types.
**1990 revised.
NA: Not available.
SOURCE: Health Insurance Association of America, Annual Survey of Health Insurance Companies, Blue Cross/Blue Shield, and Group Health Association of America, Inc.

Table 2.10a

Private Health Insurance Premiums of Insurance Companies, Self-Insured, HMOs, and Blue Cross/Blue Shield (Billions)

Type of Insurer	1990	1991	1992
All Insurers	$235.8	$255.5	$281.3
Insurance companies	112.9	116.4	125.0
Group	100.2	103.0	110.4
Fully insured	44.8	44.0	45.5
ASO	37.2	44.1	49.0
MPP	18.3	15.0	15.9
Individual	12.7	13.3	14.6
Blue Cross/Blue Shield	62.6	67.1	70.9
Self-Insured	60.3	69.2	76.8
HMO	43.6	54.2	67.1
Blue Cross/Blue Shield	5.5	6.6	9.5
Insurance companies	6.5	8.4	9.9
Other	31.6	39.2	47.7

SOURCE: Health Insurance Association of America, Annual Survey of Health Insurance Companies.

Table 2.11

Group Health Insurance Premiums of Insurance Companies, by Type of Coverage (Billions)

Year	Total group	Hospital/ medical	Dental	Medicare supplement	Loss of income
1980	$ 36.8	$28.2	$3.2	$0.0	$5.3
1981	42.5	33.0	4.1	0.1	5.2
1982	50.0	39.6	4.8	0.1	5.5
1983	54.9	44.4	5.3	0.1	5.1
1984	60.8	49.6	5.7	0.5	5.0
1985	64.4	52.7	6.2	0.6	4.8
1986	65.9	53.0	6.2	1.8	5.0
1987	74.0	59.9	6.8	1.8	5.5
1988	87.6	71.9	7.8	2.5	5.5
1989	96.1	79.3	7.8	3.0	6.0
1990*	100.2	82.4	7.8	3.4	6.6
1991	103.0	85.0	7.6	4.2	6.2
1992	110.4	90.4	8.1	5.3	6.6

*1990 revised.
SOURCE: Health Insurance Association of America, Annual Survey of Health Insurance Companies.

Table 2.12

Group Health Insurance Premiums of Insurance Companies, by Type of Risk Management (Billions)

Year	Total group premiums	Fully insured		Administrative service only		Minimum premium plan	
		Hospital/ Medical	Loss of income	Hospital/ Medical	Loss of income	Hospital/ Medical	Loss of income
1980	$ 36.8	$23.0	$4.6	$2.4	$0.2	$6.1	$0.5
1981	42.5	22.4	4.1	4.0	0.3	10.9	0.9
1982	50.0	24.6	4.2	5.7	0.4	14.2	0.9
1983	54.9	27.5	3.8	6.1	0.5	16.2	0.9
1984	60.8	26.9	3.5	10.7	0.5	18.2	1.0
1985	64.4	27.6	3.5	13.1	0.6	18.8	0.8
1986	65.9	27.1	3.4	15.4	0.8	18.4	0.8
1987	74.0	30.7	3.7	18.7	1.0	19.1	0.7
1988	87.5	36.9	3.8	25.2	1.1	20.0	0.6
1989	96.1	39.0	4.4	30.8	1.1	20.3	0.5
1990*	100.2	40.0	4.8	35.9	1.3	17.8	0.4
1991	103.0	39.4	4.6	42.8	1.2	14.6	0.4
1992	110.4	40.8	4.7	47.8	1.2	15.4	0.5

*1990 revised.
SOURCE: Health Insurance Association of America, Annual Survey of Health Insurance Companies.

Table 2.13

Individual Health Insurance Premiums of Insurance Companies, by Type of Coverage (Billions)

Year	Total individual	Hospital/ medical	Loss of income
1980	$ 6.9	$ 4.9	$2.0
1981	6.5	4.7	1.8
1982	8.3	5.8	2.5
1983	8.3	6.3	2.0
1984	9.6	7.2	2.4
1985	10.8	7.9	2.9
1986	9.6	6.7	2.9
1987	10.1	7.0	3.1
1988	10.6	7.4	3.2
1989	11.8	8.2	3.6
1990	12.7	8.9	3.8
1991	13.3	10.0	3.3
1992	14.6	10.3	4.3

SOURCE: Health Insurance Association of America, Annual Survey of Insurance Companies.

Table 2.14

Number, Enrollment, Rank, Population, and Penetration of HMOs, by State, 1993

State	Population (thousands)	Enrollment (thousands)	Total HMOs	Penetration percentage
Massachusetts	5,985	2,312.3	16	38.6
California	30,797	11,076.8	43	36.0
Minnesota	4,460	1,433.0	10	32.1
Oregon	2,870	890.7	9	31.0
Colorado	3,382	937.1	15	27.7
Maryland	5,016	1,365.6	15	27.2
Rhode Island	1,012	265.6	3	26.2
Arizona	3,955	1,018.7	11	25.8
Wisconsin	4,193	1,170.6	25	23.8
New York	17,886	4,239.0	36	23.7
Utah	1,781	420.6	9	23.6
Hawaii	1,206	252.7	5	21.0
Connecticut	3,320	653.6	10	19.7
Ohio	10,950	2,092.9	37	19.1
Michigan	9,346	1,711.5	17	18.3
Pennsylvania	12,075	2,175.8	21	18.0
Washington	4,968	892.0	9	18.0
Illinois	11,745	2,091.8	26	17.8
Florida	13,915	2,406.8	39	17.3
Delaware	716	121.7	4	17.0
Missouri	5,298	885.6	17	16.7
New Mexico	1,599	267.1	5	16.7
New Hampshire	1,222	181.8	2	14.9
Nevada	1,226	161.6	4	13.2
New Jersey	7,981	1,008.1	8	12.6
Texas	17,391	2,149.7	26	12.4
Kentucky	3,749	416.3	6	11.1
Vermont	587	62.7	1	10.7
Oklahoma	3,122	309.1	6	9.9
Virginia	6,549	603.5	13	9.2
Georgia	7,008	581.6	9	8.3
Kansas	2,543	204.7	10	8.1
Maine	1,273	99.6	2	7.8
Indiana	5,670	432.3	14	7.6
Louisiana	4,316	315.0	10	7.3
Nebraska	1,594	114.6	6	7.2
Alabama	4,242	296.0	9	7.0
North Carolina	6,994	462.5	10	6.6
Tennessee	5,155	287.2	10	5.6
Iowa	2,755	113.4	4	4.1
South Carolina	3,691	122.0	4	3.3
South Dakota	719	20.0	1	2.8
Arkansas	2,454	67.4	4	2.7
Montana	784	10.7	1	1.4
Idaho	1,019	13.8	1	1.4
North Dakota	643	6.2	2	1.0
Mississippi	2,692	1.5	1	0.1
Total USA	252,574	46,722.5	546	18.5

Table 2.15

HMO Monthly Premiums, by Region, 1992

Region	Individual	Family
New England Connecticut, Maine, Massachusetts, New Hampshire, Rhode Island, and Vermont	$147.12	$300.73
Middle Atlantic New Jersey, New York, and Pennsylvania	$125.13	$323.29
South Atlantic Delaware, Florida, Georgia, Maryland, North Carolina, South Carolina, Virginia, and West Virginia	$124.59	$340.72
Midwest Illinois, Indiana, Iowa, Kansas, Michigan, Minnesota, Missouri, Nebraska, North Dakota, Ohio, South Dakota, and Wisconsin	$120.19	$332.17
South Central Alabama, Arkansas, Kentucky, Louisiana, Mississippi, Oklahoma, Tennessee, and Texas	$112.56	$315.87
Mountain Arizona, Colorado, Idaho, Montana, Nevada, New Mexico, Utah, and Wyoming	$118.49	$324.53
Pacific Alaska, California, Hawaii, Washington, and Oregon	$118.28	$330.53

SOURCE: Group Health Association of America, 1992

Table 2.16

Percentage of HMOs Using Various Utilization Review Measures to Control Costs

Utilization review measures	Percentage of plans using measures
Inpatient utilization review	99.8
Concurrent review of hospital stays	98.4
Discharge planning	96.9
Preadmission certification of hospital admissions	96.4
Catastrophic case management	96.1
Outpatient utilization review	95.1
Retrospective review of admissions	94.9
Referral authorization for non-plan providers	93.8
Cost/utilization feedback to physicians	90.4
Second surgical opinion	62.0

SOURCE: The InterStudy Competitive Edge, Vol. 2, 1993.

Table 2.17

Percent Change in HMO Penetration Rates, by State, 1989–1993

States	HMO penetration rates (percentage)				1992–1993 Increase or decrease (%)
	1989	1991	1992	1993	
Total all states	14	15	13	17	31
Alabama	5	7	6	7	16
Alaska	0	0	0	0	0
Arizona	24	24	23	33	43
Arkansas	2	2	3	3	0
California	31	33	35	35	0
Colorado	21	22	23	23	0
Connecticut	21	21	19	25	32
Delaware	15	17	16	17	6
Florida	11	13	15	17	13
Georgia	5	6	7	7	0
Hawaii	22	22	22	23	-5
Idaho	2	2	2	1	0
Illinois	13	13	17	16	-6
Indiana	7	6	7	7	0
Iowa	9	11	4	4	0
Kansas	9	8	9	8	-11
Kentucky	9	6	7	7	0
Louisiana	6	7	8	7	-13
Maine	3	3	4	4	0
Maryland	17	22	26	32	23
Massachusetts	25	30	29	34	17
Michigan	16	16	17	18	6
Minnesota	28	28	30	32	7
Mississippi	0	0	0	0	0
Missouri	14	14	14	14	21
Montana	0	1	1	1	0
Nebraska	6	6	7	7	0
Nevada	10	9	10	13	30
New Hampshire	10	10	12	14	17
New Jersey	10	12	14	13	-7
New Mexico	12	14	16	16	0
New York	15	17	18	21	17
North Carolina	4	5	5	7	40
North Dakota	2	1	1	1	0
Ohio	13	13	19	15	-21
Oklahoma	5	7	6	7	17
Oregon	24	26	30	32	7
Pennsylvania	12	14	15	19	27
Rhode Island	22	20	23	26	13
South Carolina	2	2	3	3	0
South Dakota	4	3	3	3	0
Tennessee	5	4	5	6	20
Texas	7	8	10	10	0
Utah	15	17	21	19	-10
Vermont	6	9	10	11	10
Virginia	6	6	7	7	0
Washington	15	14	15	15	0
West Virginia	0	0	0	0	0
Wisconsin	23	22	22	23	5
Wyoming	0	0	0	0	0

SOURCE: Group Health Association of America; HMO Market Penetration, April 1993, and Marion Merrel Dow Managed Care Digest/Update Edition 1993.

Table 2.18

Type and Number of Operating PPOs, and Covered Employees, Excluding Workers' Compensation

Type of ownership	Number of PPOs	Medical/surgical plans covered employees		Specialty only covered employees		Medical/surgical, specialty, and other covered employees	
		Total	Average	Total	Average	Total	Average
Employer/ employee coalition	8	412,200	58,886	NA	NA	412,200	58,886
HMO	16	898,399	74,867	NA	NA	898,399	74,867
Hospital	32	1,264,647	46,839	90,000	90,000	1,354,647	48,380
Hospital alliance	32	1,719,882	53,746	NA	NA	1,719,882	53,746
Independent investor	161	27,088,241	248,516	4,549,048	239,424	31,637,289	247,166
Insurance company	288	14,371,169	64,445	32,000	32,000	10,403,169	64,300
Multi-ownership	23	1,536,041	80,844	52,000	52,000	1,588,041	79,402
Physician/hospital joint venture	46	1,932,880	46,021	NA	NA	1,932,880	46,021
Physician/medical group	28	957,544	45,597	NA	NA	957,544	45,597
Third-party administrator	20	(4,620,045)	(288,753)	3,051,915	1,017,305	(1,568,130)	(82,533)
Other	27	4,382,600	199,209	321,245	80,311	4,703,845	180,917
Size of PPO with workers' compensation							
1 to 19,999	226	1,337,497	6,080	37,806	7,561	1,375,303	6,112
20,000 to 99,999	194	8,245,542	45,058	565,395	51,400	8,810,937	45,417
100,000 to 49,999	93	16,057,331	191,159	2,068,007	229,779	18,125,338	194,896
500,000 to 999,999	14	6,684,732	557,061	1,075,000	537,500	7,759,732	554,267
1,000,000+	20	22,618,456	1,256,581	4,350,000	2,175,000	26,968,456	1,348,423
Size of PPO without workers' compensation							
1 to 19,999	229	1,402,348	6,289	37,806	7,551	1,440,154	6,316
20,000 to 99,999	196	8,676,095	46,898	565,395	51,400	9,241,490	47,150
100,000 to 49,999	94	17,499,813	205,880	2,068,807	229,779	19,567,820	208,168
500,000 to 999,999	11	6,538,746	726,527	1,075,000	537,500	7,613,746	692,159
1,000,000+	14	20,826,556	1,735,546	4,350,000	2,175,000	25,176,556	1,798,325

NA: Not available.
SOURCE: SMG Marketing Group, Inc., 1993.

Table 2.19

PPO Enrollment, Number of Plans, and Enrollment as a Percentage of Population

State or territory	Number of plans 12/31/92	PPO enrollment 12/31/92	Percentage of population	Number of plans 10/31/93
Total U.S.	879	50,477,748	19.5	895
Alabama	26	1,094,952	26.5	27
Alaska	3	5,176	0.9	3
American Samoa	0	0	0.0	0
Arizona	26	5,274,414	NA	26
Arkansas	4	9,704	0.4	4
California	77	10,752,067	34.8	77
Colorado	33	1,317,134	38.0	33
Connecticut	9	75,036	2.3	10
Delaware	4	68	NA	4
District of Columbia	9	678,717	NA	9
Florida	59	3,607,528	26.7	61
Georgia	26	671,442	9.9	26
Guam	0	0	0.0	0
Hawaii	3	404,449	†	3
Idaho	1	0	0.0	1
Illinois	33	4,956,671	42.6	33
Indiana	23	2,425,270	42.8	24
Iowa	9	189,464	6.7	9
Kansas	16	405,434	16.1	17
Kentucky	10	40,426	1.1	11
Louisiana	28	724,036	16.9	28
Maine	5	6,616	0.5	5
Maryland	17	771,254	15.7	17
Masschusetts	21	334,984	5.6	21
Michigan	22	1,353,358	14.3	24
Minnesota	14	777,972	17.4	15
Mississippi	5	21,649	0.8	6
Missouri	21	675,716	13.0	21
Montana	0	0	0.0	0
Nebraska	8	558,514	NA	8
Nevada	13	275,898	20.8	13
New Hampshire	6	38,100	3.4	6
New Jersey	17	308,689	4.0	17
New Mexico	5	36,902	2.3	5
New York	19	1,947,263	10.7	20
North Carolina	23	654,086	9.6	23
North Dakota	0	0	0.0	0
N. Mariana Islands	0	0	0.0	0
Ohio	44	1,096,416	10.0	44
Oklahoma	14	193,977	6.0	14
Oregon	9	416,846	14.0	9
Pennsylvania	49	974,783	8.1	50
Puerto Rico	1	55,000	1.5	1
Rhode Island	2	13,828	1.4	2
South Carolina	10	323,930	9.0	10
South Dakota	1	7,316	1.0	1
Tennessee	29	1,359,357	27.1	29
Texas	62	2,706,441	15.3	62
U. S. Virgin Islands	0	0	0.0	0

Continued

Table 2.19 *(Continued)*

State or territory	Number of plans 12/31/92	PPO enrollment 12/31/92	Percentage of population	Number of plans 10/31/93
Utah	9	404,523	22.3	11
Vermont	1	0	NA	1
Virginia	13	581,986	9.1	14
Washington	21	1,395,219	27.2	21
West Virginia	4	36,780	2.0	4
Wisconsin	15	488,357	9.8	15
Wyoming	0	0	0.0	0

†Some plans included dependents; no percentage was calculated if this affected the state's figure significantly.
NA: Not available.
SOURCE: AMCRA Foundation.

Table 2.20

Percentage of PPOs Providing Selected Coverages, by Type of Ownership, 1992

Type	General coverage	Mental health	Pharma-ceutical	Chiro-practic	Vision	Workers' Comp	Wellness program	Long-term care	Dental	Other
Employer/employee coalition	87.5	37.5	37.5	37.5	25.0	12.5	NA	12.5	12.5	12.5
HMO	100.0	87.5	68.8	50.0	56.3	25.0	62.5	31.3	37.5	12.5
Hospital	96.9	81.3	59.4	37.5	25.0	37.5	37.5	21.9	21.9	21.9
Hospital alliance	96.9	87.5	56.3	40.6	34.4	43.8	34.4	15.6	9.4	12.5
Independent investor	81.4	83.9	54.0	66.5	55.3	68.3	28.6	37.9	53.4	46.0
Insurance company	99.0	66.0	64.2	40.3	27.1	18.1	29.9	33.7	17.7	19.1
Multi-ownership	87.0	82.6	47.8	56.5	26.1	39.1	21.7	17.4	17.4	13.0
Physician/hospital joint venture	100.0	78.3	45.7	15.2	43.5	34.8	52.2	23.9	19.6	15.2
Physician/medical group	89.3	50.0	21.4	39.3	25.0	25.0	25.0	14.3	14.3	17.9
Third-party administrator	85.0	70.0	60.0	53.0	40.0	20.0	20.0	25.0	45.0	10.0
Other	85.2	77.8	37.0	44.4	29.6	37.0	33.3	18.5	33.3	33.3

NA: Not available.
SOURCE: SMG Marketing Group Inc., 1993.

Table 2.21

Percentage of Employees Subject to Utilization Management, by Plan Type, 1991 and 1992

Method	Conventional Plans 1991	1992	Preferred Provider Organizations 1991	1992	Point-of-Service Plans 1991	1992
Preadmission (inpatient)	80	78	90	88	85	92
Utilization review	71	72	84	83	84	96
Mandatory second opinion (surgery)	46	40	53	47	55	59
Large claims management	71	73	87	84	89	96
Ambulatory surgery (incentive)	39	31	48	44	48	31
Penalty for non-urgent emergency	35	35	43	51	69	65
Mental health	50	NA	61	NA	86	NA

NA: Not available.
SOURCE: 1992 HIAA Employers Survey.

Table 2.22

Supplemental Medical Insurance of Medicare over 65 Population, by Age

Age group	Percentage of enrollees	Total	Medicare only	Private individual purchase	Private employer purchase	Private both	Medicaid	Medicare and other
Total	100.0	29,176	3,324	10,725	9,621	1,467	3,459	581
65–69 years	29.4	8,570	954	2,817	3,553	498	676	72
70–74 years	27.2	7,931	817	3,034	2,842	442	702	95
75–79 years	20.0	5,840	633	2,319	1,826	264	666	131
80–84 years	13.4	3,897	460	1,579	946	167	626	119
85 years/over	10.1	2,938	460	975	454	96	790	164
Insurance percentage share								
Total		100.0	11.4	36.8	33.0	5.0	11.9	2.0
65–69 years		100.0	11.1	32.9	41.5	5.8	7.9	0.8
70–74 years		100.0	10.3	38.3	35.8	5.6	8.9	1.2
75–79 years		100.0	10.8	39.7	31.6	4.5	11.4	2.2
80–84 years		100.0	11.8	40.5	24.3	4.3	16.1	3.1
85 years/over		100.0	15.7	33.2	15.5	3.3	26.9	5.6

SOURCE: U. S. Department of Health and Human Services, HCFA Review Spring 1993.

Table 2.23

Number of Employees and Insured Employees by Establishment, by Employment-Size Class in Major Groups, 1992

Major group	Total number of employees (millions)	Total number of establishments	Establishment size by number of employees						Number of employees age 18–64 (millions)
			Under 20 (millions)	20–49 (millions)	50–99 (millions)	100–499 (millions)	500–999 (millions)	1,000 or more (millions)	
Total	135,784	2,001	1,284	276	164	161	31	25	125.1
Self-employed	12,400	NA	NA	NA	NA	NA	NA	NA	12.4
Government	19,367	NA	NA	NA	NA	NA	NA	NA	19.4
Agricultural, forestry and fishing	14,735	87	45	5	6	11	8	1	2.2
Mining	103,710	1,533	930	243	143	135	22	19	0.7
Construction	13,218	103	70	7	6	40	1	5	5.5
Manufacturing	353	15	9	3	3	0	0	0	20.2
Transportation and public utilities	2,407	44	29	4	3	4	0	0	6.6
Wholesale trade	344	84	80	4	0	0	0	0	4.2
Retail trade	474	90	84	5	1	0	0	0	19.4
Finance, insurance and real estate	129	12	10	1	1	0	0	0	6.9
Services	399	22	16	4	1	1	0	0	27.8
Unclassified establishments	15	11	11	0	0	0	0	0	NA

NOTE: Services includes business, repair, personal, entertainment, recreation, and professional services.

NA: Not available.

SOURCE: Bureau of the Census, County Business Patterns, February 1994, and January 1994 EBRI Analysis of the March 1993 CPS.

Chapter 3

PUBLIC HEALTH CARE COVERAGE: EXPENDITURES AND ENROLLMENT

◆ Federal, State, and Local Health Care Programs

In 1992, HCFA estimated that all levels of government combined spent $377 billion to fund medical and health care services, research, and medical facility construction. The government share represented nearly 46 percent of the total national health expenditure.

Government health expenditures increased by over 16 percent between 1991 and 1992, compared with 7 percent for total public and private expenditures. Per capita government expenditures were $1,442 for 1992. HCFA projects a government expenditure of nearly $880 billion by the year 2000.

◆ Federal Programs

The majority of federal health spending is for health services provided to six major groups: low-income individuals and others eligible for Medicaid, those over age 65 (Medicare), military personnel and their dependents, veterans, federal civilian employees, and Native Americans.

Medicare

Effective since July 1, 1966, Medicare is a federally administered program that provides hospital and medical insurance protection to persons age 65 and older, disabled persons under age 65 who receive cash benefits under Social Security or Railroad Retirement programs, and people of all ages with chronic kidney disease. Since 1973, aliens and some federal civil service employees and annuitants have been eligible to enroll by paying a monthly premium.

Many aged or disabled persons who are covered by Medicare also are covered by Medicaid. Where this dual coverage exists, most state Medicaid programs pay the Medicare premiums, deductibles, and copayments and, in some cases, pay for services not covered by Medicare.

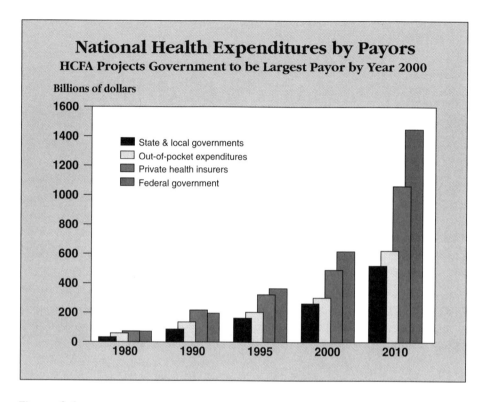

National Health Expenditures by Payors
HCFA Projects Government to be Largest Payor by Year 2000

Billions of dollars

Legend:
- State & local governments
- Out-of-pocket expenditures
- Private health insurers
- Federal government

Figure 3.1

SOURCE: Health Care Reform Project, April 1993.

Medicare consists of compulsory hospitalization insurance (HI), called Part A, and voluntary supplementary medical insurance (SMI), called Part B, which pays for physicians' services, medical services, and supplies not covered under Part A. Part A is financed by contributions from employers, employees, and participants; Part B is voluntary and is financed by monthly premiums paid by those who enroll and by the federal government.

In 1992, 407,495 physicians, 52.2 percent of the total number practicing in the United States, participated in Medicare.

On January 1, 1994, Medicare's Part A deductible rose from $676 to $696. The monthly Part B premium also increased, from $36.60 to $41.10. For 1994, the daily coinsurance amount was $174 for the 61st day of hospitalization through the 90th day and $87 for the 21st through the 100th day of extended care in a skilled nursing facility. The part B deductible remained at $100.

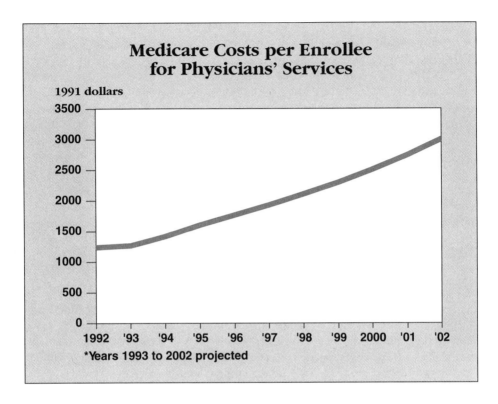

Figure 3.2

SOURCE: Medicare Board of Trustees Report 1993.

Blue Cross/Blue Shield plans and several other independent organizations serve as fiscal intermediaries for the government.

More than 6,100 hospitals have an agreement to participate under the Medicare prospective payment system (PPS). Exceptions include psychiatric and children's hospitals, hospitals for long-term care and rehabilitation, and medical facilities that have an approved waiver.

Enrollment in the Medicare program increased from 35.6 million persons in 1992 to 36.2 million persons in 1993. Medicare spending for personal health care grew 10.6 percent in 1993. Nearly $143 billion was paid by the federal government on behalf of Medicare enrollees in 1993; according to HCFA, approximately 30 percent of these Medicare funds are spent taking care of elderly people during their last year of life. Hospital and physician services, the two major components of the Medicare personal health care bill, increased over 11 percent each (Table 3.6).

With an increase in this country's population and longer life expectancies, the Medicare program enrollment will continue to climb in the coming years. HCFA projects Medicare expenditures of $191.0 billion in 1995 and $327.6 billion in 2000, a 71 percent increase by the end of the decade. Indeed, HCFA indicates that by 2050 there will be 69 million people age 65 years or older who will be eligible for Medicare. Of this number, 15 million will be age 85 or older.

Medicaid

Administered by each state according to federal requirements and guidelines, Medicaid is financed from both state and federal funds. It provides medical assistance to persons who are eligible for cash assistance programs such as Aid to Families of Dependent Children (AFDC) and Supplemental Security Income (SSI). Medicaid benefits also may be available to other persons who have enough income for basic living expenses but cannot afford to pay for their medical care.

States have broad discretion in covering different groups under their Medicaid programs as well as financial criteria for Medicaid eligiblity. To be eligible for federal funds, however, states must provide Medicaid coverage for the majority of those individuals who receive federally assisted income-maintenance payments and related groups not receiving cash payments.

In order to qualify for federal matching funds, the law requires that state programs include inpatient and outpatient hospital services, laboratory and x-ray services, and skilled nursing and home health services for individuals age 21 and older. Services such as periodic screening, diagnosis, and treatment, family planning for children under age 21, and physicians' services also must be provided. While state participation in Medicaid is optional, all 50 states participate.

As indicated in Table 3.4, the Medicaid program paid $101.7 billion for services given to 33.4 million recipients in 1993.

Projections by HCFA indicate an aggregate Medicaid growth averaging 15.5 percent per year through 1995, amounting to outlays of $154.1 billion. The projection for the second half of the decade shows a slowing of annual growth to 9.6 percent, ending the decade with a projected $359.8 billion on Medicaid spending.

Utilization of Medicare Services

Over 36 million Americans received services paid for by Medicare in 1993. HCFA data for fiscal year 1993 shows that Medicare paid almost $143 billion

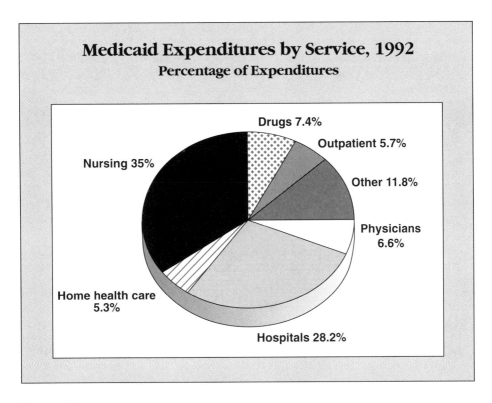

Medicaid Expenditures by Service, 1992
Percentage of Expenditures

Drugs 7.4%

Outpatient 5.7%

Nursing 35%

Other 11.8%

Physicians 6.6%

Home health care 5.3%

Hospitals 28.2%

Figure 3.3

SOURCE: HCFA. Division of Medicaid Statistics, unpublished data.

to recipients. The average Medicare benefit payment per enrollee was $3,940 for fiscal year 1993.

It is estimated that if expenditures continue at the current rate with no significant changes in the program, total trust fund disbursements for Medicare will reach $189 billion by fiscal year 1995 and might exceed $310 billion by the year 2000.

Utilization of Medicaid

There were an estimated 38 million persons eligible for Medicaid in 1993. Of these, 33.4 million received at least some service under the program. Total outlays for the Medicaid program were $76.9 billion in 1991; $97.1 for 1992; and $101.7 billion in 1993, plus administrative costs. Federal outlays for the Medicaid program increased 47 percent between 1992 and 1993.

The largest premium outlays to Medicaid-approved state qualified and provisional health maintenance organizations was paid to HMOs in the states of California, Florida, and Alabama. Provisional HMOs in North Carolina, Minnesota and the District of Columbia combined received over $400 million in 1992 (Table 3.5).

Medicaid Enrollment in Managed Care Programs

In 1993, Medicaid beneficiaries were less likely than the general population to enroll in managed care plans. For example, 5 percent (1.7 million) of Medicaid beneficiaries are enrolled in HMOs, compared with more than 19 percent of the general population. (According to the GHAA, only about 20 percent of HMOs have Medicaid contracts.)

◆ Other Government Services

Federal Civilian Employees

The Federal Employees Health Benefits Program (FEHBP) provides voluntary health insurance coverage for approximately 8.4 million federal government employees: 2.4 million active employees, 1.7 million annuitants, and 4.3 million dependents. Approximately 87 percent of all federal employees and annuitants were enrolled in FEHBP in 1993; the remaining 13 percent were either ineligible or had waived FEHBP coverage. The annual cost is an estimated $14.5 billion in 1993.

Employees covered by FEHBP choose among competing health plans with varying levels of benefits and premiums during an annual open enrollment period. The FEHBP offers three major types of plans: government-wide plans that, beginning in 1990, include only a service benefit plan administered by the National Blue Cross and Blue Shield Association; employee organization plans that are sponsored by employee organizations or unions and are open only to employees or annuitants who become members of the sponsoring organization; and comprehensive medical plans, or HMOs, that offer health care by designated plan physicians, hospitals, and other providers in designated geographic locations. There are approximately 347 HMOs in FEHBP, 35 of which offer two options.

The federal government and enrollees jointly finance the program through premium payments, with the government paying approximately 75 percent of the average of all plan premiums. The Office of Personnel Management (OPM) administers FEHBP.

59

Military Personnel and Dependents

■ Treatment at any Department of Defense medical facility is available to all active and retired military personnel and their dependents. The Civilian Health and Medical Program for the Uniformed Services (CHAMPUS) covers military families unable to use government medical facilities because of distance, overcrowding, or unavailability of appropriate medical treatment. ■ After a deductible is met, CHAMPUS pays for medical care. Retired military personnel, their dependents, and dependents of deceased personnel are compensated by CHAMPUS if they are not eligible for Medicare. ■ The Office of Defense Health Affairs projects $4.7 billion in benefits for over 5 million eligible personnel in the year 2000.		Billions of dollars	Eligibles
	1996	4,152	5,367,830
	1997	4,484	5,264,114
	1998	4,295	5,173,265
	1999	4,505	5,099,834
	2000	4,728	5,030,603
	2001	4,963	4,972,720

Figure 3.4

SOURCE: Office of Assistant Secretary of Defense, Health Affairs.

In addition to federal payment of the employer contributions under these programs, the government also incurs administrative expenses for the operation of on-site health care facilities for federal civilian employees.

Veterans' Medical Care

The government budgeted $3.4 billion for Veterans Administration (VA) medical care and research in 1993. The Veterans Administration operates 154 medical centers for the care of individuals who served honorably in the armed forces. Patients with service-related ailments receive top priority.

Characteristically, users of the VA medical system are older; often, they are members of minority groups. (However, minority and female users tend to be younger than the general system user.) VA medical system users also have less education than veterans in general regardless of gender, race, ethnicity, age, or period of service. Only half are married, compared with nearly 80 percent of all other veterans. They also are more likely to have served during the Korean conflict than veterans in general; and officers are relatively rare among them. About two-fifths are eligible for service-connected disability compensation, including nearly half of those under 35.

Indian Health Services

More than $2.3 billion in federal funds was spent in 1993 to provide medical care and health services for approximately 1.8 million Native Americans, including Alaskan natives.

Table 3.1

Medicare Enrollment and Benefit Payments, Fiscal Years 1967–1993

Year	Hospital and/or medical insurance Parts A and B		Hospital insurance Part A		Supplementary medical insurance Part B	
	Enrolled persons (millions)	Benefit payments (billions)	Enrolled persons (millions)	Benefit payments (billions)	Enrolled persons (millions)	Benefit payments (billions)
All enrollees						
1967	19.5	$ 3.1	19.5	$ 2.5	17.9	$ 0.7
1968	19.8	5.1	19.8	3.7	18.8	1.4
1969	20.1	6.3	10.0	4.7	19.2	1.6
1970	20.5	6.8	20.4	4.8	19.6	1.9
1971	20.9	7.5	20.7	5.4	19.9	2.1
1972	21.3	8.4	21.1	6.1	20.4	2.3
1973	23.5	9.0	23.3	6.6	22.5	2.4
1974	24.2	10.7	23.9	7.8	23.2	2.9
1975	25.0	14.1	24.6	10.4	23.9	3.8
1976	25.7	16.9	25.3	12.2	24.6	4.7
1977	26.5	20.8	26.1	14.9	25.4	5.9
1978	27.1	24.3	26.8	17.4	26.1	6.9
1979	27.9	28.1	27.5	19.9	26.8	8.3
1980	28.5	33.9	28.1	23.8	27.4	10.1
1981	29.1	41.2	28.6	28.9	27.9	12.3
1982	29.5	49.2	29.1	34.3	28.4	14.8
1983	30.1	55.6	29.6	37.1	28.9	17.5
1984	30.5	60.9	30.0	41.5	29.4	19.5
1985	31.1	69.5	30.6	47.7	29.9	21.8
1986	31.8	74.1	31.2	48.8	30.6	25.2
1987	32.4	79.8	31.9	49.8	31.2	29.9
1988	32.9	85.5	32.4	51.8	31.6	33.7
1989	33.6	94.1	33.1	57.2	32.1	36.9
1990	34.2	107.2	33.7	65.7	32.6	41.5
1991	34.9	114.0	34.4	68.5	33.2	45.5
1992	35.6	129.2	36.2	80.6	35.4	48.6
1993	36.3	142.9	NA	NA	NA	NA
Enrollees age 65 and older						
1967	19.5	3.2	19.5	2.5	17.9	0.7
1968	19.8	5.1	19.7	3.7	18.8	1.3
1969	20.1	6.3	20.1	4.7	19.2	1.6
1970	20.5	6.8	20.4	4.8	19.6	1.9
1971	20.9	7.4	20.7	5.4	19.9	2.1
1972	21.3	8.3	21.2	6.1	20.4	2.3
1973	21.8	9.0	21.6	6.6	20.9	2.4
1974	22.3	9.6	21.9	7.1	21.4	2.5
1975	22.8	12.7	22.5	9.4	21.9	3.3
1976	23.3	15.1	22.9	11.0	22.4	4.4
1977	23.8	18.6	23.5	13.3	22.9	5.0
1978	24.4	21.0	23.9	15.4	23.5	5.8
1979	24.9	24.4	24.6	17.5	24.1	6.9
1980	25.5	29.4	25.1	20.9	24.7	8.5
1981	26.1	35.9	25.6	25.5	25.2	10.4
1982	26.5	42.6	26.1	30.2	25.7	12.4

Continued

62

Table 3.1 *(Continued)*

Year	Hospital and/or medical insurance Parts A and B		Hospital insurance Part A		Supplementary medical insurance Part B	
	Enrolled persons (millions)	Benefit payments (billions)	Enrolled persons (millions)	Benefit payments (billions)	Enrolled persons (millions)	Benefit payments (billions)
1983	27.1	$ 48.4	26.7	$33.6	26.3	$14.8
1984	27.6	53.6	27.1	36.8	26.8	16.8
1985	28.2	64.5	27.7	42.4	27.3	19.1
1986	28.8	65.5	28.3	43.4	27.9	22.1
1987	29.4	70.6	28.8	44.2	28.3	26.4
1988	29.9	75.9	29.3	46.1	28.8	29.8
1989	30.4	83.4	29.9	50.7	29.2	32.7
1990	30.9	85.1	30.5	58.3	29.7	36.8
1991	31.5	101.0	31.1	60.8	30.2	40.2
1992	33.0	114.4	32.6	71.6	32.0	42.8
1993	NA	NA	NA	NA	NA	NA

NOTE: Totals may not add because of rounding.
NA: Not available.
SOURCE: Department of Health and Human Services, Health Care Financing Administration, Bureau of Data Management and Strategy.

Table 3.2

Beneficiaries, Age 65 and Older, Enrolled in Medicare, by Age, Race, and Gender, 1991 (Millions)

Age	Hospital and supplemental medical insurance	Hospital insurance	Supplemental medical insurance
Men			
Age 65–69	4.8	4.8	4.4
Age 70–74	3.6	3.5	3.4
Age 75–79	2.5	2.5	2.5
Age 80–84	1.5	1.5	1.4
Age 85 & older	1.1	1.0	1.0
Women			
Age 65–69	5.8	5.7	5.4
Age 70–74	4.7	4.6	4.6
Age 75–79	3.8	3.7	3.7
Age 80–84	2.7	2.7	2.7
Age 85 & older	2.6	2.6	2.5
White			
Men			
Age 65–69	4.1	4.0	3.7
Age 70–74	3.1	3.1	3.0
Age 75–79	2.2	2.2	2.2
Age 80–84	1.3	1.3	1.3
Age 85 & older	0.9	0.9	0.9
Women			
Age 65–69	4.8	4.8	4.6
Age 70–74	4.1	4.0	3.9
Age 75–79	3.3	3.3	3.3
Age 80–84	2.4	2.4	2.4
Age 85 & older	2.3	2.3	2.5
Other			
Men			
Age 65–69	0.5	0.5	0.5
Age 70–74	0.3	0.3	0.3
Age 75–79	0.2	0.2	0.2
Age 80–84	0.1	0.1	0.1
Age 85 & older	0.1	0.1	0.1
Women			
Age 65–69	0.7	0.7	0.7
Age 70–74	0.5	0.5	0.5
Age 75–79	0.4	0.3	0.4
Age 80–84	0.2	0.2	0.2
Age 85 & older	0.2	0.2	0.2

NOTE: Numbers do not add due to rounding.
SOURCE: U. S. Department of Health and Human Services, Health Care Financing Administration.

Table 3.3

Medicare and Medicaid Expenditures, 1991 and 1992 (Billions)

Type of expenditures	1991		1992	
	Medicare	Medicaid	Medicare	Medicaid
Health services and supplies	$122.9	$98.2	$137.7	$129.3
Personal health care	120.3	94.1	135.0	124.6
Hospital care	74.3	40.6	82.1	57.5
Physician services	33.9	6.7	39.1	8.3
Dental services	NA	0.9	NA	1.2
Other professional services	3.5	2.8	4.0	3.6
Home health care	3.6	2.6	4.3	3.3
Drugs and other medical non-durables	NA	6.1	NA	7.3
Vision products and other medical durables	2.4	NA	2.8	NA
Nursing home care	2.6	28.7	2.7	34.4
Other personal health care	NA	5.7	NA	9.1
Program administration	2.6	4.2	2.7	4.7
Percent of national programs' expenditures				
Health services and supplies	17.2	13.8	17.3	16.3
Personal health care	18.5	14.5	18.6	17.1
Hospital care	26.1	14.2	25.3	17.7
Physician services	24.6	4.8	25.7	5.5
Dental services	NA	2.5	NA	3.2
Other professional services	9.7	7.9	9.9	8.9
Home health care	42.8	31.0	41.9	32.4
Drugs and other medical non-durables	NA	10.2	NA	11.2
Vision products and other medical durables	19.4	NA	21.2	NA
Nursing home care	4.3	48.2	4.1	51.8
Other personal health care	NA	41.4	NA	51.8
Program administration	6.1	9.8	6.0	10.5

NA: Not available.
SOURCE: Health Care Financing Review, Fall 1992.

Table 3.3a

Medicare and Medicaid Expenditures Projected for 1995 and 2000 (Billions)

Type of expenditures	1995		2000	
	Medicare	Medicaid	Medicare	Medicaid
Health services and supplies	$191.0	$202.2	$327.6	$359.8
Personal health care	187.8	195.5	323.3	348.6
Hospital care	113.6	91.8	191.0	162.1
Physician services	55.7	13.5	104.1	24.9
Dental services	NA	1.7	NA	2.5
Other professional services	5.5	6.1	9.0	12.5
Home health care	5.9	6.8	9.0	15.8
Drugs and other medical non-durables	NA	11.1	NA	19.5
Vision products and other medical durables	3.8	NA	5.8	NA
Nursing home care	3.2	46.9	4.4	72.1
Other personal health care	NA	17.6	NA	39.2
Program administration	3.2	6.6	4.3	11.2
Percent of national programs' expenditures				
Health services and supplies	17.8	18.9	19.3	21.2
Personal health care	19.0	19.8	20.6	22.2
Hospital care	25.8	20.8	27.2	23.1
Physician services	27.0	6.5	30.2	7.2
Dental services	NA	3.6	NA	4.0
Other professional services	9.9	11.1	10.8	15.2
Home health care	35.9	41.5	29.5	51.9
Drugs and other medical non-durables	NA	13.2	NA	15.6
Vision products and other medical durables	22.2	NA	23.2	NA
Nursing home care	3.9	51.6	3.5	49.0
Other personal health care	NA	56.1	NA	72.4
Program administration	5.9	11.2	5.7	13.3

NA: Not available.
SOURCE: Health Care Financing Review, Fall 1992.

Table 3.4

Medicaid Recipients and Benefits Paid by Federal and State Governments*

Fiscal year	Poverty population	Annual recipients (millions)	Total annual benefits paid (billions)	Age 65 and over		Dependent children		All others	
				Annual recipients (millions)	Annual benefits paid (billions)	Annual recipients (millions)	Annual benefits paid (billions)	Annual recipients (millions)	Annual benefits paid (billions)
1972	24.6	19.6	$ 6.3	3.3	$ 1.9	11.1	$ 2.1	2.3	$ 2.3
1973	22.9	19.6	8.7	3.5	3.2	12.7	2.9	3.4	2.5
1974	23.4	21.5	9.9	3.7	3.7	13.9	3.4	3.9	2.9
1975	25.9	22.0	12.2	3.6	4.4	14.1	4.2	4.3	3.6
1976	24.9	22.8	14.1	3.6	4.9	14.7	4.7	4.5	4.5
1977	24.7	22.8	16.2	3.6	5.5	14.4	5.2	4.8	5.5
1978	24.5	22.0	17.9	3.4	6.3	14.1	5.4	4.6	6.3
1979	25.4	21.5	20.5	3.4	7.1	13.7	5.9	4.5	7.5
1980	29.3	21.6	23.3	3.4	8.7	14.2	6.3	4.4	8.2
1981	31.9	22.0	27.2	3.4	9.9	14.8	7.3	4.4	10.1
1982	34.4	21.6	29.4	3.2	10.7	14.9	7.6	4.3	11.1
1983	35.3	21.6	32.4	3.4	11.9	15.1	8.3	4.1	12.1
1984	33.7	21.6	33.9	3.2	12.8	15.3	8.4	4.1	12.7
1985	33.1	21.8	37.5	3.1	14.1	15.3	9.2	3.4	14.3
1986	32.4	22.5	41.1	3.1	15.1	15.7	10.1	3.7	15.9
1987	32.5	23.2	45.1	3.3	16.1	15.6	11.1	4.1	17.8
1988	31.7	22.9	48.7	3.2	17.1	15.5	11.7	4.2	19.8
1989	31.5	23.5	54.1	3.1	18.5	15.7	13.8	4.8	21.5
1990	33.6	25.3	64.8	3.2	21.5	17.2	17.6	5.0	25.4
1991	35.7	28.2	76.9	3.4	25.4	18.7	22.0	5.9	29.3
1992	36.9	32.1	97.1	4.7	27.2	16.1	23.2	11.3	26.7
1993	38.0**	33.4	101.7	3.9	31.5	18.3	16.5	11.2	53.7

*Excluding territories and possessions.
**Estimate.
NOTE: Numbers may not add to totals because of rounding. Excludes premium and per capita amounts and state expenditures not eligible for federal matching funds.
SOURCES: U. S. Department of Health and Human Services, Health Care Financing Administration, Medicaid Statistics Branch; U. S. Department of Commerce, Bureau of the Census (for data on poverty population).

Table 3.5

Premiums Paid by State to Qualified and Provisional Health Maintenance Organizations for Medicaid Recipients, Fiscal Year 1992

State	Qualified HMOs		Provisional HMOs	
	Persons in Medicaid program	Premiums paid	Persons in Medicaid program	Premiums paid
Alabama	0	$ 250,008,698	0	$0
California	355,280	271,153,844	103,038	58,000,276
District of Columbia	21,357	20,830,230	92,472	102,449,037
Florida	187,837	245,918,750	0	0
Illinois	155,784	120,854,422	0	0
Indiana	869	595,987	0	0
Michigan	209,305	188,265,237	13,994	8,732,812
Minnesota	5,471	5,950,351	106,812	131,729,359
New Hampshire	4,703	3,564,401	0	0
New Jersey	2,711	2,588,018	0	0
New York	15,093	11,960,990	0	0
North Carolina	4,717	4,091,948	0	0
Ohio	27,442	27,296,111	194,997	194,133,568
Oregon	736	1,257,724	0	0
Washington	42,898	24,430,234	0	0
Wisconsin	76,976	63,330,401	0	0
Total	**1,111,179**	**$1,242,097,346**	**511,313**	**$495,045,052**

SOURCE: Health Care Financing Administration, Medicaid Statistics Branch.

Table 3.6

Medicare Enrollees and Benefit Payments by State, 1992 and 1993

State	Benefit payments (thousands)		Medicare enrollees	
	1992	1993	1992	1993
Alabama	$ 2,100,140	$ 2,460,573	606,983	618,246
Alaska	81,727	97,340	27,279	30,098
Arizona	2,076,849	2,178,377	534,067	553,500
Arkansas	1,309,391	130,641	404,687	409,902
California	15,652,577	16,487,553	3,434,524	3,503,796
Colorado	1,242,210	1,429,580	383,560	396,453
Connecticut	1,953,460	2,052,656	485,299	491,055
Delaware	266,962	368,391	93,120	95,539
District of Columbia	1,112,051	1,111,826	78,441	78,496
Florida	10,351,327	11,721,985	2,447,906	2,493,700
Georgia	2,864,106	3,301,647	771,347	790,781
Hawaii	404,329	472,706	136,507	141,124
Idaho	299,869	341,832	139,119	142,309
Illinois	5,564,774	6,136,399	1,579,230	1,593,485
Indiana	2,454,767	2,876,565	790,985	802,572
Iowa	1,241,751	1,305,372	466,860	469,081
Kansas	1,160,530	1,350,204	373,408	376,481
Kentucky	1,787,513	1,958,777	555,198	564,958
Louisana	2,318,049	2,607,035	553,299	562,561
Maine	513,553	561,490	190,932	194,376
Maryland	2,262,085	2,469,631	567,667	578,311
Massachusetts	3,779,672	4,487,227	897,540	911,420
Michigan	4,641,997	5,171,403	1,287,741	1,308,694
Minnesota	1,942,733	2,106,232	608,201	615,327
Mississippi	1,234,661	1,327,867	378,257	383,922
Missouri	2,673,985	3,122,092	805,024	814,200
Montana	307,276	369,612	123,008	125,084
Nebraska	631,275	689,410	242,929	244,825
Nevada	598,224	663,596	159,164	169,614
New Hampshire	428,024	462,196	145,018	148,442
New Jersey	4,188,080	4,749,335	1,130,236	1,143,658
New Mexico	489,277	556,534	192,341	198,466
New York	10,268,609	11,447,774	2,573,080	2,594,326
North Carolina	3,005,797	3,242,292	945,314	971,209
North Dakota	352,161	347,160	101,123	101,920
Ohio	5,720,970	6,086,116	1,603,389	1,626,085
Oklahoma	1,471,347	1,545,624	466,655	472,900
Oregon	1,356,953	1,443,639	443,961	452,353
Pennsylvania	8,365,352	9,270,961	2,019,052	2,039,305
Rhode Island	587,786	628,236	163,602	164,910
South Carolina	1,243,924	1,440,252	468,267	481,173
South Dakota	275,842	331,448	113,217	114,514
Tennessee	2,894,511	3,251,676	722,847	737,910
Texas	6,978,035	8,007,117	1,925,526	1,973,343
Utah	426,940	590,761	171,434	176,799
Vermont	200,092	227,995	77,785	79,351
Virginia	2,226,413	2,420,279	760,930	779,006
Washington	2,145,409	2,166,637	645,448	657,780
West Virginia	931,431	1,017,016	317,682	321,949
Wisconsin	2,125,566	2,305,182	735,709	744,796
Wyoming	97,803	138,637	55,326	59,921
Puerto Rico	555,523	709,145	446,172	456,525
Other outlying areas	5,416	13,232	301,776	317,205
Totals	$129,179,077	$142,933,727	35,649,173	36,270,936

SOURCE: Health Care Financing Administration.

Table 3.7

Total Medicare Population and Enrollment of Medicare Population in HMOs, July 1993

State	Medicare population	Medicare HMO enrollees	
		Enrollees	**Percentage**
Total United States	34,853,000	1,691,385	4.9
Alabama	606,000	0	0.0
Alaska	28,000	0	0.0
Arizona	538,000	118,379	22.0
Arkansas	404,000	0	0.0
California	3,421,000	671,318	19.6
Colorado	382,000	37,550	9.8
Connecticut	483,000	0	0.0
Delaware	93,000	0	0.0
District of Columbia	78,000	0	0.0
Florida	2,455,000	317,658	12.9
Georgia	771,000	0	0.0
Hawaii	136,000	12,501	9.2
Idaho	139,000	0	0.0
Illinois	1,574,000	57,776	3.7
Indiana	789,000	2,562	0.3
Iowa	465,000	0	0.0
Kansas	373,000	2,418	0.6
Kentucky	554,000	2,795	0.5
Louisiana	551,000	0	0.0
Maine	190,000	0	0.0
Maryland	567,000	713	0.1
Massachusetts	895,000	28,408	3.2
Michigan	1,282,000	6,918	0.5
Minnesota	606,000	55,721	9.2
Mississippi	378,000	0	0.0
Missouri	804,000	14,159	1.8
Montana	123,000	0	0.0
Nebraska	242,000	3,273	1.4
Nevada	161,000	22,933	14.2
New Hampshire	145,000	0	0.0
New Jersey	1,126,000	0	0.0
New Mexico	192,000	17,552	9.1
New York	2,556,000	71,092	2.8
North Carolina	944,000	0	0.0
North Dakota	101,000	0	0.0
Ohio	1,598,000	16,335	1.0
Oklahoma	466,000	8,383	1.8
Oregon	445,000	85,681	19.3
Pennsylvania	2,014,000	26,102	1.3
Rhode Island	163,000	11,719	7.2
South Carolina	468,000	0	0.0
South Dakota	113,000	0	0.0
Tennessee	722,000	0	0.0
Texas	1,923,000	41,817	2.2
Utah	171,000	0	0.0
Vermont	77,000	0	0.0
Virginia	760,000	300	0.0
Washington	645,000	57,322	8.9
West Virginia	317,000	0	0.0
Wisconsin	734,000	0	0.0
Wyoming	55,000	0	0.0

SOURCE: HCFA Review, Fall 1993.

Table 3.8

Medicaid Recipients by Payment and Selected Types of Service, by State, 1993

State	Total recipients	Total payments	General hospital	Mental hospital	Nursing facilities
Alabama	521,539	$ 1,191,818,404	$ 235,494,909	$ 20,292,291	$ 330,831,471
Alaska	65,079	217,399,377	42,464,396	10,514,178	39,431,012
Arizona	404,030	211,910,126	92,571,877	22,270,130	14,882,146
Arkansas	339,451	997,814,499	196,843,283	46,262,738	252,632,040
California	4,833,824	9,649,517,851	3,427,053,505	10,610,917	1,953,247,360
Colorado	280,664	911,335,406	236,678,396	22,142,441	215,772,303
Connecticut	333,685	1,825,047,783	254,642,985	35,735,244	730,872,734
Delaware	68,934	251,564,500	59,512,456	0	59,310,789
District of Columbia	120,256	554,518,849	165,309,652	11,850,494	136,357,227
Florida	1,744,945	4,131,305,669	1,137,783,315	14,456,571	979,942,401
Georgia	955,262	2,440,618,176	683,445,887	0	539,960,199
Hawaii	109,970	292,508,880	61,264,734	0	106,102,876
Idaho	99,515	300,629,716	62,838,652	1,693,877	66,733,616
Illinois	1,395,566	4,625,248,849	1,740,182,245	30,839,446	1,152,589,566
Indiana	564,952	2,353,934,283	490,172,631	54,715,558	664,290,328
Iowa	289,211	895,794,880	191,556,031	4,193,033	224,206,682
Kansas	242,896	701,670,756	121,455,313	37,768,080	206,332,604
Kentucky	617,759	1,706,895,310	342,477,130	35,714,571	334,016,080
Louisiana	751,242	2,873,044,183	1,037,623,098	66,784,772	522,116,659
Maine	168,812	712,571,930	160,541,656	16,361,653	207,906,588
Maryland	444,673	1,720,670,090	550,874,628	78,948,400	399,081933
Massachusetts	764,933	2,725,602,358	626,218,001	19,861,846	1,023,325,395
Michigan	1,171,548	3,077,140,677	804,095,155	61,573,332	641,548,929
Minnesota	425,478	1,929,619,868	243,143,456	21,744,712	752,478,321
Mississippi	504,498	895,491,469	234,412,802	9,045,902	175,407,923
Missouri	609,386	1,548,325,871	359,969,649	362,745	417,837,538
Montana	89,041	287,428,709	51,953,287	20,150,790	82,240,817
Nebraska	164,663	552,803,728	116,721,021	9,439,249	176,820,544
Nevada	88,428	300,920,807	88,609,063	8,834,849	58,892,323
New Hampshire	79,332	380,342,519	31,584,583	8,676,365	159,340,131
New Jersey	793,634	3,485,064,908	965,518,721	69,947,468	943,580,091
New Mexico	240,690	542,592,891	131,597,506	24,727,355	99,290,872
New York	2,742,494	17,557,088,944	3,928,284,712	1,015,770,384	4,022,385,547
North Carolina	898,416	2,451,957,053	552,860,283	32,392,255	575,418,390
North Dakota	62,087	272,713,407	42,255,583	4,197,086	91,660,250
Ohio	1,490,983	4,666,662,717	991,846,356	0	1,476,416,961
Oklahoma	386,531	1,043,449,614	243,548,656	51,704,018	236,543,853
Oregon	325,233	831,015,325	97,665,850	20,671,143	152,756,357
Pennsylvania	1,223,080	3,886,201,196	946,826,125	107,619,371	1,364,734,300
Rhode Island	191,138	709,789,379	156,611,316	0	203,383,296
South Carolina	470,416	1,249,311,570	352,376,783	45,250,697	203,359,820
South Dakota	69,606	263,859,418	54,567,055	5,071,817	77,700,905
Tennessee	908,943	1,977,468,671	341,138,342	25,784,872	517,042,863
Texas	2,308,443	5,574,649,490	1,677,627,367	0	1,048,264,392
Utah	149,131	408,458,430	117,357,776	18,159	74,159,612
Vermont	80,564	234,897,152	32,107,670	827,117	64,472,716
Virginia	575,929	1,622,885,677	390,091,912	15,444,481	359,414,970
Washington	633,364	1,537,056,515	326,958,760	9,739,150	431,207,405
West Virginia	347,014	1,056,113,210	175,671,192	13,216,395	164,325,868
Wisconsin	471,103	1,786,328,158	270,464,167	37,334,528	666,122,408
Wyoming	46,262	125,448,070	33,495,251	221,970	34,072,704
Total	33,432,025	$101,708,889,399	$257,341,424,825	$2,150,782,450	$25,430,822,115

Source: HCFA Medicaid Statistical Information System (MSIS).

Table 3.9

Hospital Expenditures under Workers' Compensation, 1960–1993 (Millions)

Year	Total	State and local expenditures		Federal expenditures	
		Hospital	Physicians	Hospital	Physicians
1960	$ 410	$ 152	$ 250	$ 5	$ 3
1965	568	210	345	7	6
1970	999	525	448	15	11
1975	1,946	1,014	866	38	28
1980	3,581	1,882	1,582	85	32
1981	3,980	2,101	1,748	95	36
1982	4,506	2,381	1,960	120	45
1983	4,943	2,604	2,122	159	58
1984	5,555	2,952	2,379	164	60
1985	6,470	3,477	2,771	163	59
1986	7,368	3,994	3,148	167	59
1987	8,394	4,575	3,565	188	66
1988	9,773	5,329	4,153	215	76
1989	11,504	6,284	4,897	239	84
1990	13,019	7,119	5,548	260	92
1991	14,428	7,887	6,146	292	103
1992	15,671	8,617	6,715	317	112
1993*	17,677	9,684	7,547	330	116

*Estimate.
NOTE: Data revised back to 1978.
SOURCE: Health Care Financing Administration.

Chapter 4

MEDICAL CARE COSTS

◆ National Health Expenditures (NHE)

NHE represent total private and public spending for personal health care, medical research, construction of medical facilities, insurance, and administration. NHE includes government-sponsored public health programs.

National health spending is estimated to reach $819.9 billion, or $3,098 per person, in 1992, a 9.1 percent increase over 1991. Public spending amounted to 46 percent of all health care costs in 1992, 2 percent higher than in 1991. HCFA has projected 1993's total health spending at $903.3 billion; HCFA predicts that health spending will top $1.8 trillion by the year 2000.

More than 30 years ago, in 1961, NHE constituted 5 percent of the GDP. It has increased steadily over the years, reaching 13.6 percent in 1992 (Table 4.3).

The Cost of Personal Health Care

Hospital care, totalling $324.2 billion in 1992, continued to represent the largest share of personal health spending (44.6 percent). Consumers paid 4.6 percent of these hospital services out-of-pocket in 1992, down from 3.4 percent in 1991. The cost of physicians' services was the next highest at $151.8 billion (Table 4.1).

According to HCFA, nursing home care, another index of the aging population, cost $66.3 billion in 1992, an 11 percent increase over 1991. Medicare contributed only $2.7 billion to this total, and Medicaid paid a little over one-half ($34.4 billion) of these expenses. The remaining cost of financing long-term care fell almost exclusively on the patients and their families ($26.2 billion). Private long-term care insurance, still in its infancy, paid only $700 million in long-term care costs.

Personal Health Care Expenditures (PHCE)

PHCE represent private and public spending for direct health and medical services and products for individuals. PHCE for 1992 rose to $727.1 billion (a 10 percent increase over 1991) and accounted for almost 89 percent of the NHE.

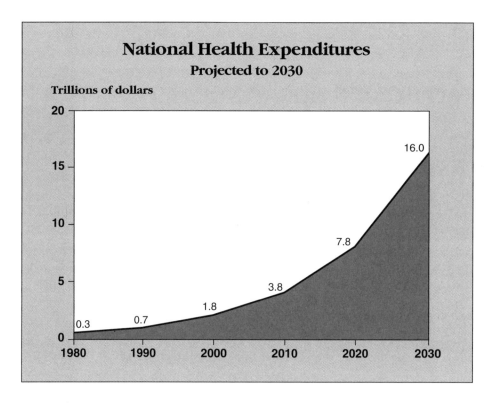

Figure 4.1

SOURCE: Health Care Financing Administration.

The increase is attributable to price inflation, both economy-wide and industry-specific, and the growth in population.

PHCE includes expenditures for hospital care, professional services, drugs and medical sundries, and nursing home care. Expenditures for medical research, construction of medical facilities, public health activities such as disease prevention and control, and the net cost of health insurance are not included in the total.

Between 1983 and 1993, the consumer price index (CPI) for physician fees increased an average of 7 percent per year. This was a higher rate of growth than that of the overall CPI, which rose at an average rate of 4.4 percent per year. Over the course of a decade, physician fees outpaced general inflation by more than 50 percent.

Inflation and industry-specific price inflation together accounted for 69 percent of the increase, while population growth accounted for 10 percent and inten-

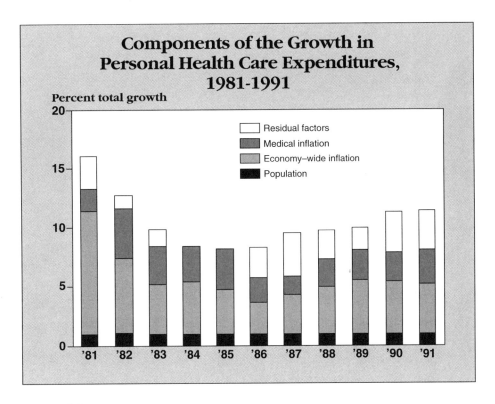

Components of the Growth in Personal Health Care Expenditures, 1981-1991

Percent total growth

Legend:
- Residual factors
- Medical inflation
- Economy–wide inflation
- Population

Figure 4.2

SOURCE: HCFA. Revised data December 13, 1993.

sity, 21 percent. (HCFA defines intensity as anything that causes changes in use per capita expenditure.) Among the factors that spurred growth in PHCE over the past three decades was the large increase in population in the 1960s and the implementation of Medicare and Medicaid, programs that increased access to health care for the elderly and poor.

Nevertheless, high economy-wide inflation during the decade that began in 1970 seemed to have the greatest effect on PHCE, and this continued into the 1980s, when medical-specific prices affected health expenditures more than they had during the previous two decades.

The use of technology helps drive up health costs. Lasers, fiberoptics, and other new technologies are in constant use in medical diagnosis and treatment.

Per capita expenditures were $3,098 in 1992, 10.2 percent more than the 1991 figure of $2,868 (Table 4.2).

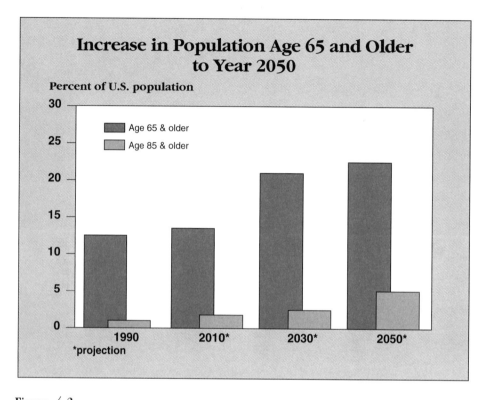

Figure 4.3

SOURCE: U. S. Department of Commerce, Bureau of the Census, Current Population Survey.

The largest portion (78.5 percent) of the personal health care dollar derives from third-party sources. Private health insurance, philanthropy, industry, and the government paid $571 billion of all expenditures for personal health care in 1992.

Personal Consumption Expenditures (PCE), published by the U.S. Department of Commerce, measure private medical care payments. Monies from Medicare, Workers' Compensation and Temporary Disability Insurance are treated as transfer payments and are included in PCE.

Again in 1993, overall inflation was the single largest contributor to rising health care costs. Growth in population accounts for about 10 percent of the rise, and the combination of the two accounts for more than half the total increase in PHCE in all but four years of the decade.

Two factors, excess medical price inflation and the residual, account for the remaining portion of health care cost growth. Excess medical price is the in-

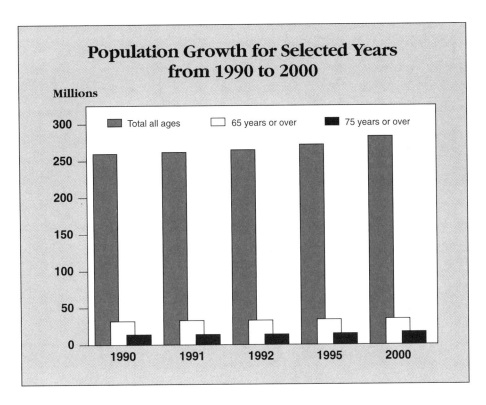

Population Growth for Selected Years from 1990 to 2000

Millions

Legend: ▨ Total all ages ☐ 65 years or over ■ 75 years or over

Years: 1990, 1991, 1992, 1995, 2000

Figure 4.4

SOURCE: HCFA Review.

crease in health services that exceeded the economywide inflation rate. The residual amount, ranging from 1.2 percent to 38.5 percent of the increase in PHCE in the decade, is sometimes considered the measure of technology utilization. Residual reflects a variety of cost related factors beyond technology including additional spending on more complex cases, an aging population, hard-to-treat illnesses such as AIDS and substance abuse, and cost increases attributable to changes in medical practice, including changes related to advances in the use of technology.

PCE and PHCE differ because of different accounting practices. PCE for medical care in 1992 was $704.6 billion, which represents 17 percent of the total spent by Americans on all personal needs. As a proportion of the public's disposable income, these expenditures were 15.7 percent in 1992, up from 15.4 percent in 1991 (Table 4.7).

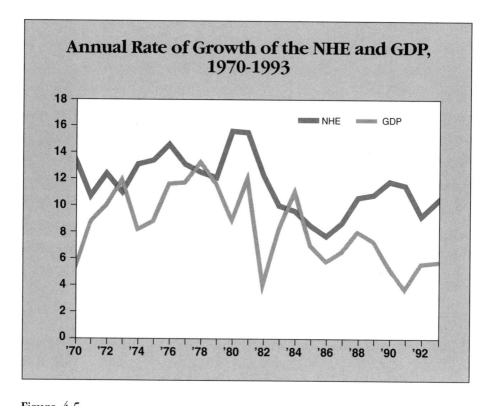

Annual Rate of Growth of the NHE and GDP, 1970-1993

Figure 4.5

*NOTE: 1993 is estimated.
SOURCE: U. S. Department of Commerce, Health Care Financing Administration.

Consumer Price Index (CPI)

The CPI measures the average change in the prices paid by urban consumers for a fixed market basket of consumption goods and services ranging from oranges to computers. The CPI compares what the market basket of goods and services cost consumers this month with what the same market basket cost a month, a year, or even 10 years ago.

According to the 1993 CPI, medical prices increased by 4.6 percent from 1992, compared with a 2.5 percent increase for all items (Table 4.8).

Individual components of the medical care index have differed in their rates of increase, but hospital room rates have risen most rapidly.

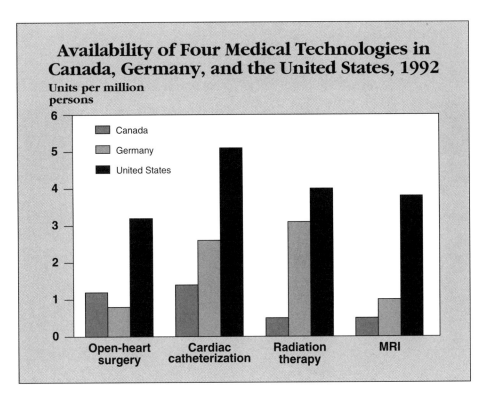

Availability of Four Medical Technologies in Canada, Germany, and the United States, 1992

Units per million persons

Legend:
- Canada
- Germany
- United States

Categories: Open-heart surgery, Cardiac catheterization, Radiation therapy, MRI

Figure 4.6

SOURCE: Health Affairs, Fall 1989.

Hospital Statistics

Community Hospitals   In 1992, the average expense to the hospital for treating a patient in a community hospital was $819.83 per inpatient day, almost a 9 percent increase over 1991. State by state, the average cost per inpatient day in 1992 varied considerably, from a low of $474.21 in Montana to a high of $1,133.50 in California.

In 1992, the average length of time a patient remained in a community hospital was 7.1 days. But the average length of stay varied by area, from a low of 5.1 days in Oregon and Utah to a high of 11.3 in North Dakota. The average cost of a stay in a community hospital in 1992 was $5,794.43, an 8 percent increase over 1991.

Operating costs of community hospitals were $282.5 billion in 1992, which is a 15 percent increase over the $245.1 billion spent in 1991. The American

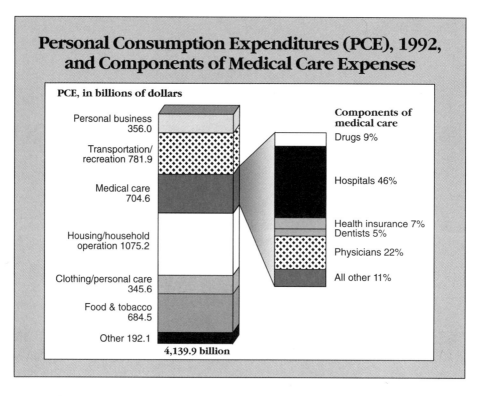

Personal Consumption Expenditures (PCE), 1992, and Components of Medical Care Expenses

PCE, in billions of dollars

Personal business 356.0

Transportation/recreation 781.9

Medical care 704.6

Housing/household operation 1075.2

Clothing/personal care 345.6

Food & tobacco 684.5

Other 192.1

4,139.9 billion

Components of medical care

Drugs 9%

Hospitals 46%

Health insurance 7%
Dentists 5%

Physicians 22%

All other 11%

Figure 4.7

SOURCE: U. S. Department of Commerce, Survey of Current Business, August 1993.

Hospital Association (AHA) reports that labor costs reached $155 billion in 1992, representing 55 percent of total community hospital expenditures.

During the past decade, hospitals have broadened the range of alternative services they offer. These changes reflect advances in technology, greater emphasis on nonacute care as a result of new payment systems, and medical care that allows a greater choice for the patient.

Freestanding Outpatient Surgery Centers There were 1,690 active freestanding outpatient surgery centers in the United States in 1992, about 40 percent of which perform fewer than 1,000 procedures per year; this is in contrast to hospitals and hospital centers that perform more than 3,500 procedures per year.

Psychiatric Hospitals The nation's 775 nonfederal mental hospitals (142,099 beds) were 80 percent occupied in 1992, with a 25.3 percent increase in admissions between 1982 and 1992. Psychiatric hospitals have in-

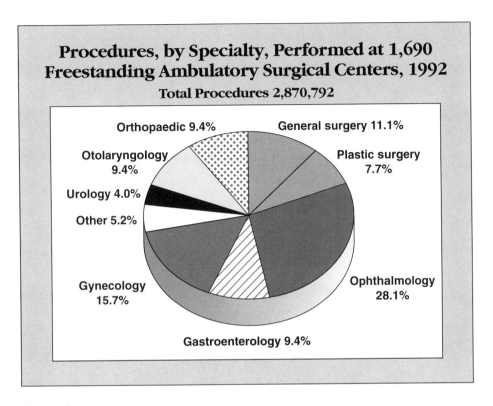

Procedures, by Specialty, Performed at 1,690 Freestanding Ambulatory Surgical Centers, 1992
Total Procedures 2,870,792

Orthopaedic 9.4%

General surgery 11.1%

Otolaryngology 9.4%

Plastic surgery 7.7%

Urology 4.0%

Other 5.2%

Gynecology 15.7%

Ophthalmology 28.1%

Gastroenterology 9.4%

Figure 4.8

SOURCE: American College of Surgeons, Socio-Economic Factbook 1994.

creased in number (249) during the 10-year period. According to *Hospital Statistics*, it cost almost $14 billion to operate facilities devoted to mental health care in the United States in 1992.

Emergency Rooms A survey conducted by *Medical Economics* in 1991 indicated that an attending physician charged $51 for an average emergency room visit, $257 for cardiopulmonary resuscitation, and $190 for the first hour of critical care.

Professional Fees

Surgical Charges Surgical charges vary considerably by geographic region and by metropolitan and nonmetropolitan areas. Table 4.12, containing data from a 1993 survey by *Medical Economics*, shows fees for a number of common surgical procedures and emergency medical procedures across the United States.

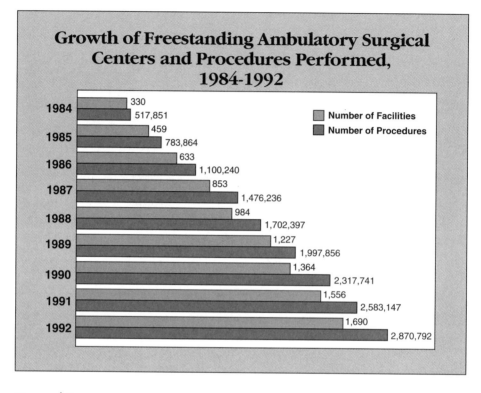

Growth of Freestanding Ambulatory Surgical Centers and Procedures Performed, 1984-1992

Number of Facilities
Number of Procedures

1984 — 330 / 517,851
1985 — 459 / 783,864
1986 — 633 / 1,100,240
1987 — 853 / 1,476,236
1988 — 984 / 1,702,397
1989 — 1,227 / 1,997,856
1990 — 1,364 / 2,317,741
1991 — 1,556 / 2,583,147
1992 — 1,690 / 2,870,792

Figure 4.8a

SOURCE: American College of Surgeons.

HIAA data on charges for selected surgical procedures for 1993 by geographic areas of the United States show considerable variation.

Physicians Physicians' fees vary considerably by type of practice and specialty, type of visit, and region of the United States. In 1993, the median charges for an initial office visit and an office revisit were highest for specialists and for physicians practicing in the western states. The physicians' index of the CPI decreased from 6.3 percent in 1992 to 4.3 percent in 1993.

Health Services Firms Offices and clinics of doctors of medicine accounted for nearly 50 percent of all taxable health services receipts in 1991, reaching $122.5 billion and increasing 6.4 percent from the previous year. Over 40 percent of these receipts are yielded by patient services provided in the doctor's office or clinic; nearly one-quarter was from hospital inpatient services. Offices and clinics of dentists gained 4.4 percent from 1990 to $29.7 billion in 1991.

Ten Most Frequently Performed Operative Procedures for Patients Discharged from Short-Stay Hospitals, 1992

Procedure	Number (thousands)	Rate per 1,000 population
Total procedures	23,403	93.4
Episiotomy	1,684	6.8
Cardiac catheterization	1,000	4.0
Cesarean	933	3.7
Repair of obstetric laceration	795	3.2
Artificial rupture of membranes	775	3.1
Cholecystectomy	571	2.3
Hysterectomy	546	2.2
Oophorectomy/salpingo-oophorectomy	458	1.8
Open reduction of fracture	418	1.7
Coronary artery bypass	407	1.6

Figure 4.9

SOURCE: U. S. Department Health and Human Services, National Center for Health Statistics.

Charges for Selected Surgical Procedures, by Geographic Area, 1993

Procedure	New York City	Philadelphia	Atlanta	Chicago	Denver	Dallas	Los Angeles
Excision of breast lesion (lumpectomy) 19120	$1,402	$ 717	$ 662	$ 756	$ 495	$ 647	$ 843
Cesarean section 59510	4,807	2,707	2,895	2,999	2,594	2,444	3,350
Abdominal hysterectomy 58150	4,854	2,704	2,555	3,230	1,884	2,339	3,161
Oophorectomy 58940	2,760	1,940	1,691	1,838	1,123	1,415	1,907
Salpingo-oophorectomy 58720	3,086	1,905	1,882	2,128	1,209	1,637	1,814
Coronary bypass (triple) 33512	7,223	6,610	5,783	6,424	5,307	5,727	6,134
Appendectomy 44950	1,882	1,142	1,140	1,361	965	1,183	1,430
Cholecystectomy 47605	2,825	1,709	1,811	2,140	1,627	1,793	2,271

Figure 4.10

SOURCE: HIAA, Prevailing Healthcare Charges System, 1993.

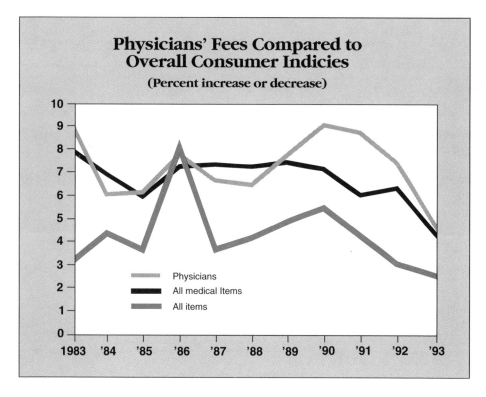

Figure 4.11

SOURCE: U. S. Department of Labor, Bureau of Labor Statistics.

Private insurance payments were the source of 40 percent of the total receipts for offices and clinics of doctors of medicine while Medicare and Medicaid payments combined amounted to 30 percent of total receipts. Direct patient payments were the source of nearly half of all receipts for offices and clinics of dentists. Nursing and personal care facilities' receipts increased in 1991 to $28.8 billion, 9.1 percent over 1990; hospitals (other than nonprofit) had receipts of $31.5 billion in 1991, an increase of 8.5 percent from 1990. Receipts for home health care and kidney dialysis centers rose 19.1 and 18.3 percent, respectively (Table 4.21).

◆ The Cost of Mental Illness and Drug Abuse

In 1989, 3.2 million adult Americans experienced some form of mental disorder. According to *Mental Health United States: 1992,* published by the U.S. Department of Health and Human Services, 2.6 million of these adult Americans

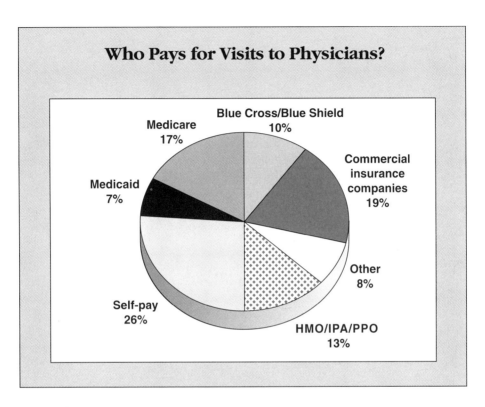

Figure 4.12

SOURCE: NCHS, Advancedata No. 237, 12/93.

Median Fees for Mental Health Treatments

Type of Psychiatric Treatment or Psychotherapy Session	Median Fee
Individual psychotherapy in office (45-50 minutes)	$115
Individual psychotherapy in hospital (45-50 minutes)	120
Family therapy session	125
Psychiatric diagnostic interview	150
Initial consultation in office, comprehensive	131
Initial consultation in hospital, comprehensive	151
Group psychotherapy, per person	50

Figure 4.13

SOURCE: *Medical Economics*, October 11, 1993.

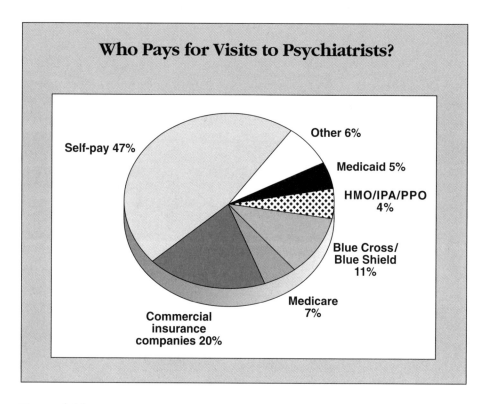

Who Pays for Visits to Psychiatrists?

Self-pay 47%

Other 6%

Medicaid 5%

HMO/IPA/PPO 4%

Blue Cross/ Blue Shield 11%

Medicare 7%

Commercial insurance companies 20%

Figure 4.14

SOURCE: NCHS, Advancedata No. 237, 12/93.

were limited in their capacity to work or function normally in the workplace by their disease. There were 1.3 million males and 1.9 million females diagnosed as mentally ill. More men are diagnosed as schizophrenics each year, while more women who are mentally ill present with a diagnosis of affective psychosis, the most prevalent mental disorder in the United States.

According to the National Mental Health Association, 68 percent of people with diagnosable mental disorders receive some ambulatory medical treatment, 22 percent actually visit a mental health specialist, and 10 percent consult a general family practitioner. A large majority of the recorded psychiatric admissions each year are actually readmissions.

In a 1992 survey of employers, HIAA found that the majority of conventional, PPO, and HMO plans cover outpatient and inpatient mental health, drug treatment, and treatment for alcohol problems.

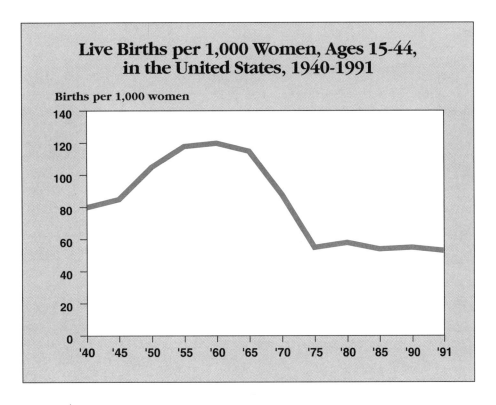

Live Births per 1,000 Women, Ages 15-44, in the United States, 1940-1991

Births per 1,000 women

Figure 4.15

SOURCE: U. S. Department of Health and Human Services, National Center for Health Statistics.

◆ The Cost of Accidents

Medical expense costs incurred through accidents totaled $399 billion in 1993.

◆ International Health Care Expenditure

According to the Organization for Economic Cooperation and Development (OECD), the United States allocates a greater proportion of its GDP to health care than any other country. In 1991, the United States spent $2,868 on each citizen, while Canada spent $2,149, West Germany $2,088, and the United Kingdom $1,162 (all in American dollars).

The Cost of Workplace Injuries

Condition	Percentage of claims	Average cost per claim
Back strain	31	$23,916
Other sprains/strains	19	13,611
Concussion/bruises	11	12,055
Fracture	11	23,138
Laceration/puncture	10	9,722
Dislocation/crushing	3	47,249
Burn	3	12,833
Hernia	3	24,499
Infection/inflammation	2	13,805
Amputation	1	40,249
Cumulative injury	1	29,166
Occupational disease	1	31,305

Figure 4.16

SOURCE: National Council on Compensation Insurance.

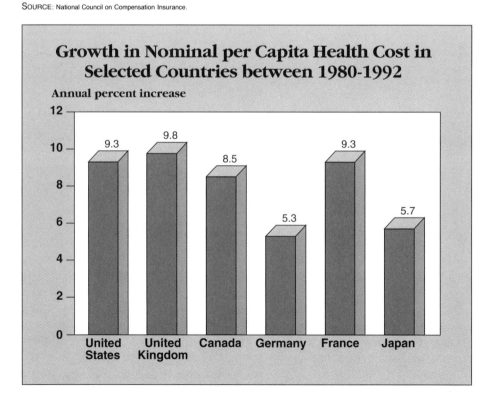

Figure 4.17

SOURCE: OECD Health Data.

In 1991, the United States spent more on total health care than any other country, however, per capita health care costs between 1990 and 1991 grew more rapidly in Germany than in any other country in the free world. France held it's nominal per capita health care spending to a mere 3 percent increase. Even with a per capita increase of 12 percent, the U.S. rate of increase was the second lowest among selected industrialized countries.

Table 4.1

National Health Expenditure, 1992 and 1993

1992* Type of expenditure	Total	Private All private funds	Private Consumer Total	Private Consumer Out of pocket	Private Consumer Private insurance	Private Other	Government Total	Government Federal	Government State and local
Total NHE	$819.9	$443.5	$408.0	$155.9	$252.1	$35.5	$376.5	$258.9	$117.5
Health services and supplies	794.5	433.9	408.0	155.9	252.1	25.9	360.7	246.4	114.3
Personal health care	727.1	397.7	372.5	155.9	216.6	25.2	329.3	237.6	91.7
Hospital care	324.2	135.5	119.3	14.9	104.3	16.3	188.7	137.7	51.0
Physician services	151.8	94.4	94.3	27.4	66.9	0.1	57.4	46.4	11.0
Dental services	38.7	37.3	37.3	20.3	17	NA	1.4	0.8	0.6
Other professional services	40.2	31.0	26.5	10.5	16	4.5	9.2	6.8	2.3
Home health care	10.3	2.6	1.9	1.2	0.7	0.7	7.7	6.1	1.6
Drugs and other medical durables	65.1	56.6	56.6	46.9	9.7	NA	8.5	4.4	4.1
Vision products and other medical durables	13.0	9.7	9.7	8.5	1.2	NA	3.3	3.0	0.3
Nursing home care	66.3	28.0	26.9	26.2	0.7	1.1	38.3	23.4	14.9
Other personal health care	17.5	2.6	NA	NA	NA	2.6	14.9	9.0	5.9
Program administration and net cost of private health insurance	45.1	36.1	35.5	NA	35.5	0.6	9.0	5.8	3.2
Government public health activities	22.4	NA	NA	NA	NA	NA	22.4	2.9	19.4
Research and construction	25.4	9.6	NA	NA	NA	9.6	15.8	12.5	3.2
Research	14.2	1.0	NA	NA	NA	1.0	13.3	11.5	1.7
Construction	11.2	8.7	NA	NA	NA	8.7	2.5	1.0	1.5

1993** Type of expenditure	Total	Private All private funds	Private Consumer Total	Private Consumer Out of pocket	Private Consumer Private insurance	Private Other	Government Total	Government Federal	Government State and local
Total NHE	$903.3	$482.2	$443.6	$169.9	$273.7	$38.6	$421.1	$290.0	$131.1
Health services and supplies	875.9	472.0	443.6	169.9	273.7	28.4	403.8	276.2	127.6
Personal health care	803.7	434.0	406.2	169.9	236.3	27.7	369.8	266.6	103.1
Hospital care	358.8	148.7	130.8	16.4	114.5	17.8	210.1	153.3	56.8
Physician services	167.3	102.5	102.4	29.8	72.6	0.1	64.8	52.5	12.3
Dental services	41.0	39.5	39.5	21.6	17.9	NA	1.5	0.8	0.7
Other professional services	44.9	34.4	29.4	11.6	17.8	5.0	10.5	7.8	2.7
Home health care	12.3	3.0	2.2	1.4	0.8	0.8	9.3	7.3	2.0
Drugs and other medical durables	70.9	61.2	61.2	50.6	10.6	NA	9.7	5.0	4.6
Vision products and other medical durables	13.9	10.2	10.2	9.0	1.2	NA	3.7	3.3	0.4
Nursing home care	74.3	31.7	30.4	29.7	0.7	1.3	42.6	26.0	16.6
Other personal health care	20.4	2.8	NA	NA	NA	2.8	17.5	10.6	7.0
Program administration and net cost of private health insurance	48.0	38.1	37.4	NA	37.4	0.7	9.9	6.3	3.6
Government public health activities	24.2	NA	NA	NA	NA	NA	24.2	3.3	20.9
Research and construction	27.4	10.2	NA	NA	NA	10.2	17.2	13.8	3.4
Research	15.7	1.0	NA	NA	NA	1.0	14.6	12.8	1.9
Construction	11.7	9.1	NA	NA	NA	9.1	2.6	1.0	1.6

*1992 is estimated.
**1993 is projected.
NA: Not available.
SOURCE: Health Care Financing Administration.

Table 4.2

National Health Expenditure Aggregate, per Capita, Percentage Distribution and Percentage Change, by Source of Funds, Selected Calendar Years

Item	1980	1985	1990	1991	1992*	1993**
National health expenditure	$250.1	$420.1	$666.2	$751.8	$819.9	$903.3
Private	143.9	245.2	383.6	421.8	443.5	482.2
Public	105.2	174.9	282.6	330.0	376.5	421.1
Federal	72.0	123.4	195.4	222.9	258.9	290.0
State and local	33.2	51.5	87.3	107.1	117.5	131.1
U. S. population (millions)	235.2	247.1	259.6	262.1	264.7	267.5
Gross national product (billions)	$2,732.0	$40,154.0	$5,524.5	$5,737.1	$6,045.8	$6,378.1
Per capita amount						
National health expenditure	$1,064.0	$1,700.0	$2,566.0	$2,868.0	$3,098.0	$3,380.0
Private	617.0	992.0	1,478.0	1,609.0	1,675.0	1,805.0
Public	447.0	708.0	1,089.0	1,259.0	1,422.0	1,576.0
Federal	306.0	500.0	753.0	850.0	978.0	1,085.0
State and local	141.0	208.0	336.0	408.0	444.0	490.0
Percentage distribution						
National health expenditure	100.0	100.0	100.0	100.0	100.1	100.0
Private	58.0	57.4	57.6	57.8	54.1	53.4
Public	42.0	41.6	42.4	42.2	45.9	46.6
Federal	28.8	29.4	29.3	28.8	31.6	32.1
State and local	13.3	12.2	13.1	13.4	14.3	14.5
Percentage of gross domestic product						
National health expenditure	9.2	10.5	12.1	13.1	13.6	14.2

*Estimated.
**Projected.
SOURCE: U. S. Department of Health and Human Services, Health Care Financing Administration, Office of the Actuary.

Table 4.3

National Health Expenditures, Gross National Product, and Gross Domestic Product, 1950–1993

Calendar year	Amount of NHE (billions)	Rate of growth of NHE (%)	Gross national product (billions)	Rate of growth of GNP (%)	Gross domestic product (billions)	Rate of growth of GDP (%)	NHE as percent of GNP (%)	NHE as percent of GDP (%)
1950	$ 12.7	NA	$ 288.0	NA	NA	NA	4.4	NA
1955	17.7	39.4	406.0	40.9	NA	NA	4.4	NA
1960	27.1	53.1	516.6	26.9	$ 513.4	NA	5.3	5.3
1961	29.1	7.4	535.4	3.7	531.8	3.6	5.4	5.5
1962	31.6	8.6	575.8	7.7	571.6	7.5	5.5	5.5
1963	34.4	8.9	607.7	5.6	603.1	5.5	5.7	5.7
1964	38.1	10.8	653.0	7.1	648.0	7.4	5.9	5.9
1965	41.6	9.2	708.1	8.5	702.7	8.4	5.9	5.9
1966	45.9	10.3	774.9	9.5	769.8	9.6	5.9	6.0
1967	51.7	12.6	819.8	5.7	814.3	5.8	6.3	6.4
1968	58.5	13.2	895.5	10.1	889.3	9.2	6.6	6.6
1969	65.7	12.3	965.3	7.4	959.5	7.9	6.8	6.9
1970	74.4	13.2	1,017.1	5.4	1,010.7	5.3	7.3	7.4
1971	82.3	10.6	1,104.9	8.6	1,097.5	8.6	7.5	7.6
1972	92.4	12.3	1,215.7	9.9	1,207.0	9.9	7.6	7.7
1973	102.5	10.9	1,362.3	12.0	1,349.6	11.8	7.5	7.6
1974	116.1	13.0	1,474.3	8.4	1,458.6	8.1	7.9	8.0
1975	132.9	13.3	1,599.1	8.5	1,585.9	8.7	8.3	8.4
1976	152.2	14.5	1,785.5	11.6	1,768.4	11.5	8.5	8.6
1977	172.0	13.0	1,994.6	11.7	1,974.1	11.6	8.6	8.7
1978	193.4	12.4	2,254.5	13.0	2,232.7	13.1	8.6	8.7
1979	216.6	12.0	2,520.8	11.5	2,488.6	11.5	8.6	8.7
1980	250.1	15.5	2,732.0	8.9	2,708.0	8.8	9.2	9.2
1981	288.5	15.4	3,063.8	11.8	3,030.6	11.9	9.5	9.5
1982	323.8	12.2	3,179.8	3.7	3,149.6	3.9	10.2	10.3
1983	356.1	9.9	3,434.4	7.6	3,405.0	8.1	10.5	10.5
1984	389.9	9.5	2,801.5	10.8	3,777.2	10.9	10.3	10.3
1985	422.6	8.4	4,015.0	6.4	4,039.0	6.9	10.5	10.5
1986	454.9	7.6	4,277.7	5.4	4,269.0	5.7	10.7	10.7
1987	494.2	8.6	4,544.5	6.7	4,540.0	6.4	10.9	10.9
1988	546.0	10.5	4,908.2	7.9	4,900.0	7.9	11.2	11.1
1989	604.3	10.7	5,248.2	6.7	5,251.0	7.2	11.6	11.5
1990	666.2	10.2	5,524.5	6.2	5,522.0	5.2	12.1	12.1
1991	751.8	12.8	5,737.1	3.9	5,722.9	3.6	13.1	13.1
1992*	819.9	9.1	6,045.8	5.4	6,038.5	5.5	13.6	13.6
1993**	903.3	10.2	6,378.1	5.5	6,377.9	5.6	14.2	14.2

*Estimated.
**Projected.
NOTE: Gross National Product equals Gross Domestic Product plus net receipts of factor income from the rest of the world.
NA: Not available.
SOURCES: U. S. Department of Health and Human Services, Health Care Financing Administration, U. S. Department of Commerce, Survey of Current Business, various issues.

Table 4.4

Personal Health Care Expenditures, by Source of Payment, 1960–1993 (Billions)

Year	Total personal health care expenditures	Consumer				State and local	Government funds		
		Consumer payments	Out of pocket	Private health insurance	Other private funds		Total federal	Medicare	Medicaid
1960	23.9	18.4	13.4	5.1	0.4	2.9	2.1	NA	NA
1961	25.3	19.4	13.7	5.7	0.5	3.2	2.3	NA	NA
1962	27.3	21.1	14.6	6.3	0.5	3.3	2.6	NA	NA
1963	29.8	22.8	15.9	6.9	0.5	3.7	2.8	NA	NA
1964	32.8	25.5	17.7	7.8	0.6	3.9	2.8	NA	NA
1965	35.6	27.7	19.0	8.7	0.8	4.3	2.9	NA	NA
1966	39.4	28.4	19.3	9.1	0.9	4.8	5.4	1.6	1.3
1967	44.7	28.5	18.9	9.6	1.0	5.5	9.7	4.9	1.5
1968	51.0	32.1	21.2	10.9	1.1	6.0	11.3	5.9	1.8
1969	57.1	35.9	23.1	12.9	1.5	6.7	13.1	6.8	2.2
1970	64.9	40.8	25.6	15.2	1.7	7.8	14.7	7.2	2.7
1971	71.3	44.1	27.1	17.0	1.9	8.5	16.9	8.1	3.7
1972	79.4	48.5	29.8	18.7	2.1	9.7	19.0	8.8	4.4
1973	88.6	54.1	32.9	21.2	2.5	11.2	21.1	10.2	4.7
1974	101.6	61.1	35.6	25.1	3.0	12.4	25.9	12.8	6.0
1975	116.6	68.4	38.5	29.9	3.5	14.4	30.9	15.7	7.1
1976	132.8	77.6	42.5	35.1	4.1	14.6	36.7	18.9	8.7
1977	149.2	87.1	46.3	40.8	4.7	16.8	41.2	22.1	9.4
1978	167.4	96.9	50.2	46.7	5.0	18.6	46.9	25.8	10.2
1979	189.3	108.8	54.1	54.7	5.6	20.9	53.8	30.1	11.9
1980	219.4	124.8	59.5	65.3	7.6	23.6	63.5	36.4	13.7
1981	254.8	144.3	67.2	77.1	8.9	26.7	74.9	43.9	16.3
1982	286.4	162.6	74.2	88.5	10.2	29.5	84.0	51.4	16.5
1983	314.9	178.7	81.4	97.4	10.9	31.8	93.4	58.4	18.2
1984	341.2	194.1	87.7	106.3	11.4	33.9	101.8	64.4	19.2
1985	369.7	208.4	94.4	114.2	12.9	36.6	111.7	70.2	21.9
1986	400.8	225.3	100.9	124.4	13.9	41.4	120.1	75.1	23.9
1987	439.3	246.9	108.8	138.1	14.9	46.9	130.4	81.3	26.4
1988	482.8	273.5	118.5	154.9	16.8	50.9	141.7	88.4	29.4
1989	530.9	296.8	126.2	170.6	18.9	56.3	158.8	100.4	33.6
1990	591.5	327.7	136.5	191.2	21.5	65.3	177.0	108.4	40.7
1991	660.2	353.5	144.3	209.3	23.4	79.1	204.1	120.2	53.5
1992	727.1	372.5	155.9	216.6	25.2	91.7	258.9	135.0	70.8
1993*	803.7	406.2	169.9	236.3	27.7	103.1	290.0	150.0	81.2

*Personal health care expenditures are estimated.

NA: Not available.

SOURCE: U. S. Department of Health and Human Services, Health Care Financing Administration.

Table 4.5

Personal Consumption Expenditures, by Type of Expenditure, 1985–1993 (Billions)

	1985	1986	1987	1988	1989	1990*	1991*	1992*	1993
Total expenditures	2,629.9	2,797.4	3,009.4	3,296.1	3,523.1	3,761.2	3,902.4	4,136.9	4,378.2
Food and tobacco	503.8	533.6	566.4	569.8	605.6	648.2	666.8	678.0	700.3
Housing	403.3	434.2	468.9	484.2	514.4	547.5	574.9	601.3	629.0
Medical care	327.5	357.6	399.0	487.7	536.4	597.8	646.6	705.1	760.5
Drugs and sundries**	36.0	39.2	42.3	50.8	55.0	60.6	64.4	66.3	69.0
Physicians	73.5	80.6	94.0	110.6	121.6	133.8	143.6	156.4	165.5
Dentists	21.5	22.8	25.0	27.9	30.0	31.6	32.9	35.9	38.6
Private hospitals and sanitariums	140.2	152.4	166.3	221.5	243.1	268.4	295.8	322.8	346.8
Health insurance	21.6	22.4	25.3	26.4	31.2	36.6	35.1	39.8	46.2
Medical care and hospitalization	17.7	18.5	20.1	21.5	26.3	30.8	31.0	34.2	37.1
Income loss (disability)	2.3	2.5	2.6	2.2	2.0	2.3	1.7	2.0	2.4
Workers' compensation	1.7	1.5	2.7	2.7	3.0	3.4	2.4	3.6	6.6
Transportation	359.5	366.3	379.7	413.2	437.3	453.9	433.6	466.3	504.2
Household operation	334.1	347.5	363.3	398.9	422.6	437.3	453.0	476.7	508.2
Recreation	185.7	201.2	223.2	246.8	266.0	285.7	298.2	318.2	339.9
Personal business	169.9	192.5	215.4	255.0	272.2	296.0	326.0	354.0	373.3
Clothing, acessories, and jewelry	193.3	207.2	222.3	231.8	248.7	259.3	264.2	281.7	293.9
Religious and welfare activities	57.1	62.9	68.1	86.0	92.7	101.6	105.6	116.9	123.0
Private education and research	43.3	46.6	50.9	71.5	79.4	86.2	92.2	98.9	105.5
Personal care	38.8	41.4	44.5	51.4	55.8	59.2	60.9	63.4	65.8
Foreign travel and other	13.1	6.5	7.7	−0.3	−8.0	−11.4	−19.7	−23.6	−25.4

*1990, 1991 and 1992 have been revised.
**Includes opthalmic products and orthopedic appliances.
SOURCE: U. S. Department of Commerce, Bureau of Economic Analysis, Survey of Current Business, various issues and July 1994.

Table 4.6

Personal Consumption Expenditures for Medical Care, by Type of Service, 1950–1992 (Billions)

Year	Total medical care	Hospital services	Percentage of total medical care	Physicians' services	Percentage of total medical care	Drugs, sundries, and appliances	Percentage of total medical care	Dentists' services	Percentage of total medical care	Net cost of health insurance	Percentage of total medical care	All other medical care	Percentage of total medical care
1950	$ 8.8	$ 2.1	24	$ 2.6	30	$ 2.2	25	$ 1.0	11	$ 0.3	3	$ 0.8	9
1955	13.4	3.4	25	3.8	28	3.0	22	1.5	11	0.6	4	1.1	8
1960	20.6	5.6	27	5.8	28	4.7	23	2.0	10	0.8	4	1.8	9
1965	31.6	8.9	28	8.5	27	6.4	20	2.8	9	1.3	4	3.7	12
1966	34.3	10.1	29	9.1	27	6.7	20	3.0	9	1.4	4	4.0	12
1967	37.1	11.8	32	10.0	27	7.0	19	3.4	9	1.3	4	3.7	10
1968	42.5	14.1	33	10.9	26	7.8	18	3.7	9	2.0	5	4.1	10
1969	48.3	17.0	35	12.4	26	8.6	18	4.3	9	1.9	4	4.3	8
1970	55.0	19.7	36	14.0	25	10.0	18	4.9	9	2.1	4	4.3	8
1971	60.9	23.2	38	15.3	25	10.5	17	5.1	8	2.6	4	4.2	7
1972	67.6	25.9	38	16.6	25	11.5	17	5.6	8	3.5	5	4.5	7
1973	75.1	28.8	38	18.4	25	12.5	17	6.6	9	3.6	5	5.2	7
1974	84.3	33.7	40	20.3	24	13.6	16	7.3	9	3.6	4	5.8	7
1975	96.9	40.1	41	23.5	24	14.9	15	8.2	8	3.2	3	7.0	7
1976	109.9	46.6	42	25.8	23	16.3	15	9.3	8	3.6	3	8.4	8
1977	126.5	53.3	42	29.6	23	17.4	14	10.3	8	5.4	4	10.4	8
1978	141.0	61.0	43	32.3	23	19.2	14	11.3	8	4.7	3	12.4	9
1979	160.6	70.0	44	36.3	23	21.6	13	12.3	8	5.6	3	14.8	9
1980	185.7	82.0	44	42.0	23	23.5	13	13.7	7	6.9	4	17.6	9
1981	217.3	96.8	45	49.0	23	25.8	12	16.1	7	7.6	3	22.0	10
1982	242.7	110.3	45	54.4	22	27.6	11	17.4	7	8.8	4	24.1	10
1983	266.5	119.6	45	61.1	23	30.3	11	18.5	7	11.0	4	25.8	10
1984	296.1	130.6	44	67.1	23	33.0	11	19.8	7	15.2	5	30.4	10
1985	327.5	140.2	43	73.5	22	36.0	11	21.5	6	21.6	7	34.7	11
1986	357.6	152.4	43	80.6	23	39.2	11	22.8	6	22.4	6	40.2	11
1987	399.0	166.3	42	94.0	24	41.7	10	25.0	6	25.3	6	46.6	12
1988	487.7	190.9	39	110.6	23	50.8	10	27.9	6	26.4	5	81.1	17
1989	536.4	209.5	39	121.6	23	55.0	10	30.0	6	31.2	6	89.1	17
1990	595.9	231.0	39	134.2	23	60.3	10	32.2	5	35.6	6	102.6	17
1991	656.0	255.2	39	148.1	23	64.6	10	34.5	5	38.3	6	115.3	18
1992	704.6	279.6	39	153.1	22	65.9	9	36.4	5	45.9	7	123.7	18

NOTE: These data exclude private expenditures in federal, state, city, and other governmental hospitals and nursing homes. In most cases, the sum of the items does not equal the total medical care because of rounding.

NOTE: 1988, 1989, 1990 data have been revised.

Table 4.7

Personal Consumption Expenditures for Medical Care as Percentages of Disposable Personal Income and Total Personal Consumption Expenditures, 1950–1992 (Billions)

Year	Personal consumption expenditures for medical care	Total personal consumption expenditures (billions)	Medical care as percentage of total personal consumption expenditures	Disposable personal income (billions)	Medical care as percentage of disposable personal income
1950	$ 8.8	$ 192.1	4.6	$ 207.5	4.3
1955	13.4	257.9	5.2	278.8	4.8
1960	20.6	330.7	6.2	358.9	5.7
1965	31.6	440.7	7.2	486.8	6.5
1970	55.0	640.0	8.6	715.6	7.7
1971	60.9	691.6	8.8	776.8	7.8
1972	67.6	757.6	9.0	839.6	8.1
1973	75.1	837.2	9.0	949.8	7.9
1974	84.3	916.5	9.2	1,038.3	8.1
1975	96.9	1,012.8	9.6	1,142.8	8.5
1976	109.9	1,129.3	9.7	1,248.7	8.8
1977	126.5	1,257.2	10.1	1,375.3	9.2
1978	141.0	1,403.5	10.0	1,546.4	9.1
1979	160.6	1,566.8	10.3	1,724.5	9.3
1980	185.7	1,732.6	10.7	1,914.3	9.7
1981	217.3	1,915.1	11.3	2,121.8	10.2
1982	242.7	2,050.7	11.8	2,261.4	10.7
1983	266.5	2,234.5	11.9	2,428.1	11.0
1984	296.1	2,430.5	12.2	2,668.6	11.1
1985	327.5	2,629.9	12.3	2,838.7	11.4
1986	357.6	2,797.4	12.8	3,013.3	11.8
1987	399.0	3,009.4	13.3	3,194.7	12.5
1988	487.7	3,296.1	14.8	3,548.2	13.7
1989	536.4	3,523.1	15.2	3,787.0	14.2
1990*	597.8	3,761.2	15.9	4,050.5	14.8
1991*	651.7	3,906.4	16.7	4,230.5	15.4
1992	704.6	4,139.9	17.0	4,500.2	15.7

*Data have been revised.

NOTE: Includes all expenses for health insurance except loss of income type coverage.

SOURCE: U. S. Department of Commerce, Bureau of Economic Analysis, Survey of Current Business, various issues, and Health Insurance Association of America.

Table 4.8

Average Annual Percentage Change in Consumer Price Index, All Urban Consumers, 1969–1993

Year	All items	All medical care items	Physicians' services	Dental services	Hospital room	Medical care commodities	Prescription drugs	Internal and respiratory over-the-counter drugs
1969	5.5	8.2	7.0	7.2	13.6	0.9	1.3	1.0
1970	5.7	7.0	7.5	5.7	12.9	2.4	1.7	2.7
1971	4.4	7.4	7.0	6.4	12.3	1.7	0.0	3.8
1972	3.2	3.5	3.0	4.1	6.4	0.2	−0.4	0.9
1973	6.2	4.5	3.4	3.2	5.0	0.2	−0.2	1.1
1974	11.0	10.4	9.2	7.6	10.5	3.6	2.3	4.5
1975	9.1	12.6	12.1	10.4	17.1	8.3	6.2	10.7
1976	5.8	10.1	11.2	6.2	13.8	6.0	5.3	6.8
1977	6.5	9.9	9.3	7.6	11.5	6.5	6.1	6.9
1978	7.6	8.5	8.4	7.1	11.1	7.0	7.7	7.1
1979	11.3	9.8	9.1	8.3	11.3	7.1	7.8	7.4
1980	13.5	11.3	10.5	11.9	13.1	9.3	9.2	10.1
1981	10.3	10.7	11.0	9.6	14.9	11.0	11.4	12.4
1982	6.2	11.8	9.4	7.6	15.7	10.3	11.6	10.8
1983	3.2	8.7	7.8	6.8	11.3	8.6	11.0	7.5
1984	4.3	6.0	6.9	8.1	8.3	7.3	9.6	6.2
1985	3.6	6.1	5.9	6.2	5.9	7.2	9.5	5.4
1986	1.9	7.7	7.2	5.6	6.0	6.6	8.6	4.9
1987	3.6	6.6	7.3	6.8	7.2	6.7	8.0	5.3
1988	4.1	6.4	7.2	6.8	9.3	6.8	8.0	5.6
1989	4.8	7.7	7.4	6.3	10.3	7.8	8.7	6.1
1990	5.4	9.0	7.1	6.6	10.9	8.4	10.0	5.1
1991	4.2	8.6	6.0	7.4	9.4	8.2	9.9	4.5
1992	3.0	7.4	6.3	6.8	8.8	6.4	7.5	3.8
1993	2.5	4.6	4.3	4.5	5.5	3.0	4.0	1.1

SOURCE: U. S. Department of Labor, Bureau of Labor Statistics, CPI detailed report, various issues.

Table 4.9

Community Hospital Statistics, by State, 1992

State	Number of hospitals	Hospital beds	Occupancy rate	Admissions	Average cost to hospital per day*	Average length of stay	Average cost to hospital per stay*
United States	5,292	920,943	65.6	31,033,557	$ 819.83	7.1	$5,794.43
Alabama	116	18,614	61.9	603,907	728.94	7.0	5,080.13
Alaska	16	1,281	53.5	37,842	1,115.85	6.6	7,455.75
Arizona	60	9,355	60.7	392,563	1,050.64	5.3	5,502.00
Arkansas	87	11,047	59.5	344,768	633.25	7.0	4,376.30
California	436	78,388	62.4	3,081,455	1,133.50	5.9	6,626.25
Colorado	71	10,100	61.4	344,164	904.28	6.6	5,932.86
Connecticut	35	9,210	75.0	350,267	1,012.24	7.2	7,241.24
Delaware	8	2,083	71.6	82,403	919.97	6.8	6,123.48
District of Columbia	11	4,384	74.5	162,446	1,124.20	7.4	8,217.88
Florida	223	51,024	61.3	1,645,258	885.58	6.9	6,092.04
Georgia	159	26,346	65.3	861,296	720.86	7.3	5,237.54
Hawaii	20	2,877	82.6	97,542	761.02	8.9	6,875.60
Idaho	41	3,333	57.6	100,137	618.04	7.0	4,346.24
Illinois	210	45,472	64.4	1,496,933	848.82	7.2	6,048.01
Indiana	113	21,457	59.3	711,017	821.76	6.5	5,305.32
Iowa	121	14,024	59.0	363,594	588.35	8.3	4,920.46
Kansas	134	11,436	54.7	292,182	661.03	7.8	5,114.73
Kentucky	107	16,045	63.0	530,388	674.18	7.0	4,652.45
Louisiana	135	18,714	58.3	609,574	836.25	6.6	5,457.23
Maine	39	4,558	67.9	147,844	674.15	7.7	5,142.23
Maryland	49	13,143	75.4	565,803	805.91	6.4	5,139.34
Massachusetts	102	21,725	72.6	835,982	937.05	6.9	6,381.28
Michigan	170	31,686	64.6	1,061,850	846.63	7.0	5,898.84
Minnesota	145	18,812	66.8	524,834	618.09	8.8	5,456.08
Mississippi	100	12,445	59.8	368,363	515.92	7.4	3,807.47
Missouri	133	23,973	60.3	718,011	791.61	7.4	5,789.10
Montana	53	4,275	65.0	101,991	474.21	10.0	4,704.20
Nebraska	90	8,443	56.4	181,198	600.30	9.6	5,713.51
Nevada	21	3,534	61.0	129,628	951.76	6.0	5,777.78
New Hampshire	27	3,401	66.2	116,338	776.03	7.1	5,480.01
New Jersey	97	31,192	79.7	1,124,199	736.58	8.1	5,909.46
New Mexico	38	4,188	54.9	842,549	949.60	5.4	5,094.48
New York	231	76,171	84.3	2,374,102	743.53	9.9	7,315.98
North Carolina	117	22,412	71.6	796,131	710.78	7.4	5,217.01
North Dakota	47	4,429	64.8	1,049,392	484.37	11.3	5,301.73
Ohio	192	42,263	60.8	9,397,751	875.48	6.5	5,649.09
Oklahoma	110	12,001	55.9	372,607	740.34	6.6	4,846.98
Oregon	63	7,494	54.5	296,018	1,011.40	5.1	5,111.55
Pennsylvania	232	51,895	72.7	1,817,708	792.78	7.6	5,954.72
Rhode Island	12	3,110	76.9	131,203	800.92	6.7	5,355.24
South Carolina	68	11,339	68.6	396,865	782.04	7.2	5,616.99
South Dakota	52	4,269	62.2	95,375	457.24	10.2	4,652.82
Tennessee	131	23,230	61.7	769,117	796.46	6.8	5,392.35
Texas	414	58,511	56.4	1,971,186	932.89	6.1	5,666.26
Utah	42	4,346	55.2	173,336	1,036.30	5.1	5,104.36
Vermont	15	1,679	65.0	56,852	726.21	7.0	5,046.12
Virginia	98	19,657	65.7	700,148	774.41	6.8	5,226.13
Washington	90	11,901	62.2	500,856	974.24	5.4	5,238.49
West Virginia	57	8,184	64.2	278,245	654.62	6.9	4,496.09
Wisconsin	128	18,356	63.7	587,256	674.03	7.3	4,909.49
Wyoming	26	2,131	51.0	45,980	515.44	8.6	4,370.00

*Reported by hospital as expense.

SOURCE: American Hospital Association, Hospital Statistics (1993–94 edition).

Table 4.10

Hospital Admissions, Emergency Room Visits, and Outpatient Hospital Visits, 1991

State	Hospital admissions per 1,000 population	Emergency room visits per 1,000 population	Outpatient hospital visits per 1,000 population
Alabama	158	426	750
Alaska	108	435	549
Arizona	125	352	564
Arkansas	160	406	384
California	112	307	1,135
Colorado	118	310	934
Connecticut	115	386	979
Delaware	138	405	1,105
District of Columbia	329	736	1,186
Florida	137	364	590
Georgia	153	469	641
Hawaii	107	294	1,190
Idaho	103	298	872
Illinois	141	269	1,109
Indiana	136	372	1,194
Iowa	146	340	1,323
Kansas	135	320	917
Kentucky	157	448	856
Louisiana	156	431	953
Maine	127	506	1,168
Maryland	132	328	624
Massachusetts	145	466	1,307
Michigan	120	345	1,387
Minnesota	128	277	804
Mississippi	169	400	419
Missouri	155	372	959
Montana	143	320	862
Nebraska	135	253	837
Nevada	108	246	604
New Hampshire	125	441	1,034
New Jersey	152	320	915
New Mexico	126	335	1,056
New York	136	389	1,314
North Carolina	131	388	602
North Dakota	171	325	623
Ohio	146	432	1,173
Oklahoma	137	351	473
Oregon	113	340	864
Pennsylvania	159	434	1,404
Rhode Island	137	514	827
South Carolina	132	410	631
South Dakota	164	298	841
Tennessee	174	465	739
Texas	131	309	536
Utah	110	335	1,287
Vermont	116	349	916
Virginia	129	371	716
Washington	113	351	757
West Virginia	167	552	1,089
Wisconsin	129	313	989
Wyoming	121	401	807

SOURCE: Derived from calculations of data from American Hospital Association, Hospital Statistics 1992–93, Statistical Abstract of the United States.

Table 4.11

Uncompensated Care in Community Hospitals in the United States, 1992

State	Total hospital expenses	Total uncompensated care expenses	Percent of total expenses
Alabama	$ 4,086,622,574	$ 351,095,842	8.6
Alaska	401,380,374	24,375,358	5.3
Arizona	2,924,553,364	145,956,397	5.0
Arkansas	2,078,393,611	151,972,830	7.3
California	27,255,420,107	1,749,206,487	6.4
Colorado	2,860,279,542	190,349,245	6.7
Connecticut	3,467,126,174	162,233,546	4.7
Delaware	695,064,204	67,321,716	9.7
District of Columbia	1,664,359,132	148,142,380	8.9
Florida	13,361,078,111	889,185,169	6.7
Georgia	6,182,514,812	529,333,725	8.6
Hawaii	897,093,295	32,924,191	3.7
Idaho	656,825,560	23,330,207	3.6
Illinois	12,341,995,519	690,349,440	5.6
Indiana	5,456,248,094	277,941,471	5.1
Iowa	2,630,265,281	114,462,867	4.4
Kansas	2,132,860,975	79,861,499	3.7
Kentucky	3,418,428,285	171,836,095	5.0
Louisiana	4,439,389,185	221,501,951	5.0
Maine	1,068,878,523	52,460,151	4.9
Maryland	3,894,755,053	321,800,126	8.3
Massachusetts	7,545,886,252	515,229,143	6.6
Michigan	9,491,078,611	320,909,086	3.4
Minnesota	3,993,236,555	95,883,389	2.4
Mississippi	1,934,194,933	162,207,782	8.4
Missouri	5,920,997,644	333,946,598	5.6
Montana	678,887,326	23,828,891	3.5
Nebraska	1,497,934,068	36,484,993	2.4
Nevada	971,586,380	64,441,467	6.6
New Hampshire	930,544,682	49,940,964	5.4
New Jersey	8,386,411,634	809,838,266	9.7
New Mexico	1,134,693,048	91,097,559	8.0
New York	23,250,575,351	1,111,077,206	4.8
North Carolina	5,662,315,777	371,039,914	6.6
North Dakota	702,579,544	15,359,749	2.2
Ohio	11,684,546,771	548,945,499	4.7
Oklahoma	2,471,315,088	174,384,524	7.1
Oregon	2,289,319,126	129,882,254	5.7
Pennsylvania	14,880,670,092	412,588,861	2.8
Rhode Island	993,525,479	34,564,000	3.5
South Carolina	2,967,399,569	231,851,479	7.8
South Dakota	603,750,072	16,035,925	2.7
Tennessee	5,585,607,871	370,874,408	6.6
Texas	15,135,425,847	1,566,829,829	10.4
Utah	1,339,348,032	51,850,984	3.9
Vermont	426,750,160	17,802,967	4.2
Virginia	5,017,519,686	325,204,129	6.5
Washington	4,045,619,836	158,806,874	3.9
West Virginia	1,802,943,821	118,024,511	6.5
Wisconsin	4,226,548,968	113,825,059	2.7
Wyoming	310,121,743	26,505,671	8.5
Total	**$248,094,865,721**	**$14,691,902,692**	**5.9**

NOTE: Medical services for the uninsured account for 70 percent of uncompensated care, while people with coverage who do not pay their deductibles account for the remaining 30 percent.

SOURCE: American Hospital Association, 1992 Annual Survey.

Table 4.12

Median Physicians' Fees for Selected Surgical Procedures, by Specialty, 1993

Specialty	Fees	Specialty	Fees
General surgery		**Neurosurgery**	
Appendectomy	$1,000	Cranioplasty	$2,847
Cholecystectomy	1,503	Craniotomy for evacuation of hematoma	3,615
Inguinal hernia (unilateral)	974	Neuroplasty (median nerve)	1,000
Modified radical mastectomy	1,800	Discectomy, anterior including osteophytectomy,	
Subtotal gastrectomy without vagotomy	2,119	cervical, single interspace	3,275
Laparoscopy, surgical; cholecystectomy	2,000	Laminectomy, lumbar, more than two vertebral	
Excision of cyst fibroadenoma from breast		segments	3,500
tissue, several lesions	550		
		Plastic surgery	
Obstetrics/Gynecology		Complete rhinoplasty	$3,000
Complete obstetrical care (usual or routine)	$2,000	Rhytidectomy, forehead	2,410
Total hysterectomy	2,197	Dermabrasion, segmental, facial scar	751
Laparoscopy with fulguration of oviducts	1,000	Excision of benign lesion	144
Dilation and curettage (therapeutic for abortion)	600	Blepharoplasty upper eyelids bilateral	1,500
Complete OB care with Cesarean section	2,400	Reduction mammoplasty, bilateral	4,500
Dilation and curettage, in hospital (diagnostic)	572	Suction-assisted lipectomy, trunk	1,750
		Mammoplasty, augmentation with prosthetic	
Thoracic surgery		implant, bilateral	3,000
Diagnostic flexible bronchoscopy	$ 451		
Lobectomy	2,501	**Orthopedic surgery**	
Esophagoscopy (dilation)	473	Colles fracture, closed manipulation	$ 545
Thoracentesis	175	Arthrocentesis of knee	69
Abdominal aortic aneurysm repair	3,357	Knee arthroscopy with meniscectomy	1,926
		Lumbar arthrodesis, single interspace	3,461
Cardiovascular surgery		Diagnostic knee arthroscopy	844
Replacement of aortic valve, with		Total knee arthroplasty	4,142
cardiopulmonary bypass	$5,000	Total hip arthroplasty	4,200
Insertion of permanent pacemaker with		Open treatment of hip fracture with internal	
transvenous electrodes, ventricular	1,550	fixation	2,392
Coronary artery bypass, with three coronary			
grafts	5,486	**Psychiatrists**	
		Individual psychotherapy, in office, 45–50	
Cardiologists		minutes	$115
Cardiac catheterization	$1,200	Individual psychotherapy, in hospital, 45–50	
Echocardiography (complete)	553	minutes	120
		Family psychotherapy, conjoint psychotherapy	125
		Psychiatric diagnostic interview	150

SOURCE: Medical Economics, October 11, 1993. Reprinted by permission.

Table 4.13

Expenditures for Hospital Care, Physicians' Services, and Prescription Drugs, by Region, 1991

Region and state	Total (millions)	Hospital care (millions)	Physician services (millions)	Prescription drugs (millions)
United States	$473,320	$286,053	$150,891	$36,377
New England	27,878	17,289	8,455	2,134
Connecticut	6,844	4,089	2,236	520
Maine	1,966	1,257	547	162
Massachusetts	14,402	9,097	4,244	1,061
New Hampshire	1,917	1,129	641	146
Rhode Island	1,924	1,215	543	166
Vermont	824	502	243	79
Mideast	92,461	59,448	26,298	6,715
Delaware	1,379	800	488	91
District of Columbia	3,4040	2,641	666	93
Maryland	9,323	5,210	3,284	829
New Jersey	14,647	8,829	4,569	1,249
New York	38,533	25,345	10,611	2,577
Pennsylvania	25,178	16,622	6,680	1,876
Great Lakes	77,434	48,089	22,933	6,412
Illinois	21,234	13,792	5,731	1,711
Indiana	9,749	6,024	2,890	835
Michigan	19,383	10,663	5,141	15,798
Ohio	20,335	12,628	6,094	1,613
Wisconsin	8,733	4,981	3,077	675
Plains	33,228	20,129	10,648	2,451
Iowa	4,631	2,933	1,294	404
Kansas	4,307	2,545	1,404	358
Minnesota	8,726	4,607	3,571	548
Missouri	10,226	6,660	2,815	751
Nebraska	2,794	1,789	779	227
North Dakota	1,322	976	442	84
South Dakota	1,221	799	342	80
Southeast	109,951	66,357	34,342	9,252
Alabama	7,494	4,521	2,296	677
Arkansas	3,968	2,359	1,241	368
Florida	27,047	15,210	9,881	1,956
Georgia	12,476	7,603	3,902	971
Kentucky	6,362	3,908	1,814	639
Louisiana	8,335	5,277	2,400	658
Mississippi	3,732	2,425	923	384
North Carolina	10,987	6,795	3,200	992
South Carolina	5,547	3,614	1,455	479
Tennessee	9,948	6,239	2,865	844
Virginia	10,825	6,407	3,464	955
West Virginia	3,299	2,000	900	329
Southwest	44,018	26,287	14,245	3,486
Arizona	6,420	3,615	2,321	3,486
New Mexico	2,448	1,570	699	179
Oklahoma	4,929	3,046	1,471	442
Texas	30,222	18,086	9,754	2,382

Continued

Table 4.13 *(Continued)*

Region and state	Total (millions)	Hospital care (millions)	Physician services (millions)	Prescription drugs (millions)
Rocky Mountain	$ 11,682	$ 7,043	$ 3,810	$ 829
Colorado	6,100	3,614	2,122	364
Idaho	1,282	762	397	123
Montana	1,164	736	314	87
Utah	2,539	1,510	822	207
Wyoming	598	394	155	49
Far West	76,668	41,411	630,159	5,097
Alaska	1,027	659	312	56
California	57,141	31,128	23,108	3,904
Hawaii	2,144	1,287	719	137
Nevada	2,274	1,195	945	135
Oregon	4,597	2,565	1,738	297
Washington	8,486	4,581	3,336	568

NOTE: Numbers do not add due to rounding.
SOURCE: Health Care Financing Administration, Office of the Actuary.

Table 4.14

Costs of Tests Frequently Performed on Pregnant Women, 1993

City	Amniocentesis	Oxytocin stress	Fetal monitoring
New York	$347	$146	$ 77
Chicago	239	155	152
Washington	341	207	144
Los Angeles	201	101	168
Denver	150	63	155
Houston	222	100	110
Miami	298	79	160
Philadelphia	286	119	195
Boston	238	136	99
New Orleans	192	73	87
Minneapolis	133	83	121

SOURCE: HIAA Surgical Prevailing Healthcare Charges System.

Table 4.15

Number of Office Visits by Physician Specialty, 1990–1991

Specialty	Number of visits (000)		Percentage distribution		Percentage change between 1990–1991
	1990	1991	1990	1991	
All visits	704,604	669,689	100.0	100.0	−5.0
General and family practice	209,788	164,857	29.8	24.6	−21.4
Internal medicine	96,622	102,923	13.7	15.4	6.5
Pediatrics	81,148	74,646	11.5	11.1	−8.0
Obstetrics and gynecology	61,243	56,834	8.7	8.5	−7.2
Ophthalmology	43,842	41,207	6.2	6.2	−6.0
Orthopedic surgery	32,917	35,932	4.7	5.4	9.2
Dermatology	24,009	29,659	3.4	4.4	23.5
General surgery	22,402	21,285	3.2	3.2	−5.0
Otolarngology	17,959	19,101	2.5	2.9	6.4
Psychiatry	20,963	15,720	3.0	2.3	−25.0
Urological surgery	9,546	12,758	1.4	1.9	33.6
Cardiovascular diseases	11,240	11,629	1.6	1.7	3.5
Neurology	6,228	6,798	0.9	1.0	9.2
All other specialties	66,969	76,341	9.5	11.4	14.5

SOURCE: National Center for Health Statistics, March 1993.

Table 4.16

Number of Visits for Selected Diagnostic Tests Ordered by Physicians, 1992

Diagnostic test	Number of visits (thousands)	Percentage distribution of visits
All vists	669,689	100.0
None	236,035	35.2
Blood pressure	289,153	43.2
Urinalysis	54,194	12.7
EKG-resting	19,020	2.8
EKG-exercise	2,661	0.4
Mammogram	11,558	1.7
Chest X-ray	16,307	2.4
Other radiology	36,864	5.5
Allergy testing	1,445	0.2
Spirometry	2,486	0.4
Pap test	28,313	4.2
Strep throat test	13,650	2.0
HIV serology	1,362	0.2
Cholesterol measure	26,932	4.0
Other lab test	114,274	17.1
Hearing test	9,282	1.4
Visual acuity	40,374	6.0
Mental status exam	8,664	1.3
Other	67,757	10.1

SOURCE: National Center for Health Statistics, March 1993.

Table 4.17

Physicians' Fees for Office Visit with New Patients, by Region and Specialty, 1993

Georgraphic area	GP/FP	INT MED	Surgery	Pediatrics	OB/GYN
All physicians	$ 59	$116	$ 85	$71	$ 93
New England	NA	120	105	NA	NA
Middle Atlantic	58	156	105	78	109
East North Central	59	102	72	60	77
West North Central	55	109	58	NA	NA
South Atlantic	53	105	71	70	92
East South Central	52	106	69	NA	NA
West South Central	56	102	77	59	NA
Mountain	60	NA	74	NA	NA
Pacific	73	139	112	84	113

NA: Not available.
SOURCE: Physician Marketplace Statistics 1993.

Table 4.18

Managed Care Patient Visits by Specialty, 1992

Specialty	Median visits per week		Percentage of total weekly visits to physicians	
	HMOs	PPOs	HMOs	PPOs
Cardiologists	9	6	11	9
Cardiovascular surgeons	8	4	11	7
Family practitioners	25	14	24	13
General practitioners	15	14	19	16
General surgeons	9	7	14	11
Internists	17	9	17	10
Neurosurgeons	8	5	10	9
OBG specialists	22	15	24	20
Ophthalmologists	11	8	14	9
Orthopedic surgeons	13	10	17	10
Pediatricians	35	24	28	22
Plastic surgeons	6	7	13	13
Thoracic surgeons	5	3	13	4
Urologists	12	9	15	10
All surgical specialties	11	9	18	14
All non-surgical specialties*	14	12	19	14
All doctors	14	11	19	14

*Excludes FPs and GPs. Medians exclude physicians with no HMO or PPO affiliations.
SOURCE: Medical Economics Magazine.

Table 4.19

Average Annual Health Plan Cost per Employee, by Region and by Industry, 1986–1993

	1993	1992	1991	1990	1989	1988	1987	1986
By Region								
Pacific	NA	NA	$3,659	$3,260	$2,943	$2,426	$2,246	$2,173
Mountain	NA	NA	3,262	2,998	2,703	2,330	1,910	1,815
North Central	NA	NA	3,546	3,234	2,822	2,570	2,065	2,046
South Central	NA	NA	3,256	2,983	2,511	2,303	1,913	1,784
New England	NA	NA	3,918	3,361	2,896	2,216	2,063	1,828
Mid-Atlantic	NA	NA	4,066	3,553	2,972	2,307	1,974	1,898
South Atlantic	NA	NA	3,412	2,955	2,408	2,108	1,782	1,692
West	$3,620	$3,437	NA	NA	NA	NA	NA	NA
Midwest	4,020	3,675	NA	NA	NA	NA	NA	NA
Northeast	4,267	3,877	NA	NA	NA	NA	NA	NA
South	3,262	3,061	NA	NA	NA	NA	NA	NA
By Industry								
Consumer products	NA	NA	3,661	3,250	2,602	2,317	1,848	2,089
Manufacturing	3,991	3,729	3,861	3,426	2,961	2,549	2,127	1,929
Mining, construction	NA	NA	4,252	3,922	3,127	2,775	2,050	2,127
Energy, petroleum	NA	NA	4,039	3,863	3,117	3,110	2,217	2,024
Wholesale/retail	2,938	2,743	2,891	2,494	2,208	1,915	1,762	1,518
Services	3,681	3,379	NA	NA	NA	NA	NA	NA
Tech professional	NA	NA	3,113	2,961	2,558	2,010	1,906	2,135
Utilities	NA	NA	4,591	4,363	3,452	2,977	2,375	2,175
Transportation	NA	NA	4,186	3,238	2,632	2,648	2,281	1,905
Health services	NA	NA	3,149	2,665	2,299	2,073	1,693	1,748
Financial services	4,067	3,694	3,479	2,850	2,413	2,031	1,675	1,549
Communications	NA	NA	4,044	3,616	3,584	2,994	2,152	1,866
Government	4,219	3,872	3,546	3,239	2,836	2,434	2,071	1,906
Education	NA	NA	3,447	3,227	2,915	1,940	1,874	1,900
Insurance	NA	NA	3,577	3,180	2,675	2,273	1,861	1,811
Transportation/utilities/ communications	4,639	4,234	NA	NA	NA	NA	NA	NA
Healthcare	3,242	3,056	NA	NA	NA	NA	NA	NA
Other	3,690	3,407	3,534	3,247	2,759	2,187	1,937	1,899
Total, all responding employees	3,781	3,502	3,605	3,217	2,748	2,354	1,985	1,857

NOTE 1: 1986 through 1991 data are comparable.
NOTE 2: 1992 and 1993 data are comparable.
NA: Not available.
SOURCE: Previous Foster Higgins Health Care Benefits Surveys, and current 1993 Foster Higgins Health Care Benefits Survey.

Table 4.20

Type of Health Insurance Plan, Enrollment, and Cost per Plan Type, by Region, Industry, and Size of Employer, 1993

Region	Percentage of employees offering at least one type				Percentage of employees enrolled in plans				Cost for each employee by plan type			
	Traditional	PPO	POS	HMO	Traditional	PPO	POS	HMO	Traditional	PPO	POS	HMO
All respondents	**57**	**24**	**4**	**22**	**48**	**27**	**7**	**19**	**$3,268**	**$3,145**	**$3,000**	**$3,075**
West	35	24	9	36	28	31	11	31	3,238	3,887	2,849	2,772
Midwest	66	25	1	17	49	31	5	15	3,665	2,884	3,338	3,390
Northeast	77	5	0	24	66	8	6	20	3,522	3,668	3,463	3,161
South	48	43	7	12	43	36	7	14	2,647	3,007	2,665	3,010
Industry												
Manufacturing	55	29	9	10	61	19	7	13	3,242	3,714	ID	3,162
Wholesale/retail	66	18	0	25	55	28	4	13	2,689	2,367	ID	2,633
Services	50	26	7	26	41	30	9	19	3,075	3,530	ID	3,037
Transportation/utilities/communications	70	11	0	30	57	14	10	19	3,518	ID	ID	3,213
Healthcare	34	39	1	27	27	51	4	17	3,125	2,611	ID	3,086
Finance	59	5	2	42	33	26	10	31	3,832	3,355	ID	2,887
Government	70	23	5	16	39	21	7	34	3,784	3,255	ID	3,311
Other	64	21	0	26	49	33	3	16	3,508	ID	ID	ID
Size of employer												
10–49 employees	55	20	3	27	54	23	2	21	2,722	ID	ID	ID
50–199	64	32	8	4	59	35	6	1	2,911	ID	ID	ID
200–499	51	47	3	11	44	46	2	7	3,185	2,513	ID	3,428
500–999	66	33	17	37	50	23	13	13	3,069	3,300	ID	2,929
1,000–4,999	71	37	11	50	47	26	5	22	3,456	2,972	ID	3,075
5,000–9,999	63	45	22	66	37	27	13	23	3,409	2,763	ID	2,996
10,000–19,999	70	51	22	73	41	28	8	23	3,617	3,241	ID	3,156
20,000 or more	78	50	35	92	42	18	9	31	3,806	3,884	ID	3,229

ID: Insufficient data.

SOURCE: Foster Higgins National Survey of Employer-Sponsored Health Plans 1993.

Table 4.21

Estimated Annual Receipts of Health Services Businesses, 1985–1991 (Millions)

Type of business	1985	1986	1987	1988	1989	1990	1991
Health services (all)	$147,415	$161,882	$182,289	$203,364	$219,081	$243,048	$261,269
Offices and clinics of doctors of medicine	72,065	78,360	90,462	100,314	106,300	115,067	122,470
Offices and clinics of dentists	20,574	21,901	24,017	25,550	26,932	28,475	29,731
Offices and clinics of doctors of osteopathy	1,765	1,938	2,119	2,335	2,321	2,513	2,599
Offices and clinics of other health practiitoners	7,864	8,791	10,340	12,167	12,795	14,802	15,628
Offices and clinics of chiropractors	2,678	3,005	3,275	3,984	4,420	4,828	4,986
Offices and clinics of optometrists	2,818	3,038	3,450	3,760	3,864	4,275	4,430
Offices and clinics of podiatrists	NA	NA	NA	NA	NA	1,689	1,826
Nursing and personal care facilities	17,462	19,040	20,063	21,361	23,349	26,446	28,848
Skilled nursing care facilities	NA	NA	NA	NA	NA	21,790	23,623
Intermediate care facilities	NA	NA	NA	NA	NA	2,998	3,338
Nursing and personal care facilities, n.e.c.	NA	NA	NA	NA	NA	1,658	1,887
Hospitals	15,724	18,068	19,720	22,777	25,023	29,059	31,523
General medical and surgical hospitals	NA	NA	NA	NA	NA	22,579	24,518
Psychiatric hospitals	NA	NA	NA	NA	NA	2,095	5,436
Specialty hospitals, except psychiatric	NA	NA	NA	NA	NA	1,385	1,569
Medical and dental laboratories	5,381	6,057	7,114	8,119	8,933	9,872	10,527
Medical laboratories	3,895	4,455	5,518	6,620	7,374	8,209	8,849
Dental laboratories	1,486	1,602	1,596	1,499	1,559	1,663	1,678
Home health care services	NA	NA	NA	NA	NA	6,196	7,381
Miscellaneous health and allied services	NA	NA	NA	NA	NA	10,618	12,562
Kidney dialysis centers	NA	NA	NA	NA	NA	1,272	1,505
Specialty outpatient facilities, n.e.c.	NA	NA	NA	NA	NA	5,258	6,426

NOTE: Data reflects taxable firms. Taxable firms were considered by definition of federal income tax.
NA: Not available.
SOURCE: Health Services; U. S. Department of Commerce, Bureau of the Census.

Chapter 5

HEALTH SERVICES RESOURCES AND UTILIZATION

The number of community hospitals (defined as nonfederal, short-term, general, and special hospitals) that provide acute care to the public has been declining since 1977. They still, however, account for 81 percent of all hospitals in the United States; 93 percent of all hospital admissions are to community hospitals.

According to the 1993–94 edition of *Hospital Statistics*, published by the AHA, community hospital admissions decreased slightly to 31.0 million in 1992 from 31.1 million in 1991. During 1992, the number of beds in community hospitals fell by 3,000, the majority of the reductions occurring in rural hospitals. Hospitals reported 349 million outpatient visits in 1992, an increase of 8 percent over the previous year. This reflected a continuing trend: the use of new facilities for the treatment of both medical and psychiatric patients on an outpatient basis. (The 10 percent increase in outpatient visits reported in 1989 was the highest rate of growth in outpatient use in more than a decade; this trend, although somewhat slowed, continued from 1991 to 1992.)

Ambulatory care was increasingly an alternative to hospitalization, as evidenced by the proliferation of ambulatory care centers and of patient visits to these centers. In the United States, 81 percent of community hospitals now have organized outpatient service departments providing outpatient surgery, examination, diagnosis, and treatment of a variety of nonemergency medical conditions on an ambulatory basis. In 1992, 26 percent of reporting hospitals provided treatment for alcohol and drug abuse on an outpatient basis (Table 5.19).

Special geriatric services are offered at 4,017 community hospitals across the country; 455 of these hospitals provide Alzheimer's diagnostic/assessment services. Hospice service, providing palliative care for the dying, is available at 874 hospitals and at an increasing number of free-standing facilities across the United States. To be eligible for reimbursement by Medicare, hospices must be certified by the U.S. Department of Health and Human Services.

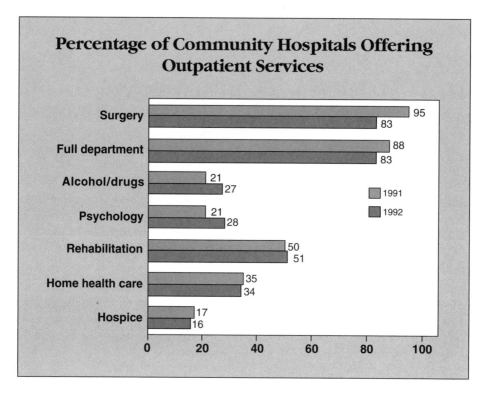

Figure 5.1

SOURCE: American Hospital Association, 1993–1994 edition.

◆ Utilization by Diagnosis

Both utilization and length of hospital stay vary according to the source of payment for medical services. The National Hospital Discharge Survey by the National Center for Health Statistics (NCHS) indicated that Medicare and Medicaid patients (14.2 million) use medical facilities more than private patients (10.1 million) and stay in the hospital for longer periods of time as well. Self-pay patients have an average stay in hospital of 5.2 days, Medicare patients average 8.6 days, Medicaid 5.6 days, and private insurance patients 4.9 days (Table 5.6).

In their 1993 data, the NCHS reported that, with the exception of obstetrical procedures for women, operations on the digestive system (5.5 million procedures) were the most common type of procedure performed on both sexes in 1991, with cardiovascular system procedures (4.1 million) next.

There were 26.7 million surgical procedures performed on women and 17.3 million on men. The majority of the surgical procedures was performed on people in the 15 to 44 age group.

According to the NCHS, the most frequent diagnoses for patients under 15 years of age were pneumonia, infectious and parasitic diseases, and fractures. Mental disorders, diseases of the genitourinary system, fractures, and heart disease were the most frequent diagnoses of patients 15 to 44 years of age, excluding females with obstetrical deliveries. Patients 45 to 64 years and 65 years and over were hospitalized most frequently for heart disease and malignant neoplasms.

The average length of stay of the 4 million women hospitalized for deliveries was 2.8 days (Table 5.7).

The most recent data from the U.S. Department of Health and Human Services reported that between 1988 and 1990, the number of discharges from short-stay hospitals with a diagnosis of HIV infection increased 54 percent to 146,000 discharges. Men 20 to 49 years of age accounted for 70 percent of all HIV discharges in 1990, down from 77 percent in 1988. The average length of stay for patients with HIV infection was twice that for all discharges (14.9 days compared with 6.4 days in 1990).

Diagnosis-Related Groups

In 1975, HCFA contracted with Yale University to develop a patient classification system to support a hospital inpatient prospective payment system for Medicare. The goal was to pay all hospitals the same fixed sum to cover all costs associated with treating a patient falling within a specific diagnosis-related group (DRG). (The underlying assumption was that hospitals that provide the necessary services efficiently will realize a net gain while those that are inefficient will find that the DRG payment does not cover their costs.) This system was tested in the early 1980s and found viable both for measuring hospital output and implementing a prospective payment system.

As more data are collected and medical technology advances, DRGs are reviewed and revised (as mandated by Congress).

◆ Physician Contacts

Collectively, people in the United States contacted their physicians either in person or by telephone more than 1.4 billion times during 1991. Women made more visits to both their doctors' offices and hospitals than men did,

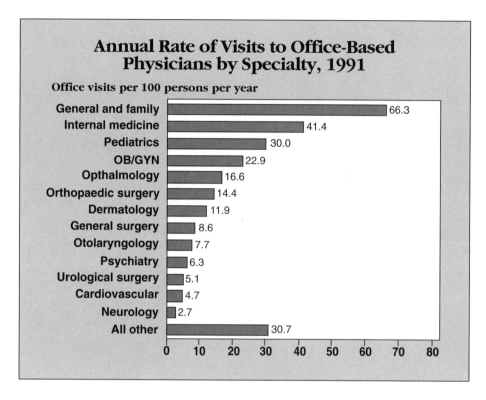

Annual Rate of Visits to Office-Based Physicians by Specialty, 1991

Office visits per 100 persons per year

Specialty	Value
General and family	66.3
Internal medicine	41.4
Pediatrics	30.0
OB/GYN	22.9
Opthalmology	16.6
Orthopaedic surgery	14.4
Dermatology	11.9
General surgery	8.6
Otolaryngology	7.7
Psychiatry	6.3
Urological surgery	5.1
Cardiovascular	4.7
Neurology	2.7
All other	30.7

Figure 5.2

SOURCE: NCHS, Health Interview Series, May 1994.

contacting physicians an average of 3.8 times in 1991. Men contacted physicians, as women did, primarily at physicians' offices, but only averaged 2.8 visits during 1991.

In 1991, general and family practitioners were visited the most, followed by pediatricians and obstetricians/gynecologists (Table 5.14). People between the ages of 25 and 44 years paid more visits to physicians than any other age group, with women making one-and-one-half more visits than males (Table 5.15).

People visited their doctors' offices almost 700 million times in 1991 and were most frequently diagnosed with diseases of the respiratory system and the nervous system. During these visits, 24 million blood pressure checks, 88 million urinalyses, and 87 million blood tests were performed. Commercial insurance companies paid for over 239 million office visits by people of all ages to their physicians in 1991, according to a May 1994 report by NCHS (Table 5.16).

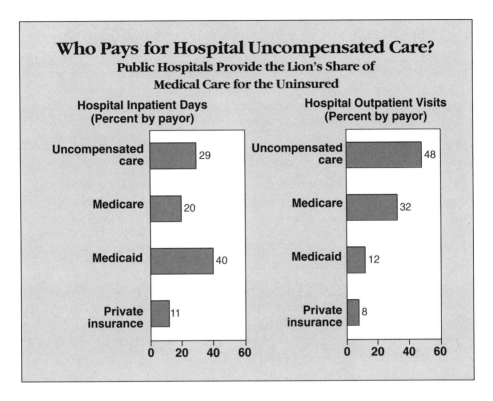

Who Pays for Hospital Uncompensated Care?
Public Hospitals Provide the Lion's Share of
Medical Care for the Uninsured

Hospital Inpatient Days
(Percent by payor)

Hospital Outpatient Visits
(Percent by payor)

Figure 5.3

SOURCE: National Association of Public Hospitals.

◆ Hospital Facilities

The number of community hospitals, especially in rural areas, has been declining for 17 years.

Since 1981, 560 community hospitals have ceased to provide inpatient acute
care services. Thirty-nine hospitals closed in 1992, down from the total of 45
closures in 1991. There were 5,292 community hospitals in operation by the
end of 1992.

The decrease in the number of hospitals was accompanied by a decline of 0.3
percent in the number of hospital beds, from 924,000 in 1991 to 921,000 in
1992 (Table 5.2).

The occupancy rate in community hospitals was 65.6 percent in 1992, and the
average length of stay dropped to 7.1 days.

Although fewer beds are available, the scope of services has increased with advances in medical technology. Hospitals offer more procedures and treatments on an outpatient basis. Occupancy in community hospitals continues to decrease partly because of expanded outpatient and ambulatory services. Since 1984, more than 25 percent of all surgeries are performed on an outpatient basis. Nearly all community hospitals, regardless of size or location, now offer some type of ambulatory surgical service.

Community hospitals continued to add additional patient services and special facilities in 1992 to administer new treatments and to utilize new technology.

Occupancy rates in private psychiatric hospitals remained at a steady 67 percent in the two-year period between 1988 and 1990. The overall length of stay dropped from 118 days in 1980 to 66 days in 1990, according to the National Association of Private Psychiatric Hospitals. Nearly half of the patients in these hospitals were diagnosed with affective disorders, including depression and manic depressive illness.

In 1991, there were 793,471 admissions to the 775 psychiatric hospitals with 142,099 hospital beds across the United States (Table 5.9).

♦ Physicians

In the 1993 *Physician Characteristics and Distribution in the United States,* the AMA listed 653,062 total physicians distributed among the different specialties. The largest number (109,017) were in internal medicine practices, followed by family practice. The largest increases were in internal medicine, family practice, pediatrics, and plastic surgery.

The majority of practicing physicians, both federal and nonfederal, saw patients and were office-based in 1992. Internal medicine, psychiatry, radiology, and pediatrics provided the most hospital-based physician administrators. Three of the same specialties, with the addition of physicians specializing in cardiovascular diseases, were more likely to engage in medical research (Table 5.12).

♦ Nursing Homes

With the increasing number of people over the age of 65, as well as children and disabled adults who require nursing home care, the number of facilities that provide long-term care with physician services and continuous professional nursing in acute care situations continues to grow each year.

In 1993, across the country, there were 15,334 nursing homes housing 1,682,701 patients; 10,580 were certified by Medicare. Medicaid patients occupied 54.8 percent of set-up beds in 1993 and provided 58.3 percent of the income. The number of hospitals reporting skilled nursing units doubled between 1981 and 1993, and the number of hospitals with other long-term-care units increased by over 50 percent. Nursing home occupancy dropped in early every age, size and ownership category in 1993.

Persons with AIDS, that is, the more than 280,000 Americans diagnosed since the early 1980s, require nursing home care sometime during the progression of their disease; special nursing facilities devoted to the care of these patients have sprung up in the past five years.

◆ Surgical Operations

According to the AHA, there were nearly 24 million surgical procedures performed in the nation's hospitals in 1992. The largest number of surgical procedures was performed in California (2.1 million) and the fewest in Alaska (34,160) (Table 5.10).

◆ Organ Transplants

Organ transplants were first performed clinically in 1953. The number and success of these often life-saving procedures grew dramatically as a result of the improvements in surgical techniques. The introduction in 1983 of cyclosporine, and in recent years several new immunosuppressive drugs, has improved survival rates in transplant patients.

There are currently 612 medical institutions in the United States that operate an organ transplant program. By the end of April 1994, there were nearly 35,000 people awaiting transplants in the United States.

It is estimated that 2,800 of the over 27,000 patients awaiting organ transplants in 1993 died due to the scarcity of transplantable organs.

According to the United Network for Organ Sharing (UNOS), 83 percent of all organ donors, both cadaveric and live, are white, 65 percent are male, and 38 percent are between 19 and 35 years of age. (In this group are many white males who have died from motor vehicle accidents or cerebrovascular accidents.)

Living heart donations take place when a lung patient receives a heart-lung transplant and then donates his or her healthy heart to another patient. (This is known as a domino transplant.) Live pancreas, lung, and liver donations are segmental transplants: the living donor gives part of his or her organ to save or improve someone else's life.

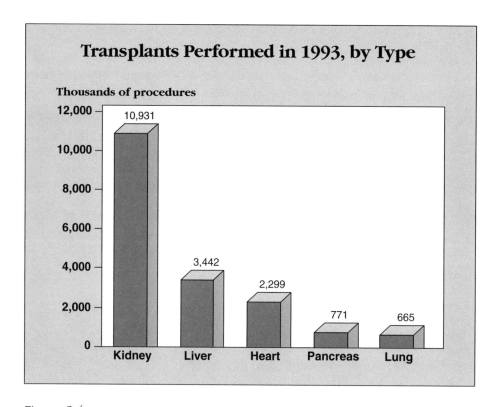

Figure 5.4

NOTE: 60 heart-lung transplants were also performed bringing the total transplants for 1993 to 18,168.
SOURCE: United Network for Organ Sharing.

Organ transplantation is the most expensive procedure in the spectrum of medical and surgical technology today. Transplant patients must take costly immunosuppressant drugs for the remainder of their lifetimes. A liver transplant, for example, can generate medical, surgical, and hospital costs of $364,200 for the first five years after the surgery.

Survival rates are increasing each year as new technology affords safer procedures for the transplant patient. At present, a person receiving a kidney transplant has an 86 percent chance of surviving for five years after surgery (Table 5.22).

Patients Awaiting Transplants, by Organ, Gender, and Age, 4/30/94

Characteristic	Kidney	Liver	Pancreas	Kidney-pancreas	Intestine	Heart	Heart-lung	Lung	Total
Total	25,848	3,347	203	948	57	2,922	202	1,360	34,887
Sex									
Female	10,964	1,577	104	422	29	537	124	773	14,530
Male	14,884	1,770	99	526	28	2,385	78	587	20,357
Total	25,848	3,347	203	948	57	2,922	202	1,360	34,887
Age									
0–5	79	278	6	0	33	83	3	6	488
6–10	108	107	2	0	8	20	6	14	265
11–18	456	107	5	0	7	43	12	68	698
19–45	16,338	1,513	175	880	7	1,042	160	743	20,858
46–64	7,436	1,122	15	68	2	1,612	21	506	10,782
65+	1,431	220	0	0	0	122	0	23	1,796
Total	25,848	3,347	203	948	57	2,922	202	1,360	34,887

Figure 5.5

SOURCE: United Network for Organ Sharing, April 1994.

118

Table 5.1

Community Hospital Statistics, 1950–1992

Year	Beds per 1,000 population	Occupancy rates (percent)	Average number of hospitalized patients per day per 1,000 population	Admissions per 1,000 population	Average length of stay (days)
1950	3.4	NA	2.5	111.4	8.1
1955	3.5	NA	2.5	117.3	7.8
1960	3.6	NA	2.7	129.2	7.6
1965	3.9	NA	3.0	138.8	7.8
1970	4.2	NA	3.3	145.6	8.2
1975	4.5	75.0	3.3	158.1	7.7
1980	4.4	75.6	3.3	162.1	7.6
1981	4.5	76.0	3.4	161.9	7.6
1982	4.5	75.3	3.4	160.2	7.6
1983	4.4	73.5	3.3	157.6	7.6
1984	4.4	69.0	3.0	151.8	7.3
1985	4.3	64.8	2.8	143.1	7.1
1986	4.1	64.3	2.7	137.0	7.1
1987	4.0	64.9	2.6	132.4	7.2
1988	3.9	65.5	2.5	128.9	7.2
1989	3.8	66.2	2.5	126.2	7.2
1990	3.7	66.8	2.5	125.4	7.2
1991	3.7	66.1	2.5	124.9	7.2
1992	3.6	65.6	2.3	122.2	7.1

NA: Not available.

SOURCE: American Hospital Association, Hospital Statistics, 1993–94 edition.

Table 5.2

Community Hospitals, Beds, Admissions, and Occupancy, 1972–1992

Year	Hospitals	Beds (thousands)	Admissions (thousands)	Occupancy (percent)
1972	5,746	879	30,709	75.4
1973	5,789	898	31,671	75.7
1974	5,875	926	32,866	75.6
1975	5,875	942	33,435	75.0
1976	5,857	956	33,979	74.6
1977	5,881	969	34,273	73.8
1978	5,851	975	34,506	73.6
1979	5,842	984	35,099	73.9
1980	5,830	988	36,143	75.6
1981	5,813	1,003	36,438	76.0
1982	5,801	1,012	36,379	75.3
1983	5,783	1,018	36,152	73.5
1984	5,759	1,017	35,155	69.0
1985	5,732	1,001	33,449	64.8
1986	5,678	978	32,379	64.3
1987	5,611	958	31,601	64.9
1988	5,533	947	31,453	65.5
1989	5,455	933	31,116	66.2
1990	5,384	927	31,181	66.8
1991	5,342	924	31,064	66.1
1992	5,292	921	31,034	65.6

SOURCE: American Hospital Association, Hospital Statistics, various editions.

Table 5.3

Short-Stay Hospital Discharges and Hospital Days, for All Causes and Causes Excluding Deliveries, by Age, Gender, and Race, 1991

	All causes				Excluding deliveries			
	Hospital discharges		Hospital days		Hospital discharges		Hospital days	
Characteristic	Number per 100 persons	Number (thousands)	Average length of stay	Number (thousands)	Number per 100 persons	Number (thousands)	Average length of stay	Number (thousands)
All persons	**10.8**	**26,873**	**6.2**	**167,226**	**9.4**	**23,487**	**6.7**	**157,065**
Age								
Under 5 years	4.3	1,421	5.8	8,231	7.3	1,421	5.8	8,231
5–17 years	3.3	1,505	5.3	7,919	3.1	1,428	5.4	7,699
18–24 years	10.3	2,531	4.4	11,197	5.9	1,443	5.4	7,837
25–44 years	9.4	7,634	5.0	38,154	6.7	5,426	5.8	31,616
45–64 years	11.7	5,517	7.0	38,544	11.7	5,505	7.0	38,501
65–74 years	24.0	4,398	7.6	33,623	24.0	4,398	7.6	33,623
75 years or over	32.2	3,867	7.6	29,556	32.2	3,867	7.6	29,556
Sex and age								
Male:								
All ages	9.0	10,854	6.8	74,134	9.0	10,854	8.8	74,134
Under 18 years	4.9	1,650	5.1	8,401	4.9	1,650	5.1	8,401
18–44 years	5.0	2,586	7.1	18,308	5.0	2,586	7.1	18,308
45–64 years	12.0	2,710	6.4	17,273	12.0	2,710	6.4	17,273
65 years and over	30.9	3,908	7.7	30,153	30.9	3,908	7.7	30,153
Female:								
All ages	12.5	16,018	5.8	93,091	9.9	12,633	6.6	82,930
Under 18 years	4.0	1,276	6.1	7,750	3.7	1,199	6.3	7,530
18–44 years	14.1	7,579	4.1	81,004	8.0	4,282	4.9	21,148
45–64 years	11.4	2,807	7.6	21,272	11.4	2,795	7.6	21,229
65 years and over	24.7	4,357	7.6	33,026	24.7	4,357	7.6	33,026
Race and age								
White:								
All ages	10.9	22,778	6.1	138,526	9.7	20,166	6.5	130,953
Under 18 years	4.3	2,284	5.2	11,981	4.3	2,237	5.3	11,839
18–44 years	9.3	8,192	4.9	,40,035	6.4	5,639	5.8	32,647
45–64 years	11.8	4,809	6.7	32,095	11.8	4,797	6.7	32,052
65 years and over	27.6	7,494	7.3	54,415	27.6	7,494	7.3	54,415
Black:								
All ages	11.1	3,420	7.0	23,872	9.2	2,827	7.7	21,750
Under 18 years	5.4	557	5.7	3,161	5.2	532	5.8	3,099
18–44 years	12.2	1,598	5.0	8,061	7.8	1,030	5.8	6,001
45–64 years	11.9	578	7.7	4,422	11.9	578	7.7	4,422
65 years and over	26.8	686	12.0	8,228	26.8	686	12.0	8,228

SOURCE: NCHS, Health Interview Survey.

Table 5.4

Number and Rate of Patients Discharged from Short-Stay Hospital Care, Average Lengths of Stay, by Gender and Age, 1991

	Discharged patients		Days of care		
	Number (thousands)	Rate per 1,000 population	Number (thousands)	Rate per 1,000 population	Average length of stay (days)
All ages, both genders	31,098	124.1	199,099	794.6	6.4
Under 15 years	2,498	45.3	12,037	218.3	4.8
Under 1 year	805	200.8	4,922	1,227.2	6.1
1–4 years	735	48.3	2,650	174.3	3.6
5–14 years	958	26.7	4,464	124.3	4.7
15–44 years	11,620	99.3	54,020	461.8	4.6
15–19 years	1,368	80.2	6,052	354.9	4.4
20–24 years	2,116	113.3	8,385	449.0	4.0
25–34 years	4,773	113.0	20,950	495.9	4.4
35–44 years	3,364	86.3	18,634	477.8	5.5
45–64 years	6,173	132.2	40,100	858.5	6.5
45–54 years	2,795	108.7	16,859	655.8	6.0
55–64 years	3,378	160.8	23,241	1,106.5	6.9
65 years and older	10,806	340.3	92,942	2,927.0	8.6
65–74 years	4,830	264.2	38,949	2,130.8	8.1
75–84 years	4,136	401.0	37,054	3,592.6	9.0
85 years and older	1,840	582.2	16,939	5,360.4	9.2
Under 17 years	2,887	46.7	14,039	227.2	4.9
17–69 years	19,741	118.2	110,695	662.6	5.6
70 years and older	8,470	390.0	74,364	3,424.4	8.8
Males					
All ages	12,478	402.7	86,930	715.2	7.0
Under 15 years	1,435	50.8	6,981	247.3	4.9
Under 1 year	466	227.3	2,792	1,360.8	6.0
1–4 years	435	55.9	1,589	204.1	3.7
5–14 years	533	29.0	2,600	141.4	4.9
15–44 years	3,248	55.9	20,698	356.5	6.4
15–19 years	362	41.6	2,318	266.5	6.4
20–24 years	400	43.0	2,315	248.6	5.8
25–34 years	1,131	54.2	7,547	361.6	6.7
35–44 years	1,355	70.5	8,518	444.2	6.3
45–64 years	3,088	137.5	20,157	897.4	6.5
45–54 years	1,363	108.8	8,305	662.8	6.1
55–64 years	1,724	173.7	11,851	1,193.5	6.9
65 years and older	4,708	368.1	39,095	3,056.5	8.3
65–74 years	2,352	293.2	18,654	2,325.3	7.9
75–84 years	1,749	449.8	14,982	3,853.4	8.6
85 years and older	607	688.8	5,460	6,197.2	9.0
Under 17 years	1,571	49.6	7,902	249.7	5.0
17–69 years	7,355	90.0	49,169	602.6	6.7
70 years and older	3,552	428.0	29,859	3,597.5	8.4

Continued

Table 5.4 *(Continued)*

	Discharged patients		Days of care		
	Number (thousands)	Rate per 1,000 population	Number (thousands)	Rate per 1,000 population	Average length of stay (days)
Females					
All ages	18,620	144.3	112,168	869.3	6.0
Under 15 years	1,064	39.5	5,056	187.9	4.8
Under 1 year	339	173.0	2,130	1,087.3	6.3
1–4 years	300	40.4	1,062	143.0	3.5
5–14 years	425	24.2	1,865	106.4	4.4
15–44 years	8,372	142.1	33,322	565.6	4.0
15–19 years	1,006	120.4	3,734	447.0	3.7
20–24 years	1,716	183.2	6,070	648.3	3.5
25–34 years	3,641	170.4	13,403	627.0	3.7
35–44 years	2,009	101.4	10,116	510.4	5.0
45–64 years	3,085	127.2	19,944	822.4	6.5
45–54 years	1,431	108.6	8,554	649.2	6.0
55–64 years	1,654	149.4	11,389	1,028.6	6.9
65 years and older	6,098	321.6	53,846	2,839.6	8.8
65–74 years	2,478	241.5	20,295	1,978.5	8.2
75–84 years	2,387	371.5	22,072	3,434.8	9.2
85 years and older	1,233	541.1	11,479	5,036.9	9.3
Under 17 years	1,316	43.7	6,137	203.6	4.7
17–69 years	12,386	144.9	61,526	719.9	5.0
70 years and older	4,918	366.5	44,505	3,317.1	9.1

SOURCE: National Center for Health Statistics, Advancedata.

Table 5.5

Procedures Performed on Patients Discharged from Short-Stay Hospitals, by Procedure, Gender, and Age, 1991 (Thousands)

Procedures Performed	Total	Male	Female	Under 15 years	15–44 years	45–64 years	65 years and older
All procedures	43,922	17,264	26,658	2,235	17,090	9,524	15,073
Operations on the nervous system	970	500	470	236	328	196	210
Operations on the endocrine system	103	28	75	NA	41	22	25
Operations on the eyes	399	189	210	25	65	85	224
Operations on the ear	129	75	54	66	36	15	13
Operations on the respiratory system	956	561	396	60	173	290	433
Operations on the cardiovascular system	4,123	2,383	1,740	148	477	176	2,022
Coronary artery bypass graft	407	296	111	NA	23	178	206
Cardiac catheterization	1,000	603	397	19	89	447	446
Operations on the hemic and lymphatic systems	392	212	180	20	77	110	185
Operations on the digestive system	5,559	2,319	3,241	221	1,571	1,400	2,367
Appendectomy	255	135	120	57	156	29	14
Cholecystectomy	571	166	404	NA	194	189	185
Repair of inguinal hernia	172	155	17	25	31	51	65
Operations on the urinary system	1,558	884	674	47	376	386	750
Operations on the male genital organs	584	584	NA	46	40	116	382
Prostatectomy	363	363	NA	NA	NA	68	295
Operations on the female genital organs	2,308	NA	2,308	8	1,624	445	231
Hysterectomy	546	NA	546	NA	322	161	63
Oophorectomy and salpingo-oophorectomy	458	NA	458	NA	248	150	59
Obstetrical procedures	6,867	NA	6,867	24	6,839	NA	NA
Cesarean section	933	NA	933	NA	931	NA	NA
Operations on the musculoskeletal system	3,323	1,710	1,614	208	1,323	798	994
Total hip replacement	117	50	67	NA	8	31	78
Operations on the integumentary system	1,324	552	773	75	488	330	431
Mastectomy	118	NA	117	NA	17	42	58

NA: Not available.
SOURCE: National Center for Health Statistics, Advancedata, March 1993.

Table 5.6

Average Length of Stay in Days for Patients Discharged from Short-Stay Hospitals, by Principal Expected Source of Payment, Region, and Age, 1991 (Millions)

Region and Age	Patients including all sources of payment	Private insurance	Medicare	Medicaid	Workers' compensation	Other government payments	Self-pay	Other payments and no charge
Total United States	6.4	4.9	8.6	5.6	5.0	5.4	5.2	5.1
Under 15 years	4.8	4.3	10.6	5.5	NA	4.7	4.3	4.4
15–44 years	4.6	4.3	8.7	4.8	4.7	4.8	4.5	4.8
45–64 years	6.5	5.9	8.1	8.6	5.0	6.9	6.4	5.5
65 years and over	8.6	7.1	8.6	9.7	7.2	8.3	9.6	6.7
Northeast	7.3	5.1	10.2	7.5	5.1	7.6	6.0	5.0
Under 15 years	5.0	4.4	23.4	5.5	NA	5.5	4.8	4.7
15–44 years	5.2	4.3	9.2	7.1	4.4	7.0	5.3	4.5
45–64 years	7.2	6.3	9.7	10.8	5.2	9.6	7.0	5.6
65 years and over	10.1	8.7	10.2	11.8	8.2	NA	15.0	7.2
Midwest	6.5	5.0	8.4	5.6	5.5	5.1	5.7	5.7
Under 15 years	4.8	4.6	6.8	5.5	NA	4.2	3.9	4.7
15–44 years	4.9	4.4	10.7	4.8	4.9	4.5	5.0	5.4
45–64 years	6.5	5.9	8.1	8.5	5.9	7.3	5.8	6.0
65 years and over	8.4	7.7	8.3	7.8	7.0	NA	9.4	8.4
South	6.2	5.0	8.2	4.9	5.0	5.6	5.1	5.0
Under 15 years	4.5	4.2	7.5	5.0	NA	4.1	4.2	5.2
15–44 years	4.5	4.5	7.8	3.9	5.1	5.1	4.5	4.7
45–64 years	6.4	5.8	7.6	7.7	4.6	6.8	6.9	5.3
65 years and over	8.3	6.9	8.3	10.7	6.3	8.4	7.8	5.5
West	5.4	4.5	7.4	4.9	4.3	4.4	3.5	4.9
Under 15 years	5.0	3.9	5.9	6.4	NA	8.8	4.1	2.8
15–44 years	4.0	3.9	6.9	3.9	3.8	3.6	3.0	4.7
45–64 years	5.8	5.5	7.5	6.7	4.7	5.2	4.9	5.4
65 years and over	7.3	5.9	7.4	7.2	NA	NA	4.4	6.2

NA: Not available.
SOURCE: National Center for Health Statistics, Health Interview Survey, 1991.

Table 5.7

Number of Women Delivering Babies, by Age, Race, and Geographic Region, Discharged from Short-Stay Hospitals, 1991

Age, race and region	Discharged patients		Days of care		
	Number (thousands)	Rate per 1,000 population	Number (thousands)	Rate per 1,000 population	Average length of stay (days)
10–54 years	3,973	49.2	11,028	136.6	2.8
Age					
10–14 years	14	1.6	33	3.8	2.4
15–44 years	3,956	67.2	10,987	186.5	2.8
15–19 years	524	62.8	1,475	176.6	2.8
20–24 years	1,041	111.2	2,794	298.4	2.7
25–29 years	1,166	113.4	3,273	318.4	2.8
30–34 years	852	76.8	2,350	211.8	2.8
35–44 years	373	18.8	1,095	55.3	2.9
45–54 years	NA	NA	NA	NA	NA
10–17 years	202	15.0	537	39.8	2.7
18–54 years	3,771	56.1	10,491	156.1	2.8
Race					
White	2,244	33.8	6,130	92.3	2.7
Black	557	51.8	1,691	157.1	3.0
All other	289	80.9	765	214.5	2.7
Race not stated	883	NA	2,442	NA	2.8
Region					
Northeast	670	41.1	2,098	182.9	3.1
Midwest	575	45.6	2,491	129.8	2.8
South	1,418	50.7	4,117	147.3	2.9
West	1,010	58.5	2,322	134.5	2.3

NA: Not available.
SOURCE: National Center for Health Statistics, Health Interview Survey, 1990.

Table 5.8

Selected Birth Statistics, by State, 1992

State	Number of live births per 1,000 population	Percentage of births in which mother received prenatal care	Percentage of low birth weight babies
Alabama	11.7	73.1	8.3
Alaska	10.4	81.4	4.9
Arizona	9.2	65.5	6.3
Arkansas	10.0	70.7	8.3
California	8.3	72.6	6.1
Colorado	9.0	76.2	7.8
Connecticut	8.5	83.6	6.9
Delaware	11.2	77.3	7.5
Florida	10.0	70.9	7.7
Georgia	12.4	72.8	8.4
Hawaii	7.4	75.4	7.1
Idaho	9.1	73.6	5.5
Illinois	11.2	78.1	7.7
Indiana	10.3	78.6	6.6
Iowa	8.4	85.2	5.4
Kansas	8.4	80.5	6.1
Kentucky	9.5	76.8	6.9
Louisiana	11.2	75.2	9.1
Maine	7.2	82.4	4.9
Maryland	10.4	82.6	8.0
Massachusetts	7.5	82.7	5.9
Michigan	11.0	79.1	7.6
Minnesota	7.4	80.8	4.9
Mississippi	12.0	75.0	9.4
Missouri	9.8	78.5	6.9
Montana	9.7	77.2	5.5
Nebraska	8.4	83.1	5.8
Nevada	8.3	71.0	7.2
New Hampshire	7.8	84.6	5.1
New Jersey	9.4	79.4	7.3
New Mexico	9.2	57.4	7.0
New York	10.3	73.5	7.7
North Carolina	11.5	75.7	8.1
North Dakota	8.8	82.5	5.0
Ohio	9.8	81.6	7.0
Oklahoma	8.9	72.4	6.5
Oregon	8.6	75.1	5.2
Pennsylvania	9.9	79.0	7.1
Rhode Island	8.8	84.1	6.2
South Carolina	12.3	67.3	9.3
South Dakota	9.9	77.9	5.4
Tennessee	10.6	76.4	8.2
Texas	8.8	66.9	7.0
Utah	7.8	84.1	5.7
Vermont	6.7	81.0	5.5
Virginia	10.2	79.6	7.1
Washington	8.7	76.8	5.6
West Virginia	9.4	73.7	6.6
Wisconsin	8.6	81.6	5.8
Wyoming	9.0	79.7	7.3

SOURCE: Northwestern National Life, Children's Health State Rankings, 1993.

Table 5.9

Total Psychiatric Hospitals, Beds, and Admissions, by State, 1992

State	Psychiatric hospitals in state	Psychiatric hospital beds	Admissions to psychiatric hosptials
Alabama	12	3,194	13,418
Alaska	3	253	2,434
Arizona	15	1,730	14,930
Arkansas	9	770	6,528
California	67	9,490	67,243
Colorado	11	1,857	11,574
Connecticut	18	2,191	9,322
Delware	3	482	2,876
District of Columbia	2	1,431	4,839
Florida	50	6,042	41,402
Georgia	26	3,509	41,145
Hawaii	1	175	809
Idaho	5	331	2,291
Illinois	26	6,383	37,263
Indiana	18	3,740	14,530
Iowa	6	1,378	6,251
Kansas	12	1,827	9,479
Kentucky	12	1,675	14,338
Louisiana	27	3,010	20,382
Maine	5	688	3,241
Maryland	16	3,312	15,290
Massachusetts	23	3,956	26,482
Michigan	19	4,787	23,211
Minnesota	8	2,982	7,982
Mississippi	7	2,436	7,996
Missouri	14	2,149	13,570
Montana	1	22	126
Nebraska	4	691	4,847
NEvada	5	408	3,945
New Hampshire	6	789	6,064
New Jersey	13	5,216	14,027
New Mexico	11	1,229	8,749
New York	43	16,712	41,994
North Carolina	21	4,154	27,342
North Dakota	1	335	1,677
Ohio	27	4,629	30,814
Oklahoma	15	1,573	12,967
Oregon	6	1,374	4,799
Pennsylvania	44	10,296	44,620
Rhode Island	3	320	2,065
South Carolina	11	1,775	10,280
South Dakota	1	60	724
Tennessee	14	2,248	18,713
Texas	65	8,880	61,916
Utah	9	859	5,365
Vermont	2	329	1,567
Virginia	23	4,165	30,590
Washington	8	1,788	8,302
West Virginia	4	585	4,479
Wisconsin	20	3,334	25,989
Wyoming	3	550	2,684
Totals	775	142,099	793,471

SOURCE: American Hospital Association, Hospital Statistics, 1993–94.

Table 5.10

Surgical Operations in Hospitals, by State, 1992

State	Operations	State	Operations
Alabama	399,402	Montana	68,204
Alaska	34,160	Nebraska	186,353
Arizona	299,216	Nevada	100,371
Arkansas	247,162	New Hampshire	88,262
California	2,088,411	New Jersey	703,437
Colorado	318,380	New Mexico	135,448
Connecticut	277,331	New York	1,647,157
Delaware	80,582	North Carolina	597,192
District of Columbia	123,477	North Dakota	79,638
Florida	1,263,224	Ohio	1,160,415
Georgia	656,441	Oklahoma	292,800
Hawaii	71,723	Oregon	258,219
Idaho	79,610	Pennsylvania	1,501,412
Illinois	1,081,547	Rhode Island	121,369
Indiana	591,545	South Carolina	317,880
Iowa	344,653	South Dakota	70,230
Kansas	240,143	Tennessee	551,988
Kentucky	409,785	Texas	1,521,977
Louisiana	418,034	Utah	138,420
Maine	126,224	Vermont	45,198
Maryland	536,101	Virginia	558,347
Massachusetts	675,967	Washington	526,643
Michigan	910,965	West Virginia	242,195
Minnesota	408,131	Wisconsin	473,581
Mississippi	235,624	Wyoming	38,325
Missouri	616,093	Total	23,958,992

SOURCE: American Hospital Association, Hospital Statistics, 1993–94.

Table 5.11

Number of Facilities and Procedures and Types of Procedures Performed at Freestanding Ambulatory Surgical Centers, 1988–1991

	1988	1989	1990	1991
Number of facilities	984	1,227	1,364	1,555
Number of procedures	1,702,397	1,997,856	2,317,741	2,586,147
Type of procedures (percentage of total)				
Ophthalmology	27.5	28.4	28.5	30.2
Gynecology	19.4	19.6	17.7	15.1
Otolaryngology	10.3	10.0	9.9	9.6
Orthopaedic surgery	9.6	9.1	9.1	9.5
General surgery	8.5	8.4	7.1	6.1
Plastic surgery	8.0	7.6	7.5	7.1
Podiatry	4.6	4.6	4.5	4.0
Urology	3.8	3.6	3.7	3.9
Gastroenterology	2.5	4.2	6.3	7.7
Dental (surgical extraction)	1.8	1.7	1.3	1.0
Neurology	0.4	0.4	0.4	0.2
Other	3.6	2.4	4.0	5.6
Total	100.0	100.0	100.0	100.0

SOURCES: SMG Marketing Group, Chicago 1992. Freestanding Outpatient Surgery Center's Directory and Report.

Table 5.12

Physicians (Federal and Nonfederal) by Selected Specialty and Activity, 1992

Specialty	Total physicians	Patient care	Office based	Hospital based	Administration	Medical-teaching	Research
Anesthesiology	28,148	27,034	19,998	3,120	266	543	237
Cardiovascular diseases	16,478	14,709	11,460	1,407	312	338	1,039
Dermatology	7,912	7,550	6,318	371	75	99	168
Radiology*	18,156	14,117	10,858	2,209	1,557	416	1,583
Emergency medicine	15,470	14,813	9,373	3,796	403	160	55
Family practice	50,969	49,269	40,479	2,555	788	702	100
Gastroenterology	7,946	7,121	5,724	538	92	171	541
General practice	20,719	20,475	18,575	1,600	337	26	43
General surgery	39,211	37,792	24,956	2,919	529	348	441
Internal medicine	109,017	99,502	65,312	8,445	2,531	1,523	5,083
Neurology	9,742	8,559	6,330	917	150	204	781
Obstetrics/gynecology	35,273	34,136	27,115	1,947	385	410	279
Pediatrics	44,881	41,482	29,110	3,851	1,104	796	1,371
Pathology	17,005	13,910	7,948	3,154	945	373	994
Opthalmology	16,433	15,970	13,752	675	86	119	240
Orthopaedic surgery	20,640	20,244	15,832	1,277	83	135	119
Nuclear medicine	1,372	1,181	736	307	52	34	81
Urology	9,452	9,214	7,688	573	73	71	72
Psychiatry	36,405	33,005	21,913	5,860	1,877	503	788

NOTE: There were 653,062 physicians in January 1992. This table only represents a selected group of this total.
*Radiology includes nuclear radiology, pediatric radiology, and vascular and interventional radiology.
SOURCE: U. S. Department of Health and Human Services, Bureau of Health Professions.

Table 5.13

Estimates and Projections of Active Physicians and Dentists (Thousands)

Year	Physicians			Dentists
	Total	Medical doctors	Osteopaths	
Historical				
1950	219.9	209.0	10.9	79.2
1955	240.2	228.6	11.6	84.4
1960	259.5	247.3	12.2	90.1
1965	288.7	277.6	11.1	96.0
1970	326.2	314.2	12.0	102.2
1975	384.4	370.4	14.0	112.0
1980	457.5	440.4	17.1	126.2
1981	466.7	448.7	18.0	129.2
1982	483.7	465.0	18.7	132.0
1983	501.2	481.5	19.7	135.1
1984	506.5	485.7	20.8	138.0
1985	520.7	498.8	21.9	140.8
1986	534.8	511.6	23.2	143.2
1987	548.5	524.1	24.4	145.5
1988	562.0	536.3	25.7	147.4
Projections				
1990	587.7	559.5	28.2	150.8
1995	645.5	611.1	34.4	156.8
2000	696.5	656.1	40.0	161.2

SOURCE: U. S. Department of Health and Human Services, Health Care Financing Administration.

132

Table 5.14

Average Total Patient Visits to Physicians per Week, by Selected Specialty, Census Division, Location, and Type of Practice, 1984–1991

	1984	1985	1986	1987	1988	1989	1990	1991
All physicians	118.1	117.1	117.7	119.3	121.1	121.6	120.9	118.4
Specialty								
General/Family practice	139.0	138.1	139.2	138.3	145.6	143.0	146.0	144.4
Internal medicine	107.7	105.2	111.1	114.5	113.0	117.9	112.0	110.7
Surgery	110.0	108.2	10.8	107.8	105.0	108.8	107.6	106.9
Pediatrics	128.7	130.8	131.9	127.4	135.1	138.1	134.0	133.5
Obstetrics/Gynecology	115.7	112.0	114.8	112.7	118.9	115.6	120.0	112.2
Census division								
New England	108.7	98.2	109.5	112.0	105.0	109.5	106.3	104.8
Middle Atlantic	114.4	110.9	110.3	109.5	113.9	116.1	111.3	110.7
East North Central	123.1	122.6	121.3	125.7	124.6	122.1	125.3	122.8
West North Central	128.6	117.6	122.0	128.9	136.0	138.2	136.2	128.7
South Atlantic	119.9	122.3	118.9	122.3	123.6	127.5	127.4	122.7
East South Central	153.8	157.5	148.9	151.1	158.4	155.4	156.1	141.7
West South Central	132.6	127.5	126.3	125.7	119.8	126.0	122.2	124.5
Mountain	114.2	109.9	111.2	115.0	118.6	120.7	111.9	120.2
Pacific	94.7	102.4	107.4	104.2	111.6	104.2	107.5	106.6
Location								
Nonmetropolitan	150.3	144.0	140.0	141.5	153.3	150.6	150.1	142.6
Metropolitan								
Fewer than 1 million	125.6	123.7	124.1	127.6	127.1	129.2	127.6	123.4
1 million and over	104.1	105.6	106.7	106.6	108.8	108.3	108.3	108.6
Type of practice								
Solo	113.7	112.3	112.2	114.0	115.6	115.1	116.0	117.6
Non-solo	122.3	121.2	122.0	123.2	124.9	125.9	123.9	118.9

SOURCE: American Medical Association, Socioeconomic Characteristics of Medical Practice 1992.

Table 5.15

Annual Rate of Office Visits by Patient's Age, Sex, and Race, 1992

Age, sex, and race	Number of visits (thousands)	Percentage distribution	Number of visits per person per year
All visits	762,045	100.0	3.0
Age			
Under 15 years	155,168	20.4	2.7
15–24 years	72.016	9.5	2.1
25–44 years	211,897	27.8	2.6
45–64 years	154,997	20.3	3.2
65–74 years	90,625	11.9	4.9
75 years and over	77,341	10.1	6.3
Sex and age			
Female	457,369	60.0	3.5
Under 15 years	74,417	9.8	2.7
15–24 years	46,629	6.1	2.7
25–44 years	143,410	18.8	3.5
45–64 years	93,353	12.3	3.7
65–74 years	51,771	6.8	5.1
75 years and over	47,790	6.3	6.2
Male	304,676	40.0	2.5
Under 15 years	80,752	10.6	2.8
15–24 years	25,387	3.3	1.5
25–44 years	68,487	9.0	1.7
45–64 years	61,644	8.1	2.6
65–74 years	38,854	5.1	4.5
75 years and over	29,552	3.9	6.4
Race and age			
White	653,851	85.8	3.1
Under 15 years	124,631	10.8	2.8
15–24 years	60,758	8.0	2.2
25–44 years	182,245	23.9	2.7
45–64 years	135,756	17.8	3.3
65–74 years	80,673	10.6	4.9
75 years and over	69,787	9.2	6.3
Black	82,599	10.8	2.6
Under 15 years	23,207	3.0	2.6
15–24 years	9,345	1.2	1.8
25–44 years	22,487	3.0	2.3
45–64 years	13,949	1.8	2.8
65–74 years	7,352	1.0	4.5
75 years and over	6,260	0.8	6.4
All other races			
Asian/Pacific Islander	22,967	3.0	NA
American Indian/Eskimo/Aleut	2,329	0.3	NA

NOTE: Numbers do not add to totals due to rounding.
NA: Not available.
SOURCE: CDC, Advance Data August 18, 1994.

Table 5.16

Office Visits by Patient's Principal Reason for Visit, 1992

Principal reason	Number of visits (thousands)	Percentage
All visits	762,045	100.0
Symptoms	441,037	57.9
General symptoms	49,099	6.4
Psychological/mental disorders	21,599	2.8
Nervous system (excluding sense organs)	23,360	3.1
Cardiovascular/lymphatic system	4,529	0.6
Eyes and ears	53,750	7.1
Respiratory system	94,637	12.4
Digestive system	35,027	4.6
Genitourinary system	34,143	4.5
Skin, hair, and nails	42,235	5.5
Musculoskeletal system	82,659	10.8
Diseases	66,528	8.7
Diagnostic, screening and preventive	113,857	14.9
Treatment	74,160	9.7
Injuries and adverse effects	23,782	3.1
Test results	7,318	1.0
Administrative	9,186	1.2
Other	26,177	3.4

NOTE: Numbers do not add to totals due to rounding.
SOURCE: CDC, Advance Data August 18, 1994.

Table 5.17

Expected Sources of Payment for Office Visits, 1992

Expected sources of payment	Visits (thousands)	Percentage
All visits	762,045	100.0
Private/commercial insurance	250,870	32.9
Medicare	151,656	19.9
HMO/other prepaid	146,338	19.2
Patient-paid	145,459	19.1
Medicaid	84,098	11.0
Other government	15,622	2.1
No charge	12,454	1.6
Other	30,327	4.0
Unknown	17,773	2.3

NOTE: Numbers do not add to totals due to rounding.
SOURCE: CDC, Advance Data August 18, 1994.

Table 5.18

Nursing Care Facilities and Utilization, by State, 1991

State	Number of certified nursing care facilities	Medicare certified nursing care facilities	Medicaid certified nursing care facilities	Population in nursing care facilities
Alabama	219	208	11	24,031
Alaska	15	8	7	1,202
Arizona	132	128	4	14,472
Arkansas	248	47	201	21,809
California	1,290	1,125	165	148,362
Colorado	204	159	45	18,506
Connecticut	240	190	50	30,962
Delaware	41	34	7	4,596
District of Columbia	16	11	5	7,008
Florida	554	490	64	80,298
Georgia	364	216	148	36,549
Hawaii	43	30	13	3,225
Idaho	70	70	0	6,318
Illinois	792	407	385	93,662
Indiana	590	263	327	50,845
Iowa	463	57	406	36,455
Kansas	415	84	331	26,155
Kentucky	282	145	137	27,874
Louisiana	327	80	247	32,072
Maine	146	23	123	9,855
Maryland	217	166	51	26,884
Massachusetts	540	346	194	56,662
Michigan	439	319	120	57,622
Minnesota	472	381	91	47,051
Mississippi	162	44	118	15,803
Missouri	469	279	190	52,060
Montana	99	90	9	7,764
Nebraska	237	50	187	19,171
Nevada	36	34	2	3,605
New Hampshire	76	18	58	8,202
New Jersey	306	227	79	47,054
New Mexico	71	24	47	6,276
New York	619	581	38	126,175
North Carolina	320	275	45	47,014
North Dakota	83	67	16	8,159
Ohio	988	552	436	93,769
Oklahoma	409	37	372	29,666
Oregon	176	108	68	18,200
Pennsylvania	690	610	80	106,454
Rhode Island	100	71	29	10,156
South Carolina	147	129	18	18,228
South Dakota	118	31	87	9,356
Tennessee	300	145	155	35,192
Texas	1,127	403	724	101,005
Utah	90	59	31	6,222
Vermont	48	21	27	4,809
Virginia	258	139	119	37,762
Washington	287	181	106	32,840
West Virginia	122	60	62	12,591
Wisconsin	418	205	213	50,345
Wyoming	38	26	12	2,679
Total	15,913	9,453	6,460	1,772,032

SOURCE: U. S. Department of Health and Human Services, Health Care Financing Administration, unpublished data.

Table 5.19

Registered Nurses, by State, 1991*

State	Number	State	Number
Alabama	24,900	Montana	5,400
Alaska	2,400	Nebraska	13,000
Arizona	24,800	Nevada	10,000
Arkansas	13,500	New Hampshire	10,300
California	179,000	New Jersey	54,600
Colorado	24,100	New Mexico	7,600
Connecticut	27,800	New York	148,600
Delaware	6,500	North Carolina	45,200
District of Columbia	10,500	North Dakota	6,200
Florida	89,100	Ohio	85,200
Georgia	38,500	Oklahoma	15,700
Hawaii	6,300	Oregon	22,000
Idaho	5,800	Pennsylvania	105,600
Illinois	85,900	Rhode Island	9,700
Indiana	40,900	South Carolina	17,200
Iowa	24,300	South Dakota	6,400
Kansas	19,900	Tennessee	30,600
Kentucky	18,600	Texas	87,800
Louisiana	19,300	Utah	9,100
Maine	10,900	Vermont	5,600
Maryland	35,700	Virginia	36,400
Massachusetts	70,600	Washington	39,400
Michigan	66,400	West Virginia	11,800
Minnesota	35,900	Wisconsin	35,900
Mississippi	13,000	Wyoming	3,000
Missouri	41,600		

*Estimates as of December 1991.
SOURCE: U. S. Department of Health and Human Services, Division of Nursing.

Table 5.20

Licensed Pharmacists in the United States, 1991–1992

State	Number	State	Number
Alabama	4,900	Nebraska	1,464
Alaska	376	Nevada	923
Arizona	4,404	New Hampshire	1,387
Arkansas	2,788	New Jersey	10,233
California	23,581	New Mexico	1,068
Colorado	4,500	New York	17,226
Connecticut	3,800	North Carolina	6,828
Delaware	802	North Dakota	1,984
District of Columbia	NA	Ohio	11,350
Florida	13,979	Oklahoma	3,975
Georgia	7,800	Oregon	3,075
Hawaii	1,068	Pennsylvania	10,912
Idaho	1,311	Rhode Island	1,376
Illinois	11,834	South Carolina	4,175
Indiana	333	South Dakota	650
Iowa	4,081	Tennessee	5,949
Kansas	3,077	Texas	756
Kentucky	4,204	Utah	1,987
Louisiana	5,200	Vermont	967
Maine	1,028	Virginia	6,234
Maryland	12,800	Washington	5,240
Massachusetts	7,987	West Virginia	2,011
Michigan	9,311	Wisconsin	5,102
Minnesota	4,927	Wyoming	997
Mississippi	2,940		
Missouri	5,965	Total	249,979
Montana	1,114		

SOURCE: Morgan Quitno, Health Care State Rankings 1993.

Table 5.21

Percentage of Community Hospitals with Selected Special Facilities and Services, Selected Years, 1982–1992

Facility	1982	1984	1986	1988	1990	1991	1992
Emergency department	94	86	95	95	94	93	82
Rehabilitation (outpatient)	33	36	38	41	52	84	81
Family planning	11	12	29	32	NA	22	21
Open-heart facility	11	11	13	14	17	17	16
X-ray therapy	20	17	18	18	20	19	17
Megavolt therapy	17	15	18	18	20	20	18
Radioactive implants	23	21	24	24	25	25	22
Organ transplantation	4	NA	5	6	10	11	10
Blood bank	72	67	73	71	69	70	62
Respiratory therapy	91	85	73	92	91	91	82
Speech pathology	37	44	50	47	46	46	46
Hemodialysis (inpatient)	23	24	28	27	27	26	25
Genetic counseling	7	8	8	8	10	10	9
Physical therapy	88	87	91	88	85	85	79
Occupational therapy	36	45	46	45	50	52	55
Psychiatric partial hospital	10	14	12	17	13	14	21
Psychiatric (outpatient)	14	21	17	17	20	20	28
Alcohol/chemical dependency	12	18	18	19	21	21	26
Home care department	13	21	35	35	36	36	34
Hospice	9	10	15	15	16	17	16
CT scanners	31	42	60	60	70	73	66
Magnetic resonance imaging	NA	NA	10	9	16	21	21
Birthing room	NA	NA	NA	NA	65	66	57
Reproductive health services	NA	NA	NA	NA	42	43	37
AIDS/ARC Inpatient Care	NA	NA	NA	NA	NA	70	64

NA: Not available.
SOURCE: American Hospital Association, Hospital Statistics, various issues.

Table 5.22

Transplantation, Initial and Follow-Up Costs, and Survival Rates, 1993 Dollars

Charge category	Heart	Liver	Kidney	Pancreas	Heart-lung	Lung	Cornea	Bone marrow
Initial cost								
Evaluation	$ 9,500	$ 9,500	$ 9,500	$ 3,100	$ 9,500	$ 9,500	$ 0	$ 9,500
Candidacy (per month)	9,200	9,200	0	0	9,200	9,200	0	9,200
Organ procurement	16,100	21,500	15,800	9,900	16,300	16,300	0	10,300
Hospital	127,900	194,800	36,900	41,400	155,100	155,100	4,400	8,000
Physician	22,600	37,200	7,500	7,800	28,700	26,300	3,600	20,000
Follow-up	16,100	23,000	10,300	1,600	19,500	19,500	0	29,500
Immunosuppressant drugs	7,700	7,700	7,700	1,200	7,700	7,700	0	7,700
Total	$209,100	$302,900	$87,700	$65,000	$246,000	$243,600	$8,000	$167,200
Per year cost following transplant								
Follow-up	9,200	16,100	4,600	700	12,600	12,600	0	21,800
Immunosuppressant drugs	5,800	5,800	5,800	900	5,800	5,800	0	5,800
Total	$15,000	$21,900	$10,400	$1,600	$18,400	$18,400	$0	$27,600
Estimated total charge for first five years, adjusted for survival	$252,600	$364,200	$124,900	$70,300	$282,800	$280,400	$8,000	$233,400
Transplantation survival rates								
One year	80	75	93	88	60	60	100	70
Five years	65	65	86	79	40	40	100	50

SOURCE: Milliman & Robertson, Inc., Cost Implications of Human Organ Transplantations, An Update: 1993.

Table 5.23

Number of Inpatient and Outpatient Admissions and Cost per Admission for Selected Conditions Based on Sample Insured Population, 1990 and 1991

Disease and ICD-9-CM Code	Inpatient 1990		Inpatient 1991	
	Number of admissions	Cost per admission	Number of admissions	Cost per admission
Angina 411.10	396	$12,420	521	$14,973
Emphysema (chronic) 492.80	13	5,273	9	9,829
Hypertension (essential) 401.90	47	4,142	54	5,366
Anxiety (generalized) 300.02	9	12,996	9	13,602
Polyps (colon) 211.30	18	6,254	16	8,496
Pneumonia (acute) 486.00	410	6,982	498	7,613
Sinusitis (with flu) 487.10	16	2,772	24	2,894
Ulcer (duodenal) 532.90	9	4,566	22	6,651
Urethritis (acute) 597.80	0	0	2	4,765
All admissions	30,939	$8,190	37,448	$8,594

	Outpatient 1990		Outpatient 1991	
	Number of claims	Cost per claim	Number of claims	Cost per claim
Angina 411.10	1,839	$241.30	2,521	$197.58
Emphysema (chronic) 492.80	1,156	143.79	1,567	88.60
Hypertension (essential) 401.90	46,222	43.32	66,323	43.68
Anxiety (generalized) 300.02	61,515	117.67	9,178	119.36
Polyps (colon) 211.30	3,073	299.53	4,920	323.68
Pneumonia (acute) 486.00	10,161	56.71	13,260	57.99
Sinusitis (with flu) 487.10	3,776	36.80	7,513	37.01
Ulcer (duodenal) 532.90	699	123.77	806	122.67
Urethritis (acute) 597.80	1,311	57.57	1,872	51.71
Total, all claims	2,666,098	$88.70	3,868,218	$90.34

SOURCE: Health Insurance Association of America, Medstat System, Inc.

Table 5.24

Comparison of the Canadian and United States' Health Care Resources and Selected Procedures, 1992

Resources	Canada	United States
Population	27,243,000	253,668,000
Hospitals		
Acute care hospital beds/ 100,000 population	439	364
Technology		
MRIs	22	2,200
CT Scanners	203	5,100
Lithotriptors	11	400
Open-heart surgery centers	33	919
Hemodialysis stations	842	28,812
Physicians		

Total non-federal physicians in
  patient care (excluding interns
  and residents)
	50,805	361,784

Population per physician in patient care	536	701
Population per specialist		
Cardiologists	44,083	21,802
Cardiovascular/thoracic surgeons	118,965	67,108
FP/GPs	1,003	4,564
General surgeons	14,226	12,307
Nephrologists	169,211	98,780
Neurosurgeons	144,143	75,858
OBG specialists	17,679	10,848
Oncologists	296,120	78,951
Ophthalmologists	28,028	19,033
Orthopedic surgeons	28,202	17,041
Otolarngologists	46,253	39,841
Pediatricians	15,010	10,047
Procedures **(total performed annually)**	Canada	United States
Arthroplasty (hip)	16,659	377,000
Cataract surgery	105,886	1,350,000
Cholecystectomy	60,764	522,000
Coronary artery bypass graft	13,775	392,000
Heart transplant	149	2,128
Kidney transplant	829	9,982
Liver transplant	271	2,952
Mastectomy	12,233	121,000
Prostatectomy	43,425	375,000

SOURCE: Medical Economics Magazine, May 24, 1993.

Chapter 6

DISABILITY, MORBIDITY, AND MORTALITY

◆Disability

DI insurance pays cash directly to insured people when injury or sickness prevents them from earning a living; benefits are provided by group and individual policies and by specific government programs. (DI is categorized as health insurance, although it functions differently from medical services insurance.) Disability rates for both acute and chronic health conditions vary by social and economic characteristics and are measured by work-loss days, restricted activity days, and disability days.

Occupational Illnesses and Injuries

The Bureau of Labor Statistics' annual survey of occupational injuries and illnesses reported that in 1992 there were approximately 6.8 million job-related injuries and illnesses in the private sector occurring at a rate of 8.9 per 100 full-time workers, up from 8.4 per 100 in 1991. (See Figure 6.1.)

The construction industry led all others with the highest injury and illness incidence rate in 1992; these included illnesses and disorders associated with trauma and with conditions due to repeated motion, pressure, or vibration (such as carpal tunnel syndrome). These workplace illnesses associated with repeated trauma made up over 60 percent of the illness cases in 1992.

Approximately 453,700 more job-related injuries were reported in the private sector in 1992 than in 1991. Manufacturing accounted for 64 percent or 292,300 of the total illness cases reported and for nearly all the increase in illnesses in 1992.

A report of the Menninger Foundation, *Predicting Which Disabled Employees Will Return to Work: The Menninger RTW Scale,* estimates that of the more than 569,000 workers who become disabled each year, approximately 48 percent return to work, many without rehabilitation. Nine percent will not return to work, regardless of rehabilitation services.

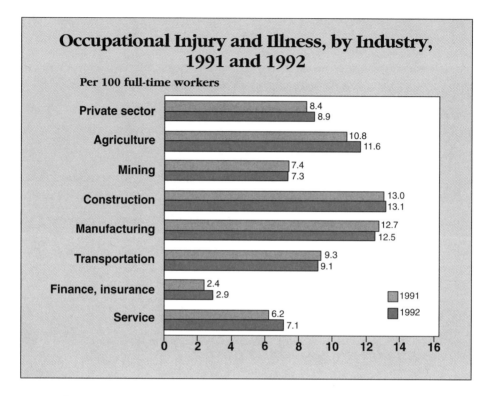

Figure 6.1

SOURCE: U. S. Department of Labor.

Workers with higher incomes have fewer days of disability resulting from acute health conditions. Males and females also have marked differences in the number of disability days they experience. Females averaged eight days and males averaged only six days of restricted activity per person in 1991.

Fatal Occupational Injuries

The incidence of fatal work injury for certain groups of workers is greater than their proportion of total employment. These groups include men; the self-employed; older workers (age 55 and older); those in farming and transportation related occupations; and those in agriculture, mining, and construction industries.

According to a 1993 Bureau of Labor Statistics report, highway vehicle accidents led all other events, accounting for 18 percent of the 6,083 fatal occupational injuries in 1992. Homicides were a close second, affecting women work-

Principal Causes of Injury as a Percentage of Total Injuries

- 25% Lifting
- 22% Slip or fall
- 9% Struck by object
- 7% Pushing and/or pulling
- 6% Stepped on/struck against object
- 5% Cut, punctured, scraped by object
- 5% Caught in/between object
- 4% Using a tool/machine
- 4% Motor vehicle
- 3% Exposed to extreme heat/cold
- 3% Holding/carrying an object
- 2% Reaching
- 1% Jumping
- 1% Repetitive motion
- 5% All other (e.g., electrocution, robbery, explosion, etc.)

Figure 6.2

SOURCE: National Council of Compensation Insurance, 1992.

ers more than men. This manner of injury and death accounted for 17 percent of fatally injured workers. The majority of fatally injured workers were 25–54 years old.

Among industry groups, agricultural crop production, special trades construction contractors (roofing and electrical work), trucking and warehousing, and local government (police and firefighters) had the largest number of fatal work injuries (Table 6.7).

Acute Conditions

Over 369 million workdays were lost as a result of all acute health conditions in 1991, a 2 percent decrease over 1990. Males lost 176 million workdays, and females lost 199 million (Table 6.2). Men were more often unable to work because of injuries, and women lost more workdays due to respiratory infections.

Return to Work Potential of Disability Cases

Predictors	Returned to work	Did not return
Age		
16–34	76%	24%
35–44	94	26
45–54	52	48
55–64	36	64
Marital Status		
Single	63%	37%
Married	48	52
Other	28	72
Cause of Disability		
Cardiovascular	54%	46%
Pulmonary	32	68
Gastrointestinal	92	8
Musculoskeletal	71	29
Neurological	23	77
Other physical	66	34

Figure 6.3

SOURCE: National Council of Compensation Insurance, 1992.

Chronic Conditions

In 1991, almost 36 million people, 14.3 percent of the U.S. civilian noninstitutionalized population (248.7 million), suffered some activity limitation because
of one or more chronic conditions; 4.3 percent of the population were unable
to carry on a major job assignment because of a long-term chronic disease or
impairment. These chronic conditions and long-term latent illnesses, difficult
to recognize and often not recorded accurately, are believed to be more prevalent than the NCHS Health Interview Survey indicates.

Workplace Injuries and Workers' Compensation Insurance

Workers' compensation insurance pays medical expenses and part of lost
wages to workers hurt on the job, whether the employee or the employer was
at fault. It is a state-mandated program and most employers are required to
carry workers' compensation coverage. The majority of the employers insure
through private insurance companies and some of the larger employers are
self-insured. According to HCFA, federal, state, and local government expenditures for workers' compensation was almost $18 billion in 1991.

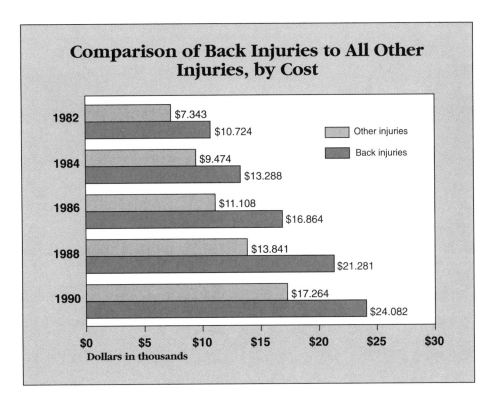

Comparison of Back Injuries to All Other Injuries, by Cost

| Other injuries |
| Back injuries |

1982 — $7.343 / $10.724
1984 — $9.474 / $13.288
1986 — $11.108 / $16.864
1988 — $13.841 / $21.281
1990 — $17.264 / $24.082

Dollars in thousands

Figure 6.4

SOURCE: National Council on Compensation Insurance, 1993.

Social Security Disability Insurance Program

The Social Security Disability Insurance Program is the largest federal income program for disabled persons. There was considerable growth in this program from 1957 to 1993.

The number of workers and dependents receiving benefits through Social Security increased from 4.9 million in 1992 to 5.3 million people in 1993. There were 3.7 million workers with disabilities who received a total of $2.4 billion in benefits through the program in 1993 (Table 6.9).

◆ Morbidity and Mortality

Expectation of life at birth for the resident population of the United States rose from 75.4 years in 1990 to 75.5 years in 1991.

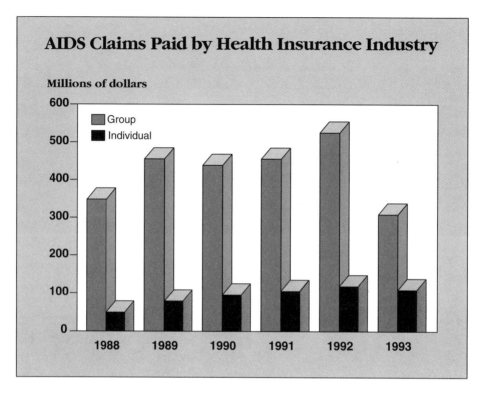

Figure 6.5

NOTE: The amount paid by commercial insurance companies for AIDS claims dropped from $644 million in 1992 to $416 million in 1993 due to advances in treatment.
SOURCE: 1993 ACLI/HIAA AIDS-Related Claims Survey.

Life expectancy at birth improved slightly for both males and females in 1991. Males born in 1991 could expect to live 72 years, and females had a life expectancy of 78.9 years (Table 6.10).

Despite medical breakthroughs and environmental changes, cancer and cardiovascular-renal diseases remain the leading causes of death. Deaths from cancer increased slightly from 200.3 per 100,000 population in 1989 to 203.2 in 1990, while deaths from heart disease, pneumonia, tuberculosis, and cerebrovascular diseases decreased, as they have done since 1960. Death rates from pneumonia and influenza increased slightly in 1990, a year of increased influenza-associated mortality in the elderly.

There were a total of 2,148,463 deaths in the United States in 1990, 19,536 fewer than in 1988 and 2,003 fewer than in 1989.

AIDS Cases in the United States, through December 1993

Area	1992		1993		Cumulative totals		
	Number of cases	Rate by population	Number of cases	Rate by population	Adults/ adolescents	Children < years old	Total
Metropolitan areas with 500,000							
or more population	39,876	24.9	89,407	55.3	302,570	4,428	306,998
Central counties	39,131	26.7	87,742	59.3	297,407	4,343	301,750
Outlying counties	745	5.6	1,665	12.1	5,163	85	5,248
Metropolitan areas with 50,000							
to 500,000 populations	4,840	10.4	11,128	23.7	33,758	501	34,259
Central counties	4,583	11.1	10,517	25.0	31,727	458	32,185
Outlying counties	257	5.1	611	11.9	2,031	43	2,074
Non-metropolitan areas	2,647	5.0	5,809	10.9	18,028	280	18,308
Total	47,572	18.4	106,949	40.8	355,936	5,228	361,164

Figure 6.6

SOURCE: CDC, HIV/AIDS Surveillance Report 9/94.

Since 1980, the age-adjusted death rate has decreased every year except 1985 and 1988, years when major influenza outbreaks increased mortality in the United States.

The downward trend in the mortality rate is in part the result of a decline in the incidence of heart and cerebrovascular diseases and atherosclerosis, which has been declining since 1960. The largest decline was for vascular disease for both males and females.

In their recent projections of age-adjusted death rates, the Social Security Administration projected a decrease in the death rate for both males and females from heart disease through the year 1995, after which it will continue to decline. Deaths per 100,000 from cancer for both genders continues to increase through the year 2010 before it is projected to decline (Tables 6.13 and 6.14).

AIDS

The death rate has been affected in the past few years by acquired immune deficiency syndrome (AIDS). The NCHS January 1993 *Advance Report of Final Mortality Statistics* listed HIV infection as the tenth leading cause of death in 1990. For the black population it ranked seventh, and for the white population, tenth. For males of all races, HIV was the eighth leading cause of death; for females, it did not rank among the ten leading causes in 1990.

HIV was the third leading cause of death for those age 25 to 44. According to ACLI and HIAA, commercial health insurance companies paid $622 million in

AIDS-related claims in 1993. Life and health insurance industries together paid in excess of $1.5 billion in AIDS-related claims in 1993.

According to the Centers for Disease Control (CDC) in Atlanta, there have been 339,250 cases of AIDS reported by December 31, 1993, with 223,490 deaths. CDC estimates that 2 million Americans are presently infected with HIV.

Mortality Data, Selected Countries

According to the OECD, France and Japan have the longest life expectancy at birth for women and men, respectively. In France a female can expect to live 80.9 years; a Japanese man may expect to live 75.9 years from the year of his birth. Icelandic peoples live longer after they reach 80 years of age than people in any other OECD country. Females may expect to live to 89 and men to 87.4 years after their eightieth birthday (Table 6.12).

Table 6.1

Restricted Activity Days, Bed Disability Days, and Work Loss Days, per Person Due to Acute Conditions, 1989–1991

	Restricted activity days			Bed disability days			Work-loss days 18 years and over		
	1989	1990	1991	1989	1990	1991	1989	1990	1991
Gender									
Male	6.9	6.0	6.4	2.9	2.6	2.6	3.0	2.7	2.7
Female	9.8	8.0	8.2	3.9	3.5	3.6	3.9	3.7	3.7
Family Income									
Under $10,000	10.6	10.5	10.7	4.9	4.7	4.8	5.1	4.3	4.9
$10,000–19,999	8.1	8.0	8.2	3.8	3.8	3.7	NA	NA	3.9
$20,000–34,999	7.6	7.2	7.3	3.4	3.2	2.9	NA	NA	2.9
$35,000 and over	6.0	6.1	6.4	2.7	2.4	2.6	NA	NA	NA
Place of Residence									
Metropolitan statistical area	7.4	7.1	7.4	3.4	3.1	3.2	3.1	3.2	3.3
Other statistical area	7.7	7.2	7.1	3.5	3.1	3.0	3.1	2.9	2.8
Age									
Under 5 years	9.6	9.5	9.9	4.5	4.5	4.2	NA	NA	NA
5–17 years	7.9	6.6	7.2	4.1	3.1	3.3	NA	NA	NA
18–24 years	7.5	7.7	7.1	3.2	3.5	3.2	3.9	4.8	3.8
25–44 years	7.1	6.6	6.8	3.0	2.8	2.8	3.6	3.2	3.2
45–66 years	5.9	5.8	6.4	2.8	2.9	2.7	2.5	2.3	2.7
65 years and older	9.9	8.7	8.8	4.2	3.2	3.6	NA	NA	NA
Race									
White	7.5	7.2	7.4	3.4	3.0	3.0	3.2	3.1	3.0
Black	7.6	6.7	7.3	3.8	3.3	3.9	4.8	3.5	4.3

NOTE: The data refer to the civilian, noninstitutional population.

NOTE: A restricted activity day is one on which a person cuts down his usual activities for the whole day because of illness or injury. A bed disability day is one in which a person stays in bed for all or most of the day because of a specific illness or injury. Family income includes the total income of each member of the family.

NA: Not available.

SOURCE: U.S. Department of Health and Human Services, National Center for Health Statistics, Current Estimates from the National Health Interview Survey, United States 1991.

Table 6.2

Total Workdays Lost by Employees, by Age, Gender, and Acute Conditions, 1990 and 1991

| | Number of work-loss days (millions) | | | | | |
| | All ages 18 or more | | Age 18 to 44 | | Age 45 or more | |
Total	1990	1991	1990	1991	1990	1991
Acute conditions	374.9	369.3	290.2	273.1	84.7	96.2
Infective/parasitic diseases	24.9	18.8	19.5	15.5	5.4	3.3
Respiratory conditions	132.7	148.7	94.7	105.5	38.1	43.2
Digestive system conditions	14.3	19.2	9.1	13.5	5.2	5.7
Injuries	125.6	103.1	105.2	76.3	20.5	26.7
All other acute conditions	16.8	26.4	13.1	20.1	3.8	6.3
Male						
All acute conditions	176.2	170.4	134.6	123.4	41.6	46.9
Infective/parasitic diseases	10.8	8.7	7.5	6.9	3.3	1.6
Respiratory conditions	56.8	59.7	36.1	42.4	20.7	17.2
Digestive system conditions	5.3	6.6	3.8	4.8	1.5	1.8
Injuries	82.3	69.8	72.1	51.6	10.3	18.1
All other acute conditions	5.9	12.7	4.6	8.1	1.3	4.7
Female						
All acute conditions	198.7	198.9	155.6	149.7	43.1	49.2
Infective/parasitic diseases	14.1	10.1	12.1	8.5	2.1	1.6
Respiratory conditions	75.9	89.1	58.7	63.1	17.2	25.9
Digestive system conditions	8.9	12.6	5.3	8.7	3.7	3.8
Injuries	43.4	33.3	33.2	24.6	10.2	8.7
All other acute conditions	10.9	14.7	8.4	11.9	2.5	1.7

NOTE: Data refer to civilian noninstitutionalized population. In some cases the sum of the items does not equal the total shown because of rounding.
A work-loss day is a day in which a currently employed person, 18 years or over, did not work at least half of his or her normal workday because of a specific illness or injury. An acute condition is one that required either medical attention or restricted activity and lasted fewer than 3 days.

SOURCE: U.S. Department of Health and Human Services, National Center for Health Statistics, Current Estimates from the National Health Interview Survey, United States, December 1992.

Table 6.3

Occupational Injuries and Illnesses, by Industry, 1992

Industry	Total cases (thousands)	Lost workday cases		Cases without lost workdays (thousands)
		Total (thousands)	With days away from work (thousands)	
Private industry total (injuries and illnesses)	6,799.4	2,953.4	2,331.1	3,846.0
Agriculture, forestry, and fishing	115.6	54.0	47.1	61.6
Mining	47.2	26.1	23.0	21.1
Construction	519.9	230.4	209.6	289.5
Manufacturing	2,213.2	953.6	623.6	1,259.6
Durable goods	1,356.0	553.5	370.6	802.5
Nondurable goods	857.1	400.1	253.0	457.1
Transportation and public utilities	487.7	272.7	227.7	215.0
Wholesale and retail trade	1,681.5	698.3	590.1	983.2
Wholesale trade	436.6	210.4	172.7	226.2
Retail trade	1,244.9	487.9	417.4	757.0
Finance, insurance, and real estate	173.7	71.1	60.4	102.7
Services	1,560.5	647.2	552.7	913.4
Private industry total (injuries)	6,342.0	2,776.1	2,226.0	3,565.9
Agriculture, forestry, and fishing	109.4	52.3	45.7	57.2
Mining	45.3	25.6	22.5	19.7
Construction	509.5	226.8	206.4	282.6
Manufacturing	1,920.8	833.7	565.9	1,087.1
Durable goods	1,184.1	488.9	336.8	695.2
Nondurable goods	736.7	344.8	229.0	391.9
Transportation and public utilities	471.0	266.1	219.3	204.9
Wholesale and retail trade	1,637.6	682.0	577.0	955.5
Wholesale trade	423.0	205.3	169.0	217.7
Retail trade	1,214.6	476.7	407.9	737.9
Finance, insurance, and real estate	157.7	64.4	55.6	93.2
Services	1,490.7	625.1	533.5	865.6
Private industry total (illnesses)	457.4	177.3	105.1	280.1
Agriculture, forestry, and fishing	6.2	1.8	1.4	4.4
Mining	19.0	0.5	0.4	1.4
Construction	10.5	3.6	3.2	6.9
Manufacturing	292.3	119.9	57.7	172.5
Durable goods	171.9	64.6	33.7	107.3
Nondurable goods	120.4	55.2	23.9	65.2
Transportation and public utilities	16.7	6.6	5.3	10.0
Wholesale and retail trade	43.9	16.2	13.2	27.7
Wholesale trade	13.6	5.1	3.7	8.6
Retail trade	30.3	11.2	9.5	19.2
Finance, insurance, and real estate	16.1	6.7	4.8	9.4
Services	69.8	22.1	19.2	47.7

NOTE: Numbers do not add due to rounding.
SOURCE: U. S. Department of Labor, BLS, PR, 12/15/93.

Table 6.4

Occupational Injuries and Illness Rates per 100 Full-Time Workers, 1984–1992

Industry/type of case	1984	1985	1986	1987	1988	1989	1990	1991	1992
Private sector									
Total cases	8.0	7.9	7.9	8.3	8.6	8.6	8.8	8.4	8.9
Lost workday cases	3.7	3.6	3.6	3.8	4.0	4.0	4.1	3.9	3.9
Lost workdays	63.4	64.9	65.8	69.9	76.1	78.7	84.0	86.5	NA
Agriculture, forestry/fishing									
Total cases	12.0	11.4	11.2	11.2	10.9	10.9	11.6	10.8	11.6
Lost workday cases	6.1	5.7	5.6	5.7	5.6	53.7	5.9	5.4	5.4
Lost workdays	90.7	91.3	93.6	94.1	101.8	100.9	112.2	108.3	NA
Mining									
Total cases	9.7	8.4	7.4	8.5	8.8	8.5	8.3	7.4	7.3
Lost workday cases	5.3	4.8	4.1	4.9	5.1	4.8	5.0	4.5	4.1
Lost workdays	160.2	145.3	125.9	144.0	152.1	137.2	119.5	129.6	NA
Construction									
Total cases	15.5	15.2	15.1	14.7	14.6	14.3	14.2	13.0	13.1
Lost workday cases	6.9	6.9	6.9	6.8	6.8	6.8	6.7	6.1	5.8
Lost workdays	128.1	134.5	134.5	135.8	142.2	143.3	147.9	148.1	NA
Manufacturing									
Total cases	10.6	10.4	10.6	13.1	13.1	13.1	13.2	12.7	12.5
Lost workday cases	4.7	4.6	4.7	5.7	5.8	5.8	5.8	5.6	5.4
Lost workdays	77.9	80.2	85.2	107.4	113.0	113.0	120.7	121.5	NA
Transportation/public utilities									
Total cases	8.8	8.6	8.2	8.4	8.9	9.2	9.6	9.3	9.1
Lost workday cases	5.2	5.0	4.8	4.9	5.1	5.3	5.5	5.4	5.1
Lost workdays	105.1	107.1	102.1	108.1	118.6	121.5	134.1	140.0	NA
Wholesale and retail trade									
Total cases	7.4	7.4	7.7	7.7	7.8	8.0	7.9	7.6	8.4
Lost workday cases	3.3	3.2	3.3	3.4	3.5	3.6	3.5	3.4	3.5
Lost workdays	50.5	50.7	54.0	46.1	60.9	63.5	65.6	72.0	NA
Finance, insurance, and real estate									
Total cases	1.9	2.0	2.0	2.0	2.0	2.0	2.4	2.4	2.9
Lost workday cases	0.9	0.9	0.9	0.9	0.9	0.9	1.1	1.1	1.2
Lost workdays	13.6	15.4	15.4	14.3	17.2	17.6	27.3	24.1	NA
Service									
Total cases	5.2	5.4	5.4	5.5	5.4	5.5	6.0	6.2	7.1
Lost workday cases	2.5	2.6	2.6	2.7	2.6	2.7	2.8	2.8	3.0
Lost workdays	41.1	45.4	45.4	45.8	47.7	51.2	56.4	60.0	NA

NA: Not available.

SOURCE: Department of Labor, Monthly Labor Review, February 1993.

Table 6.5

Selected Chronic Conditions by Gender and Age, 1991 (Thousands)

Type of condition	Male					Female				
			65 years and older					65 years and older		
	Under 45 years	45–64 years	Total	65–74 years	75 years and older	Under 45 years	45–64 years	Total	65–74 years	75 years and older
Musculoskeletal conditions										
Arthritis	2,116	4,372	4,896	2,754	2,151	2,991	6,985	9,790	5,043	4,746
Gout	310	528	552	372	181	111	309	329	128	201
Intervertebral disc disorders	1,292	1,073	402	279	123	777	995	434	290	144
Bursitis	5,870	860	111	325	82	945	1,078	622	407	216
Impairments										
Visual impairment	2,308	1,436	1,192	594	598	1,049	802	1,026	445	761
Cataracts	133	133	1,761	859	903	262	586	3,480	1,477	2,003
Glaucoma	183	304	619	333	286	108	257	1,109	508	601
Hearing impairment	3,760	4,039	4,656	2,705	1,951	2,545	2,626	5,054	2,166	468
Speech impairment	1,403	217	159	70	89	793	257	152	42	110
Paralysis of extremities	296	3,611	175	72	104	601	118	249	79	1,573
Selected digestive conditions										
Ulcer	849	570	405	213	192	818	666	413	234	179
Frequent indigestions	1,519	852	552	278	274	1,296	793	710	439	271
Gastritis or duodenitis	600	287	160	102	58	760	667	463	299	164
Enteritis or colitis	431	212	146	96	50	584	338	506	223	283
Selected genitourinary, nervous, endocrine, metabolic disorders										
Goiter	135	99	178	112	66	938	1,236	1,086	726	360
Diabetes	646	1,310	1,220	796	425	860	1,398	1,788	1,103	685
Epilepsy	548	133	95	46	143	447	122	86	59	27
Diseases of prostate	154	143	309	105	204	1,074	NA	915	NA	NA
Migraine headache	2,055	598	100	788	23	4,634	1,627	525	281	244
Selected circulatory conditions										
Heart disease	2,073	2,073	3,825	2,376	1,449	3,197	2,868	1,963	994	2,800
Hypertension	2,619	5,485	3,871	2,614	1,256	2,398	6,022	7,405	4,278	3,126
Cerebrovascular disease	86	293	863	519	344	103	465	1,046	547	499
Selected respiratory conditions										
Chronic bronchitis	3,578	942	640	460	180	4,840	1,600	949	569	380
Asthma	4,548	762	414	270	135	4,139	1,159	731	417	296
Hay Fever	8,187	2,218	963	665	298	8,803	2,833	1,245	789	456
Emphysema	12	389	657	432	225	52	212	324	167	157

NA: Not available.
SOURCE: National Center for Health Statistics, Health Interview Survey, December 1992.

Table 6.6

Percentage of Nonfatal Occupational Injuries and Illnesses Involving Days Away from Work, by Selected Injury or Illness, Characteristic, and Industry, 1992

Characteristic	Private industry	Agriculture, forestry and fishing	Mining	Construction	Manufacturing	Transporation, and public utilities	Wholesale trade	Retail trade	Finance, insurance, and real estate	Services
Total: 2,331,100 cases	100	100	100	100	100	100	100	100	100	100
Nature of injury, illness:										
Sprains, strains	43.9	38.0	41.4	37.7	39.8	50.5	46.7	41.3	40.1	50.1
Bruises, contusions	9.6	8.0	10.7	7.8	7.4	10.5	10.2	10.5	8.2	9.4
Cuts, lacerations	7.4	9.5	5.9	9.2	8.1	4.3	6.9	11.1	6.8	4.7
Fractures	6.2	6.9	11.1	10.0	6.1	6.5	6.5	5.0	7.4	5.0
Heat burns	1.8	0.6	1.3	1.2	1.5	0.6	1.0	3.9	0.7	1.6
Carpel tunnel syndrome	1.4	0.5	0.3	0.5	2.8	0.7	0.8	0.9	3.2	1.0
Chemical burns	0.7	0.7	0.9	0.6	0.9	0.5	0.6	0.6	0.5	0.6
Amputations	0.5	1.4	0.8	0.5	1.0	0.2	0.6	0.3	0.4	0.2
Multiple injuries	2.9	3.1	6.4	3.4	2.8	3.1	3.1	2.7	2.9	2.7
All other	25.7	30.3	21.2	29.1	27.7	23.1	23.8	23.6	29.7	24.7
Source of injury, illness:										
Chemicals, chemical products	2.0	2.1	5.8	1.5	2.5	1.2	1.9	1.6	2.3	1.9
Containers	15.1	11.9	5.8	5.7	15.1	20.4	23.9	22.2	12.2	9.3
Furniture, fixtures	4.2	0.7	0.6	1.7	3.0	2.3	2.9	2.9	6.6	5.9
Machinery	6.9	8.2	12.2	6.6	11.1	2.9	6.3	6.3	5.0	4.3
Parts and materials	11.1	7.4	17.6	25.0	16.5	9.3	12.5	12.5	5.9	4.2
Worker motion or position	13.4	12.4	4.9	10.3	17.3	12.9	10.9	10.9	16.1	12.8
Floor, ground surface	14.8	14.8	13.9	17.2	10.1	15.1	13.6	13.6	24.3	16.5
Tools, instruments, equipment	6.3	9.1	8.5	10.8	6.7	3.9	4.1	4.1	5.2	5.1
Vehicles	6.7	6.7	6.1	4.3	4.3	16.6	11.3	11.3	5.0	6.1
Health care patient	4.5	NA	NA	NA	NA	0.8	NA	NA	0.3	18.8
All other	15.1	26.8	24.5	16.9	13.3	14.6	12.7	12.7	17.2	15.1

NOTE: Numbers do not add to totals due to rounding.

NA: Not available.

SOURCE: U. S. Department of Labor, Bureau of Labor Statistics, April 1994.

Table 6.7

Fatal Work Injuries, by Selected Worker Characteristics, 1993

Characteristic	Number	Percentage
Total fatalities	6,271	100
Employment status		
Wage and salaried workers	4,981	79
Self-employed	1,290	21
Sex and age		
Men	5,970	92
Women	481	8
Both sexes:		
Under 16 years	29	NA
16 to 17 years	39	1
18 to 19 years	101	2
20 to 24 years	502	8
25 to 34 years	1,510	24
35 to 44 years	1,576	25
45 to 54 years	1,193	19
55 to 64 years	801	13
65 years and over	514	8
Race		
White	6,106	81
Black	664	11
Asian or Pacific Islander	190	3
Hispanic (may be of any race)	640	10
American Indian, Aleut, Eskimo	47	1
Other	263	4

NA: Not available.
SOURCE: Bureau of Labor Statistics 1994.

Table 6.8

Fatal Occupational Injuries by Occupation, 1993

Occupation	Fatalities	
	Number	**Percentage**
Total fatalities	6,271	100
Managerial and professional specialty	681	11
Executive, administrative and mangerial	427	7
Professional specialty	254	4
Technical, sales, and administrative support	842	13
Technicians and related support	167	3
Airplane pilots and navigators	104	2
Sales occupations	556	9
Administrative support occupations, including clerical	119	2
Service occupations	539	9
Protective service	288	5
Firefighting and fire prevention, including supervisors	39	1
Police and detectives, including supervisors	149	2
Guards, including supervisors		
Farming, forestry, and fishing	961	15
Farming occupations and managers	409	7
Ohter agricultural and related occupations	214	3
Farm workers, including supervisors	209	3
Forestry and logging occupations	142	2
Timber cutting and logging occupations	124	2
Fishers, hunters, and trappers	91	1
Fishers	79	1
Precision production, craft, and repair	1,095	17
Mechanics and repairers	317	5
Construction trades	565	9
Carpenters	96	2
Electricians	78	1
Electrical power installers and repairers	42	1
Structural metal workers	34	1
Operators, fabricators, and laborers	1,959	31
Machine operators, assemblers, and inspectors	205	3
Transportation and material moving occupations	1,182	19
Motor vehicle operators	917	15
Truck drivers	731	12
Driver-sales workers	41	1
Taxicab drivers and chauffeurs	113	2
Material moving equipment operators	180	3
Handlers, equipment cleaners, helpers, and laborers	572	9
Construction laborers	218	3
Other laborers	202	3
Military occupations (resident armed forces)	121	2

NOTE: Numbers do not add to total due to rounding.
SOURCE: Bureau of Labor Statistics, 1994.

Table 6.9

Growth in the Social Security Disability Program, 1957–1993

Year	Total	Disabled workers	Wives and husbands	Children
People paid				
1957	149,850	149,850	NA	NA
1960	687,451	456,371	76,599	155,481
1970	2,664,995	1,492,948	283,447	888,600
1980	4,682,172	2,861,253	462,204	1,358,715
1985	3,907,169	2,656,500	305,528	945,141
1986	3,993,279	2,727,388	300,592	965,301
1987	4,044,724	2,785,885	290,895	967,944
1988	4,074,300	2,830,284	280,821	963,195
1989	4,128,827	2,894,364	271,488	961,975
1990	4,265,981	3,011,294	265,890	988,797
1991	4,513,040	3,194,938	266,219	1,051,883
1992	4,889,696	3,467,783	270,674	1,151,239
1993	5,253,566	3,725,966	272,759	1,254,841
Benefits paid (thousands)				
1957	$ 10,904	$ 10,904	$ NA	$ NA
1960	48,000	40,668	2,636	4,697
1970	242,400	196,010	12,060	34,330
1980	1,261,723	1,060,792	51,065	149,866
1985	1,459,906	1,285,386	40,507	134,014
1986	1,506,584	1,330,577	39,456	136,551
1987	1,596,707	1,415,825	39,205	141,677
1988	1,682,887	1,498,637	38,878	145,373
1989	1,799,655	1,609,780	39,148	150,727
1990	1,970,108	1,768,313	39,869	161,926
1991	2,164,237	1,946,823	40,792	176,622
1992	2,408,992	2,171,080	41,951	195,961
1993	2,650,575	2,390,829	42,570	217,176

NOTE: These data represent people paid and amount paid for the last month of each calendar year.

NA: Not available.

SOURCE: U. S. Department of Health and Human Services, Social Security Administration. Summer 1994.

Table 6.10

Life Expectancy at Birth, by Race and Gender, Selected Years, 1940–1991

| | All races | | | White | | | All other | | | | | |
| | | | | | | | Total | | | Black | | |
Year	Both sexes	Male	Female	Both sexes	Male	Female	Both sexes	Male	Female	Both sexes	Male	Female
1940	62.9	60.8	65.2	64.2	62.1	66.6	53.1	51.5	54.9	NA	NA	NA
1950	68.2	65.6	71.1	69.1	66.5	72.2	60.8	59.1	62.9	NA	NA	NA
1960	69.7	66.6	73.1	70.6	67.4	74.1	63.6	61.1	66.3	NA	NA	NA
1970	70.8	67.1	74.7	71.7	68.0	75.6	65.3	61.3	69.4	64.1	60.0	68.3
1975	72.6	68.8	76.6	73.4	69.5	77.3	68.0	63.7	72.4	66.8	62.4	71.3
1980	73.7	70.0	77.4	74.4	70.7	78.1	69.5	65.3	73.6	68.1	63.8	72.5
1981	74.1	70.4	77.8	74.8	71.1	78.4	70.3	66.2	74.4	68.9	64.5	73.2
1982	74.5	70.8	78.1	75.1	71.5	78.7	70.9	66.8	74.9	69.4	65.1	73.6
1983	74.6	71.0	78.1	75.2	71.6	78.7	70.9	67.0	74.7	69.4	65.2	73.5
1984	74.7	71.1	78.2	75.3	71.8	78.7	71.1	67.2	74.9	69.5	65.3	73.6
1985	74.7	71.0	78.2	75.3	71.8	78.7	71.0	67.0	74.8	69.3	65.0	73.4
1986	74.7	71.2	78.2	75.4	71.9	78.8	70.9	66.8	74.9	69.1	64.8	73.4
1987	74.9	71.4	78.3	75.6	72.1	78.9	71.0	66.9	75.0	69.1	64.7	73.4
1988	74.9	71.4	78.3	75.6	72.2	78.9	70.8	66.7	74.8	68.9	64.4	73.2
1989	75.1	71.7	78.5	75.9	72.5	79.2	70.9	66.7	74.9	68.8	64.3	73.3
1990	75.4	71.8	78.8	76.1	72.7	79.4	71.2	67.0	75.2	69.1	64.5	73.6
1991	75.5	72.0	78.9	76.3	72.9	79.6	71.5	67.3	75.5	69.3	64.6	73.8

NOTE: Values for 1981–1989 have been revised using intercensal population estimates based on the 1990 census. They are not comparable to any previous NCHS reports.

NA: Not available.

SOURCE: National Center for Health Statistics, unpublished data, July 1994.

Table 6.11

Expectation of Life at Selected Ages, by Race and Gender, United States, 1990–1992

	Expectation of life in years								
	White			Black			Other		
Age	1990	1991	1992	1990	1991	1992	1990	1991	1992
Male									
0	72.7	72.9	73.2	64.5	64.6	65.5	67.0	67.3	67.8
15	58.6	58.7	59.0	51.3	51.3	52.0	53.6	53.8	54.2
25	49.3	49.5	49.7	42.4	42.6	43.3	44.6	44.9	45.4
35	40.1	40.3	40.4	34.1	34.3	34.9	36.0	36.3	36.8
45	31.1	31.3	31.4	26.2	26.4	27.2	27.8	28.1	28.8
55	22.5	22.7	23.0	19.0	19.3	20.1	20.3	20.6	21.3
65	15.2	15.4	15.5	13.2	13.4	13.9	14.0	14.3	14.9
75	9.4	9.5	9.5	8.6	8.7	8.9	9.1	9.2	9.6
86	5.2	5.3	5.3	5.0	5.1	5.5	5.3	5.4	5.9
Female									
0	79.4	79.6	79.7	73.6	73.8	73.9	75.2	75.5	75.6
15	65.2	65.3	65.4	60.2	60.3	60.4	61.7	61.8	62.0
25	55.4	55.6	55.6	50.6	50.7	50.8	52.0	52.2	52.4
35	45.8	45.9	45.9	41.3	41.4	41.5	42.6	42.8	43.0
45	36.2	36.4	36.4	32.4	32.5	32.7	33.6	33.8	34.1
55	27.2	27.3	27.4	24.2	24.3	24.5	25.1	25.3	25.7
65	19.1	19.2	19.2	17.2	17.2	17.4	17.8	17.9	18.3
75	12.0	12.1	12.1	11.2	11.2	11.2	11.5	11.6	11.9
85	6.4	6.5	6.7	6.3	6.3	6.6	6.4	6.4	6.9
Chances per 1,000 of surviving from birth to specific age									
Male									
15	987	987	989	973	973	976	976	977	979
25	974	975	976	949	946	950	955	954	955
35	957	958	960	908	907	912	922	922	923
45	932	932	933	846	844	845	871	871	868
55	881	882	881	744	743	746	785	878	783
65	760	763	767	571	575	594	627	634	641
75	534	540	550	341	348	378	399	409	430
86	229	236	238	128	131	138	163	169	178
Female									
15	990	991	991	978	979	980	981	982	982
25	986	986	987	972	972	973	975	976	975
35	980	980	981	956	957	958	962	963	963
45	968	968	969	928	928	926	939	939	935
55	938	939	940	869	870	969	888	890	887
65	864	865	868	751	755	754	783	788	784
75	709	711	712	559	563	573	602	607	614
85	424	429	423	304	306	301	340	345	348

*1992 data are provisional.
SOURCE: Various reports from the National Center for Health Statistics, Advance Data 1994.

Table 6.12

Over 65 Population, Male and Female Life Expectancy in Selected Countries, 1991

Country	Total population (thousands)	Over 65 population (percentage)	Male life expectancy at birth (years)	Female life expectancy at birth (years)	Male life expectancy at age 80 (years)	Female life expectancy at age 80 (years)
Australia	17,086	11.2	73.9	80.0	6.8	8.6
Austria	7,718	15.1	72.5	79.0	6.6	7.6
Belgium	9,993	NA	72.4	79.1	6.1	7.9
Canada	26,639	11.5	NA	NA	NA	NA
Denmark	5,140	15.6	72.0	77.7	6.4	8.1
Finland	4,986	13.5	70.9	78.9	6.1	7.5
France	56,735	14.0	72.7	80.9	NA	NA
Germany	63,074	NA	NA	NA	NA	NA
Greece	10,140	NA	NA	NA	NA	NA
Iceland	256	10.7	75.7	75.7	7.4	9.0
Ireland	3,503	11.3	NA	NA	NA	NA
Italy	57,647	15.3	NA	NA	NA	NA
Japan	123,540	12.0	75.9	75.9	6.9	8.7
Luxembourg	381	NA	NA	NA	NA	NA
Netherlands	14,944	12.8	73.8	80.1	NA	NA
New Zealand	3,379	10.9	NA	NA	NA	NA
Norway	4,242	16.3	73.4	79.8	6.4	8.1
Portugal	9,859	13.1	70.9	77.9	NA	NA
Spain	38,959	13.4	NA	80.1	NA	NA
Sweden	8,566	17.8	74.8	80.4	6.6	8.3
Switzerland	6,796	15.0	74.0	80.9	6.8	8.5
Turkey	57,163	NA	64.1	68.4	5.2	5.9
United Kingdom	57,411	15.7	NA	78.5	NA	NA
United States	259,571	12.6	72.0	78.8	NA	NA

NA: Not available.

SOURCE: Organization for Economic Cooperation and Development (OECD), OECD Data Health File, 1992.

Table 6.13

Female Age-Adjusted Death Rates (per 100,000), by Cause of Death, Selected Years and Projected Years

Calendar year	Total	Heart disease	Cancer	Vascular disease	Violence	Respiratory disease	Infancy	Digestive disease	Diabetes mellitus	Cirrhosis (liver)	AIDS	Other
1970	803.6	308.4	141.0	144.9	45.6	38.5	24.7	19.0	21.2	10.3	0.0	50.0
1975	709.1	265.2	141.4	119.8	39.6	34.3	18.2	15.8	17.4	9.5	0.0	48.0
1980	668.1	250.1	146.0	92.1	36.0	37.0	14.5	16.8	15.1	8.8	0.0	51.7
1985	638.0	227.6	150.7	73.6	31.3	45.5	11.9	16.3	14.3	7.1	0.4	59.2
1990	620.9	206.8	153.6	61.3	30.2	52.5	10.3	15.9	13.8	6.2	3.5	66.7
1991	615.0	202.5	154.2	58.5	29.6	53.1	9.9	15.8	13.5	6.1	4.5	67.4
1992	609.5	198.4	154.4	55.9	28.9	53.6	9.5	15.7	13.2	6.0	5.5	68.2
1995	594.6	186.5	156.4	48.6	27.1	55.4	8.3	15.4	12.2	5.7	8.0	70.8
2000	573.5	168.4	159.3	38.9	24.5	58.7	6.8	15.1	10.9	5.4	10.1	75.5
2005	553.9	153.4	161.7	32.6	22.6	61.2	5.8	14.8	9.9	5.2	7.8	78.9
2010	537.0	142.6	161.5	29.2	21.7	61.7	5.3	14.5	9.4	5.1	6.5	79.4
2015	521.5	134.2	159.9	26.7	21.1	61.2	4.9	14.2	9.1	5.1	6.4	78.8
2020	506.7	126.5	158.0	24.5	20.5	60.5	4.5	13.9	8.8	5.0	6.4	78.0

SOURCE: Social Security Administration, Office of the Actuary.

Table 6.14

Male Age-Adjusted Death Rates (per 100,000), by Cause of Death, Selected Years and Projected Years

Calendar year	Total	Heart disease	Cancer	Vascular disease	Violence	Respiratory disease	Infancy	Digestive disease	Diabetes mellitus	Cirrhosis (liver)	AIDS	Other
1970	1,359.5	554.3	221.1	187.5	126.0	93.3	31.5	29.0	19.9	22.2	0.0	74.7
1975	1,237.5	491.8	229.8	156.2	113.3	87.9	22.7	23.6	17.1	21.6	0.0	73.5
1980	1,165.1	454.1	240.6	119.8	108.6	88.4	17.8	23.5	15.6	19.2	0.0	77.6
1985	1,096.4	408.5	243.2	95.1	92.2	97.7	14.8	22.5	15.2	15.7	5.5	86.0
1990	1,055.0	360.7	246.2	80.0	88.1	101.4	12.5	21.1	15.3	14.4	26.1	89.2
1991	1,047.9	353.1	247.3	76.4	86.6	101.7	11.9	20.8	15.1	14.2	31.2	89.8
1992	1,040.9	345.6	248.5	72.9	85.0	102.0	11.4	20.5	14.8	13.9	35.8	90.5
1995	1,019.3	324.4	252.1	63.5	80.6	102.9	9.9	19.6	14.1	13.1	46.4	92.6
2000	981.0	292.3	258.3	50.8	73.9	105.0	8.0	18.4	13.0	12.0	52.9	96.4
2005	934.0	265.8	263.2	42.5	69.0	106.8	6.8	17.5	12.1	11.3	39.7	99.3
2010	900.1	246.9	263.6	38.1	66.5	106.8	6.2	17.0	11.6	11.0	32.9	99.6
2015	874.0	231.9	261.1	34.8	65.1	105.9	5.7	16.6	11.2	10.9	32.0	98.7
2020	850.1	218.4	258.2	32.0	63.9	104.8	5.3	16.3	10.9	10.7	31.9	97.8

SOURCE: Social Security Administration, Office of the Actuary.

Table 6.15

Death Rates per 100,000 Population for 15 Leading Causes of Death, by Age, 1990

Cause of death	All ages	Under 1 year	1–4 years	5–14 years	15–24 years	25–34 years	35–44 years	45–54 years	55–64 years	65–74 years	75–84 years	85 years and older
All causes	863.8	971.9	46.8	24.0	99.2	139.2	223.2	473.4	1,196.9	2,648.6	6,007.2	15,327.4
Heart diseases	289.5	1,332.9	1.9	0.9	2.5	7.6	31.4	120.5	367.3	894.3	2,295.7	6,739.9
Malignant neoplasms	203.2	2.3	3.5	3.1	4.9	12.6	43.3	158.9	449.6	872.3	1,348.5	1,752.9
Cerebrovascular diseases	57.9	3.8	0.3	0.2	0.6	2.2	6.5	18.7	48.0	144.4	499.3	1,633.9
Accidents and adverse effects	37.0	23.6	17.3	10.4	43.9	37.0	31.3	29.4	34.3	46.6	100.3	257.1
Chronic obstructive pulmonary diseases	34.9	1.4	0.4	0.3	0.5	0.7	1.6	9.1	48.9	152.5	321.1	433.3
Pneumonia and influenza	32.0	16.1	1.2	0.4	0.6	1.8	3.8	7.0	18.6	59.1	253.5	1,140.0
Diabetes mellitus	19.2	NA	NA	0.1	0.3	1.6	4.0	11.3	33.0	73.5	145.2	255.0
Suicide	12.4	NA	NA	0.8	13.2	15.2	15.3	14.8	16.0	17.9	24.9	22.2
Chronic liver disease	10.4	NA	NA	NA	0.1	2.1	9.7	18.0	29.9	34.9	34.1	23.4
HIV infection	10.1	2.7	0.8	0.2	1.5	19.7	27.4	15.2	6.2	2.0	0.7	NA
Homicide	10.0	8.4	2.6	1.5	19.9	17.7	11.8	7.6	5.0	3.8	4.3	4.6
Nephritis	8.3	3.8	0.2	0.1	0.2	0.5	1.4	2.9	8.2	23.9	69.7	199.1
Septicemia	7.7	6.8	0.7	0.1	0.2	0.7	1.5	3.1	8.0	20.9	60.2	183.7
Atherosclerosis	7.3	NA	NA	NA	NA	NA	0.1	0.6	3.2	12.3	53.2	318.0
Conditions in perinatal period	7.1	443.0	0.9	0.1	NA	NA	NA	NA	NA	NA	NA	NA

NOTE: Values for 1981 and prior years cannot be compared to this table due to revisions in 1981–1989 data.

NA: Not available.

SOURCE: National Center for Health Statistics, Health Interview Survey, December 1992.

Table 6.16

Mortality from all Causes of Death among Men and Women per 100,000 in Selected Countries, 1990

Country	Men					Women				
	All Ages	Under 25	25–44	45–64	65+	All Ages	Under 25	25–44	45–64	65+
United States										
White	663.4	113.4	223.8	969.9	5838.3	398.9	64.0	90.0	556.8	4443.9
All other	876.2	183.6	428.6	1414.9	6076.2	509.9	101.4	176.0	829.2	4298.4
Total	692.8	127.0	255.4	1025.0	5861.3	415.6	71.4	104.8	594.7	4429.4
Canada	613.4	98.4	161.8	876.9	5657.1	359.0	55.7	77.7	478.7	3964.4
Denmark	708.3	81.3	185.1	1004.6	6966.2	454.3	49.4	95.1	673.6	5228.9
Finland	762.7	92.4	258.5	1204.8	6629.4	395.7	44.6	90.4	457.5	4940.7
France	634.8	101.1	223.6	1049.0	5810.7	329.3	55.5	91.2	412.3	4427.8
Germany, F.R.	682.1	87.0	163.0	971.8	7003.1	395.4	50.2	83.5	472.3	5164.9
Iceland	537.9	100.0	137.5	681.8	5425.0	354.4	34.6	65.8	513.0	4220.0
Netherlands	621.5	74.0	119.7	806.8	6437.1	363.9	48.7	73.4	442.3	4540.0
Norway	641.4	90.0	157.4	866.1	6474.0	377.6	48.1	77.5	445.0	4840.7
Sweden	569.7	74.1	139.5	725.9	6050.2	356.8	45.8	76.3	410.9	4635.2
Switzerland	599.1	102.5	178.3	744.6	6107.9	341.3	53.3	77.8	377.2	4577.9
United Kingdom										
England and Wales	650.1	88.0	131.6	919.7	6508.6	417.4	52.2	75.9	560.4	5137.5
Northern Ireland	732.9	81.7	151.4	1025.3	7202.6	464.1	51.4	85.0	640.5	5440.7
Scotland	764.6	92.3	165.8	1163.1	7246.9	491.3	48.2	90.8	725.5	5688.2
Japan	501.9	60.9	120.5	710.9	5003.1	287.0	34.6	67.3	325.7	3437.0

SOURCE: Metropolitan Life Insurance Company, Statistical Bulletin, April–June 1993.

Table 6.17

Most Common Mental Disorders as a Percentage of Population, 1993

Type of disorder	Total population	Male	Female
Affective disorders			
Major depressive episode	17.1	12.7	21.6
Manic episode	1.6	1.6	1.7
Dysthmia (frequent and severe depressed mood adolescents)	6.4	4.8	8.0
Anxiety disorders			
Panic disorder	3.5	2.0	5.0
Agoraphobia without panic (fear of being in a place where you cannot leave or get help)	5.3	3.5	7.0
Social phobia (extreme fear of speaking in public or meeting new people)	13.3	11.1	15.5
Simple phobia (fear of flying, snakes, etc.)	11.3	6.7	15.7
Generalized anxiety disorder	5.1	3.6	6.6
Substance use disorders			
Alcohol abuse	9.4	12.5	6.4
Alcohol dependence	14.1	20.1	8.2
Drug abuse	4.4	5.4	3.5
Drug dependence	7.5	9.2	5.9
Other disorders			
Antisocial personality	3.5	5.8	1.2
Non-affective psychosis (schizophrenia, delusional disorder, typical psychosis)	0.7	0.6	0.6

SOURCE: Archives of General Psychiatry, January 1994.

Table 6.18

Deaths and Fatality Rate of Patients Discharged from Short-Stay Hospitals, by Sex and Age, 1991

Age	Number in thousands			Rate per 100 discharges		
	Both sexes	Male	Female	Both sexes	Male	Female
All ages	918	471	447	3.0	3.8	2.4
Under 65 years	230	134	96	1.1	1.7	0.0
Under 15 years	20	10	10	0.8	0.7	1.0
15–44 years	56	36	20	0.5	1.1	0.2
45–64 years	154	89	65	2.5	2.9	2.1
65 years and over	688	336	351	6.4	7.1	5.8

SOURCE: CDC, National Hospital Discharge Survey, July 1993.

Table 6.19

Deaths and Fatality Rates of Patients Discharged from Short-Stay Hospitals, by Age and Selected Categories of First-Listed Diagnosis, 1991

Diagnosis	All ages	Under 65 years	65 years and over	All ages	Under 65 years	65 years and over
	Number in thousands			Rate per 100 discharges		
All deaths	918	230	688	3.0	1.1	6.4
Heart disease	207	39	168	5.6	2.9	7.1
Acute myocardial infarction	86	16	69	12.3	5.9	16.4
Congestive heart failure	60	6	54	7.9	3.9	8.9
Cardiac dysrhythmias	23	7	16	4.2	4.0	4.3
Chronic ischemic heart disease	14	NA	11	1.1	NA	1.5
Malignant neoplasms	151	52	99	9.5	7.3	11.2
Malignant neoplasms of trachea, bronchus, and lung	40	12	28	16.8	10.5	22.5
Pneumonia	82	10	72	7.6	2.0	12.3
Cerebrovascular disease	69	12	57	8.3	6.1	8.9
Injury and poisoning	41	15	27	1.5	0.8	3.0
Septicemia	40	8	32	16.7	9.7	20.2
Nephritis, nephrotic syndrome, and nephrosis	15	*	11	13.1	*	18.6

NA: Not available.
SOURCE: NCHS, National Hospital Discharge Survey, July 1993.

168

Table 6.20

AIDS Cases and Rates per 100,000 Population and Totals, by State and Age Group, 1992 and 1993

State	1992 Number of cases	1992 Rate per 100,000	1993 Number of cases	1993 Rate per 100,000	Cumulative totals Adults/ adolescents	Cumulative totals Children <13 years	Total
Alabama	440	10.6	733	17.5	2,397	44	2,441
Alaska	18	3.1	70	11.7	198	2	200
Arizona	385	10.0	1,238	31.5	3,179	14	3,193
Arkansas	278	11.6	404	16.7	1,308	22	1,330
California	8,774	28.4	18,689	59.9	65,387	366	65,753
Colorado	407	11.7	1,324	37.1	6,739	19	3,758
Connecticut	648	19.8	1,758	53.6	4,734	112	4,846
Delaware	138	20.0	375	53.6	904	10	914
District of Columbia	718	122.7	1,585	274.0	5,661	80	5,741
Florida	5,085	37.7	10,931	79.9	34,577	801	35,378
Georgia	1,374	20.3	2,789	40.3	9,816	90	9,906
Hawaii	138	11.9	359	30.6	1,313	11	1,324
Idaho	35	3.3	77	7.0	222	2	224
Illinois	1,888	16.3	2,959	25.3	11,003	142	11,145
Indiana	398	7.0	954	16.7	2,677	18	2,695
Iowa	112	4.0	202	7.2	619	7	626
Kansas	191	7.6	356	14.1	1,085	5	1,090
Kentucky	214	5.7	232	8.5	1,197	13	1,210
Louisiana	803	18.8	1,464	34.1	5,292	79	5,371
Maine	44	3.6	149	12.0	458	4	462
Maryland	1,201	24.4	2,528	50.9	7,651	172	7,823
Massachusetts	864	14.4	2,703	45.0	7,724	138	7,862
Michigan	735	7.8	1,840	19.4	5,150	66	5,216
Minnesota	217	4.9	659	14.6	1,910	13	1,923
Mississippi	262	10.0	461	17.4	1,552	21	1,573
Missouri	714	13.8	1,745	33.3	4,915	34	4,949
Montana	20	2.4	32	3.8	137	2	139
Nebraska	61	3.8	179	11.1	483	5	488
Nevada	248	18.6	638	45.9	1,758	16	1,774
New Hampshire	48	4.3	124	11.0	414	6	420
New Jersey	2,030	26.0	5,434	69.0	19,713	458	20,171
New Mexico	107	6.8	294	18.2	859	2	861
New York	8,382	46.3	17,467	96.0	67,051	1,403	68,454
North Carolina	583	8.5	1,368	19.7	4,152	76	4,228
North Dakota	9	1.4	11	1.7	39		39
Ohio	773	7.0	1,585	14.3	5,257	69	5,326
Oklahoma	271	8.5	725	22.4	1,890	15	1,905
Oregon	288	9.7	778	24.7	2,331	10	2,341
Pennsylvania	1,347	11.2	3,214	26.7	10,115	142	10,257
Rhode Island	107	10.7	348	34.8	917	11	928
South Carolina	397	11.0	1,476	40.5	3,247	38	3,285
South Dakota	8	1.1	29	4.1	64	3	67
Tennessee	408	8.1	1,203	23.6	3,037	30	3,069
Texas	2,938	16.6	7,543	41.8	24,687	217	24,904
Utah	135	7.5	264	14.2	852	20	872
Vermont	26	4.6	74	12.9	192	3	185
Virginia	781	12.2	1,625	25.0	5,079	82	5,161
Washington	262	11.0	1,564	29.8	4,986	18	5,004
West Virginia	56	3.1	106	5.8	402	5	407

Continued

Table 6.20 *(Continued)*

State	1992 Number of cases	1992 Rate per 100,000	1993 Number of cases	1993 Rate per 100,000	Cumulative totals Adults/ adolescents	Cumulative totals Children <13 years	Total
Wisconsin	230	4.6	731	14.5	1,782	21	1,803
Wyoming	5	1.1	46	9.8	103		103
Subtotal	45,904	18.0	103,533	40.1	344,217	4,937	349,154
Guam			2	1.4	13		13
Pacific Islands, U.S.					2		2
Puerto Rico	1,609	44.9	3,199	88.4	11,269	284	11,553
Virgin Islands, U.S.	11	10.7	57	55.1	161	4	162
Total*	47,572	18.4	106,949	40.8	355,936	5,228	361,164

*Total includes 277 persons whose state of residence is unknown.
SOURCE: CDC, HIV/AIDS Surveillance Report.

Table 6.21

Number and Rate of Patients with Human Immunodeficiency Virus (HIV) Discharged from Short-Stay Hospitals, by Selected Characteristics, 1989–1991

Characteristic	Numbers in thousands			Rate per 100,000 population		
	1989	1990	1991	1989	1990	1991
All HIV discharges	140	146	165	56.7	58.7	65.7
Sex						
Male	118	114	127	98.5	94.6	104.6
Female	22	32	37	17.3	24.9	29.1
Age						
Under 25 years	9	14	16	9.7	15.3	17.1
25–29 years	23	20	25	107.0	97.3	122.3
30–34 years	28	38	38	128.9	172.2	173.7
35–39 years	32	36	36	163.3	179.7	178.7
40–44 years	24	17	25	144.1	96.5	132.4
45 years and over	24	21	25	31.1	26.9	32.0
Race						
White	77	75	71	37.0	36.0	33.9
Black	45	49	62	147.8	157.3	199.8
All other	5		7	60.5		66.0
Not stated	13	19	25			
Region						
Northeast	54	66	61	106.8	129.9	120.7
Midwest	21	20	26	34.3	33.4	43.7
South	40	37	44	46.9	42.6	50.6
West	25	24	33	49.3	46.3	62.3

SOURCE: CDC, National Hospital Discharge Survey, July 1993.

HEALTH AND HEALTH CARE ACRONYMS

ACLI	American Council of Life Insurance
ADA	American Dental Association
AD&D	Accidental Death & Dismemberment Policy
AHA	American Hospital Association
AHCPR	Agency for Health Care Policy and Research
AIDS	Acquired Immune Deficiency Syndrome
AMA	American Medical Association
ANA	American Nurses Association
APA	American Pharmaceutical Association
ASO	Administrative Services Only
BCBS	Blue Cross/Blue Shield
BLS	Bureau of Labor Statistics
CDC	Centers for Disease Control
CHAMPUS	Civilian Health and Medical Program of the Uniformed Services
COB	Coordination of Benefits
COBRA	Consolidated Omnibus Budget Reconciliation Act
CON	Certificate of Need
CPI	Consumer Price Index
CPR	Cardiopulmonary Resuscitation
CPT	Current Procedural Terminology
DOL	Department of Labor
DRG	Diagnosis-Related Group
EBRI	Employee Benefit Research Institute
EOB	Explanation of Benefits
EPO	Exclusive Provider Organization
ERISA	Employee Retirement Income Security Act
FEHBP	Federal Employees Health Benefits Program
FFS	Fee for Service
GAO	General Accounting Office
GDP	Gross Domestic Product
GHAA	Group Health Association of America
GNP	Gross National Product
HCFA	Health Care Financing Administration
HCPCS	HCFA Common Procedural Coding System
HHS	U.S. Department of Health and Human Services
HIAA	Health Insurance Association of America

HIV	Human Immunosuppressant Virus
HMO	Health Maintenance Organization
ICD	International Classification of Diseases
IPA	Independent Practice Association, Individual Practice Association
LHD	Local Health Departments
LOS	Length of Stay
LTC	Long-Term Care
LTD	Long-Term Disability
MMPS	Medical Mortality Prediction System
MPP	Minimum Premium Plan
NAHDO	National Association of Health Data Organizations
NAIC	National Association of Insurance Commissioners
NCHS	National Center for Health Statistics
NCHSR	National Center for Health Services Research
NHC	National Health Council
NIH	National Institutes of Health
NIMH	National Institute of Mental Health
OBRA	Omnibus Budget Reconciliation Act
OECD	Organization for Economic Cooperation and Development
POS	Point of Service
PPO	Preferred Provider Organization
PPRC	Physician Payment Review Commission
PPS	Prospective Payment System
ProPAC	Prospective Payment Review Assessment Commission
RBRVS	Resource-Based Relative Value Scale
SHA	State Health Agency
SNF	Skilled Nursing Facility
SSA	Social Security Administration
STD	Sexually Transmitted Disease
STD	Short-Term Disability
TEFRA	Tax Equity and Fiscal Responsibility Act
TPA	Third-Party Administrator
TPP	Third-Party Payer
UCR	Usual, Customary, and Reasonable
UR	Utilization Review
WHO	World Health Organization

HISTORICAL INSURANCE FACTS

1798   U.S. Marine Hospital Service established by U.S. Congress. Compulsory deductions for hospital service were made from seamen's wages.

1847   The first insurer to issue sickness insurance was organized: The Massachusetts Health Insurance Company of Boston.

1849   New York State passed the first general insurance law.

1850s The first insurance supervisory boards were created in New Hampshire, Massachusetts, Rhode Island, and Vermont.

1850   Individual accident insurance became available in the United States with the chartering of the Franklin Health Assurance Company in Massachusetts.

1851   One of the earliest voluntary mutual protection associations, *La Société Française de Bienfaisance Mutuelle*, was organized in San Francisco. It is noteworthy for having established a hospital in 1852 to provide for its members.

1855   The first separate insurance department, independent of any established agency, was created in Massachusetts.

1859   The first full-time insurance commissioner was appointed in New York.

1863   The Travelers Insurance Company of Hartford, Connecticut, offered accident insurance for railway mishaps; then, all forms of accident protection. It was the first company to issue insurance resembling its present form.

1875   A number of mutual benefit associations, called "establishment funds," were formed for employees of a single employer. The benefits provided usually included small payments for death and disability.

1890s This period brought the promotion of many fraternal associations, assessment mutuals, and industrial insurers. Because many of these companies and associations were inadequately financed and poorly managed, many states passed legislation against them.

1890   Policies providing benefits for disability from specified diseases were first offered.

1900   Shortly after the turn of the century, disability benefits became available for substantially all diseases.

1910   Montgomery Ward & Co., Inc., replaced its "employee establishment fund" with an insured contract. This plan is generally regarded as the first group health insurance policy.

1912   The Standard Provisions Law drafted by the National Convention of Insurance Commissioners (now the NAIC) was enacted by most states. This model law sought to provide uniformity and fairness in the "operating conditions" of the health insurance contract.

1916   First noncancellable disability income contract was offered.

1917   Group accidental death and dismemberment insurance was first written.

1920s   Early in this decade, individual hospitals began offering hospital expense benefits on an individual prepaid basis.

1920s   First partial disability benefits for sickness and accident became available.

1929   The first health maintenance organization, the Ross-Loos Clinic, was established in Los Angeles, California.

1929   A group of school teachers arranged for Baylor Hospital in Dallas, Texas, to provide room, board, and specified ancillary services at a predetermined monthly cost. This plan is considered the forerunner of what later became known as the Blue Cross plans.

1929   With the depression, many companies entered a period of retrenchment in their disability income product line, particularly in the area of maintaining reasonable indemnity limits in order to avoid overinsurance.

1930s   The depression stimulated the expansion of insurance coverages through both public demand and hospitals' encouragement.

1932   First citywide Blue Cross plan was tried out with a group of hospitals in Sacramento, California.

1935   The Social Security Act (P.L. 74-241) provided for the first time grant-in-aid to states for such public health activities as maternal and child care, aid to children with disabilities, blind persons, the aged, and certain health-impaired persons.

1937   Health Service Plan Commission (Blue Cross Commission) was organized.

1938   Hospital insurance for dependents of covered persons was developed.

1938   Private insurers introduced group surgical expense benefit plans.

1939   The first Blue Shield plan (surgical-medical), called the California Physicians' Service, was developed.

1940s   During World War II, as a result of the freezing of wages, group health insurance became an important component of collective bargaining for employee benefits.

1942   Compulsory cash sickness benefits were begun by four states (Rhode Island, 1942; California, 1946; New Jersey, 1948; New York, 1949).

1943   Private insurers introduced group medical expense benefits (physicians' visits expense benefits).

1946   The Health Insurance Council, a federation of eight insurance associations was organized to give technical and practical assistance on health insurance to the providers of medical care.

1946   Blue Shield Medical Care Plans, Inc., (Blue Shield Commission) was organized.

1948   The National Labor Relations Board ruled, in a dispute between the United Steelworkers' Union and the Inland Steel Company, that the term "wages" be construed to include pension and insurance benefits. The U.S. Supreme Court upheld this ruling in a 1949 decision.

1949   Major medical expense benefits were introduced by Liberty Mutual Insurance Company to supplement basic medical care expenses.

1954   Congress introduced the disability "freeze" that stated that the quarters during which a worker is disabled are not counted in determining the number of quarters needed to be fully or currently insured under Old Age and Survivors Insurance (OASI).

1956   Disability insurance was added to the Social Security System, providing monthly cash benefits for insured persons who are totally disabled.

1957   Vision care expense benefits were introduced by private insurers, followed in 1959 by extended care facility expense benefits.

1959   Continental Casualty Company issued the first comprehensive group dental insurance plan written by an insurance company.

1960s   First disability contracts for business use appeared (overhead expense, key man).

1960s   Eligibility for disability benefits under Social Security was expanded.

1961 First state enrollment plan was made available by Connecticut to persons age 65 and older on a state basis and under special enabling legislation allowing the pooling of risks by a group of insurance companies (Associated Connecticut Health Insurance Companies).

1963 The Health Profession Educational Assistance Act (P.L. 88-129) aided training of physicians, dentists, and other public health personnel.

1964 Prescription drug expense benefits were introduced.

1964 The Nurse Training Act (P.L. 88-581) provided special federal effort for training professional nursing personnel.

1965 Social Security Amendments of 1965 (P.L. 89-97) established a Social Security hospital insurance program for the aged and a voluntary supplementary medical insurance program (Medicare) and grants to states for medical assistance programs (Medicaid).

1966 Program of governmental health insurance, Medicare, for people age 65 and older, became effective July 1.

1967 The Age Discrimination in Employment Act (ADEA) became effective.
● The act applied only to employees between the ages of 40 and 65, and the vast majority of employee benefit plans provided them with the same benefits as younger employees.
● The act contained a specific provision (Section 4(f)(2)) that stated that it was permissible for an employer to observe the terms of any bona fide employee benefit plan such as a retirement, pension or insurance plan that was not a subterfuge to evade the purposes of the act.

1971 The Insurance Medical Scientist Scholarship Fund was formed by several insurance companies, providing full scholarships for students planning careers in medical research and teaching.

1972 Social Security Amendments of 1972 (P.L. 92-603) extended health insurance benefits (Medicare) to the disabled and to end-stage renal disease patients, established Professional Standards Review Organization (PSRO) programs, expanded research and demonstrations of financing mechanisms and introduced automatic cost-of-living adjustments to disability benefits.

1972 Legislation created the Supplemental Security Income program, which federalized categorical public assistance for the aged, blind, and permanently and totally disabled.

1973 The Health Maintenance Organization Act (P.L. 93-222) assisted in the establishment and expansion of HMOs.

1974   The Employee Retirement Income Security Act (ERISA) of 1974 was signed into law. While generally thought of as a law that regulates private pension plans, the act also contains provisions relating to other employee benefit plans that have encouraged the growth of self-insurance.

1975   The National Health Planning and Resources Development Act of 1974 (P.L. 93-641) authorized major federal reorganization of health planning programs and set up the national designation of local Health Systems Areas and governing agencies.

1976   The Health Professions Educational Assistance Act of 1976 (P.L. 94-484) contained provisions requiring medical school students who receive federal scholarship aid to serve a specified period in rural and inner city areas and required that medical schools with teaching hospitals provide for a greater proportion of medical residencies in primary medicine.

1976   The Health Maintenance Organization (HMO) Amendments of 1976 (P.L. 94-460) relaxed requirements for HMOs to qualify for federal support.

1976   The National Consumer Health Information and Health Promotion Act of 1976 (P.L. 94-317) set forth national goals for health information and promotion and a systematic strategy for their achievement, stressing health education.

1977   The Medicare-Medicaid Anti-Fraud and Abuse Amendments (P.L. 95-142) amended the Social Security Act to require uniform reporting of financial data by providers, upgraded criminal penalties for fraud under Medicare-Medicaid programs, and amended certain PSRO provisions.

1978   The Health Maintenance Organization Amendments of 1978 (P.L. 95-559) set forth a three-year extension of the HMO assistance program.

1978   Title VII of the Civil Rights Act of 1964 was amended to prohibit sex discrimination on the basis of pregnancy for all employment-related purposes.

1978   ADEA of 1967 was amended to raise the mandatory retirement age from 65 to 70. The act prohibits discrimination concerning benefits to older workers. An employer may coordinate benefits with other programs—e.g., Medicare for employees over age 65—provided that total benefits are equivalent to those offered younger workers.

1981   The Omnibus Budget Reconciliation Act (OBRA) mandated significant cuts in federal expenditures for health programs, increased Medicare deductibles, removed the limit on the number of states that can apply for Medicare and Medicaid cost reimbursement waivers, and directed the Secretary of Health and Human Services to develop a model prospective reimbursement methodology for inpatient services under Medicare and Medicaid.

1982   The Tax Equity and Fiscal Responsibility Act (TEFRA) of 1982 provided Medicare recognition for any state hospital cost-control system that meets certain federal standards (including equitable treatment of all payers) and for employees aged 65–69 with employer-sponsored health insurance. It made Medicare the secondary payer, brought federal employees under Medicare, and made certain changes in the methods of hospital reimbursements under Medicare.

1983   In response to the requirement of TEFRA, a prospective payment system for hospital care of Medicare enrollees was enacted as a component of the Social Security Amendments of 1983.

1984   The Omnibus Deficit Reduction Act of 1984 (P.L. 98-369) extended Medicare as secondary payer of aged spouses of workers under age 65, froze Medicare reimbursement for physician fees, and reduced increases in hospital costs.

1984   The National Organ Transplant Act of 1984 (P.L. 98-507) established a task force on organ transplantation, authorized grants for organ procurement organizations, and established bone marrow registry demonstration and study.

1985   The Consolidated Omnibus Budget Reconciliation Act of 1985 (P.L. 99-272) required that employer group health plans offer continue coverage to workers and their dependents upon termination of employment, and to workers' spouses and dependents who would lose such coverage due to death of the worker, divorce, and Medicare eligibility; made private employer health plans primary to Medicare for active workers and their spouses who also have Medicare coverage; required that third-party payers reimburse for certain care rendered in government-run veterans and military hospitals; and established a task force to study long-term care insurance policies.

1986   The Tax Reform Act of 1986 (P.L. 99-514) removed the federal tax exemption for Blue Cross/Blue Shield organizations engaged in providing commercial-type insurance, established uniform nondiscrimination rules for group health insurance plans, and restored a partial, 25 percent tax deduction for health insurance premiums for self-employed individuals and their employees.

1986   The Omnibus Budget Reconciliation Act of 1986 (P.L. 99-509) made private employer health plans primary to Medicare for beneficiaries eligible by reason of permanent disability in cases where the disabled person is a covered dependent under a working spouse's health plan or if the disabled person returns to active employment, and revised the formula for determining Medicare's Part A deductible.

1986   ADEA for 1967 was further amended to prohibit mandating retirement at any age; employer-provided benefits for older workers must be equal to those for younger workers.

1988   The Health Maintenance Organization Amendments of 1988 (P.L. 100-51) provided greatly enhanced flexibility to federally qualified HMOs for structuring their organizations and for calculating premiums. Employers were also permitted to base their contributions to federally qualified HMOs on the projected claims experience of employees joining the HMO.

1988   The Medicare Catastrophic Coverage Act of 1988 (P.L. 100-360) represented the largest expansion in the Medicare program since its inception in 1965. Benefit changes included the elimination of all cost sharing for inpatient hospital care after the hospital deductible, a cap of $1,370 on out-of-pocket expenses for physicians' services, and minor changes in skilled nursing, home health, and respite care benefits. A phased-in outpatient drug benefit will be added to Medicare in 1991. Employers offering retiree health benefits to Medicare beneficiaries must rebate in cash or new benefits the actuarial value of the new catastrophic benefits for one year.

1988   Congress passed AIDS-related legislation appropriating funds for research, education, HIV testing, and home health demonstration projects.

1989   The Omnibus Budget Reconciliation Act of 1989, Title VI of H.R. 3299, contained a provision requiring states to extend Medicaid coverage to all pregnant women and children up to age 6 with family incomes up to 133 percent of federal poverty level ($13,380 for a family of three) by April 1, 1990. The act (P.L. 101-239) also included a three-part plan to reform the physician payment system under Medicare.

1989   The Medicare Catastrophic Coverage Act of 1988 (P.L. 100-360) was repealed.

1989   Agency for Health Care Policy and Research (AHCPR). OBRA 1989 established the AHCPR to develop guidelines, standards, performance measures, and review criteria for health care. AHCPR also promotes improvements in clinical practice, and in the organization, financing, and delivery of medically appropriate health care services.

1990   Older Workers Benefit Protection Act. This act amended existing law to provide that employers must provide older workers with benefits equal to those provided younger workers, unless the cost of providing equal benefits is greater for an older worker.

1990   Medigap Insurance Reform. As part of OBRA 1990, Congress passed a set of major reforms for states to follow in their regulation of Medicare supplement insurance. Two of the most significant provisions were (1) designating only ten Medicare supplement benefit packages as marketable and (2) requiring that all policies be guaranteed renewable.

1991   Soldiers and Sailors Relief Act Amendments. These provided that employer-provided health insurance must be reinstated for military reservists and their families upon a reservist's return from active duty, as if employment had not been interrupted.

1992   Americans with Disabilities Act (ADA). The ADA provides protections against discrimination to persons with disabilities; the protections are not intended to interfere with insurance underwriting practices, provided those practices are consistent with state law and not used intentionally to discriminate against the disabled.

1993   Family Medical and Leave Act. This act requires employers of more than five persons to allow eligible employees up to twelve weeks of leave during any twelve-month period for personal illness, birth, adoption, or illness of a spouse, child, or parent. Employers must provide the same health insurance coverage as during active employment.

GLOSSARY

A

Accident   An event that is unforeseen, unexpected, and unintended.

Accidental Bodily Injury   Physical injury sustained as the result of an accident.

Accumulation Period   Specified period during which the insured must incur eligible medical expenses that satisfy a required deductible.

Actuary   Accredited insurance mathematician who calculates premium rates, reserves, and dividends, and who prepares statistical studies and reports.

Administrative Services Only (ASO) Agreement   Contract between an insurer (or its subsidiary) and a group employer, eligible group, trustee, or other party, in which the insurer provides certain services. These services may include actuarial support, benefit plan design, claims processing, data recovery and analysis, employee benefits communication, financial advice, medical care conversions, preparation of data for reports to governmental units, and stop-loss coverage.

Adverse Selection   Tendency of those who are poorer-than-average health risks to apply for or maintain insurance coverage.

Age Limits   Stipulated minimum and maximum ages below and above which an insurance company will not accept applications or may not renew policies.

Agent   Insurance company representative licensed by the state who solicits, negotiates, or effects contracts of insurance and who provides services to the policyholder for the insurer.

Aggregate Indemnity   The maximum dollar amount that may be collected for any disability or period of disability under an insurance policy.

AIDS   Acronym for acquired immune deficiency syndrome—a disease caused by a virus that damages the body's immune system, thereby destroying its ability to fight off illness.

Allocated Benefits   Benefits for which the maximum amount payable for specific services is itemized in a group contract.

Alternate Delivery System   Provision of health services in settings that are more cost-effective than an inpatient, acute-care hospital, such as skilled and intermediary nursing facilities, hospice programs, and in-home services.

Ambulatory Care   Medical services provided on an outpatient (non-hospitalized) basis. Services may include diagnosis, treatment, surgery, and rehabilitation.

Amendment   Formal document changing the provisions of an insurance contract and signed jointly by authorized representatives of the insurer and the policyholder.

Application   Statement of relevant facts signed by an individual who is seeking insurance or by a prospective group policyholder; the application is the basis for the insurer's decision to issue a policy. The application usually is incorporated into the policy.

Approval   (1) When used in connection with the filing of policy and certificate forms and rates with a state insurance department, approval signifies the legal acceptance of the forms by the state's representative; (2) when used in connection with underwriting, approval signifies the insurer's acceptance of the risk as set forth in the application (as originally made or as modified by the insurer); (3) approval also signifies the acceptance of an offer from an applicant or policyholder in the form of a contract for new insurance, reinstatement of a terminated policy, request for a policy loan, or other event, by an officer of the company.

Assign   The transfer of one's interest (policy benefits) to another (a third party). The action is called an assignment.

Association Group   A group formed from members of a trade or professional association for group insurance under one master health insurance contract.

B

Beneficiary   Person or persons designated by a policyholder to receive insurance policy proceeds.

Benefit   Amount payable by the insurance company to a claimant, assignee, or beneficiary when the insured suffers a loss covered by the policy.

Binding Receipt   A receipt given for a premium payment accompanying the application for insurance. If the policy is approved, this binds the company to make the policy effective from the date of receipt.

Blanket Contract Contract of health insurance that covers a class of persons not individually identified. It is used for groups such as athletic teams and for employee travel policies.

Blanket Medical Expense A provision that entitles the insured person to collect up to a maximum established in the policy for all hospital and medical expenses incurred, without any limitations on individual types of medical expenses.

Blue Cross Nonprofit membership corporation providing protection against the cost of hospital care in a limited geographic area.

Blue Shield Nonprofit membership corporation providing protection against the cost of surgery and other items of medical care in a limited geographic area.

Broker Person licensed by the state who places business with several insurers; the broker, although paid a commission by the insurer, represents the insurance buyer rather than the insurance company.

Business Insurance A policy that primarily provides coverage to a business, rather than an individual. Such insurance is often purchased to indemnify a business for the loss of services in case a key employee (such as a partner) becomes disabled.

C

Capitation Method of payment for health services in which a physician or hospital is paid a fixed amount for each person served regardless of the actual number or nature of services provided.

Certificate of Insurance Document delivered to an individual that summarizes the benefits and principal provisions of a group insurance contract. May be distributed in booklet form.

Claim Demand to the insurer by or on behalf of an insured person for the payment of benefits under a policy.

Co-insurance Arrangement by which the insurer and the insured share, in a specific ratio, payment for losses covered by the policy, after the deductible is met.

Comprehensive Medical Expense Insurance Form of health insurance that provides, in one policy, protection for both basic hospital expense and major medical expense coverage.

Consideration Clause   Policy stipulation that states the basis on which an insurer issues an insurance contract—usually the statements in the applications and the payment of premium.

Contributory Plan   Group insurance plan under which the insured shares in the cost of the plan with the policyholder.

Conventional Health Plan   Plan that provides all benefits under insurance policies and issues certificates containing the insurance company's guarantees to covered persons.

Conversion Privilege   Right given to an insured person under a group insurance contract to change coverage, without evidence of medical insurability, to an individual policy upon termination of the group coverage. The conditions under which conversion can be made are defined in the master policy.

Coordination of Benefits (COB)   Method of integrating benefits payable under more than one health insurance plan so that the insured's benefits from all sources do not exceed 100 percent of allowable medical expenses or eliminate appropriate patient incentives to contain costs.

Cost Containment   Control or reduction of inefficiencies in the consumption, allocation, or production of health care services that contribute to higher than necessary costs. (Inefficiencies in consumption can occur when health services are inappropriately utilized; inefficiencies in allocation exist when health services could be delivered in less costly settings without loss of quality; and, inefficiencies in production exist when the costs of producing health services could be reduced by using a different combination of resources.)

Covered Expenses   Those specific health care charges that an insurer will consider for payment under the terms of a health insurance policy.

D

Deductible   Amount of covered expenses that must be incurred and paid by the insured before benefits become payable by the insurer.

Diagnosis-Related Groups (DRGs)   System of determining specific reimbursement fees based on the medical diagnosis of a patient.

Disability   Physical or mental condition that makes an insured person incapable of performing one or more occupational duties either temporarily (short-term), long-term, or totally (total disability).

Disability Income Insurance   Form of health insurance that provides periodic payments when an insured is unable to work as a result of illness or injury.

Dismemberment   Accidental loss of limb or sight.

Disposable Personal Income   Personal income less personal tax and nontax payments; the income available to people for spending and saving.

Double Indemnity   Payment of twice the policy's normal benefit in case of loss resulting from specified causes or under specified conditions.

Duplication of Coverage   Coverage of an insured under two or more policies for the same potential loss.

E

Earned Premium   Portion of a premium for which protection of the policy has already been provided by the insurer.

Effective Date   Date on which insurance coverage under policy begins.

Eligibility Date   Date on which a member of an insured group may apply for insurance.

Eligibility Period   Time following the eligibility date (usually 31 days) during which a member of an insured group may apply for insurance without evidence of insurability.

Eligible Employees   Employees of a group policyholder who have met the eligibility requirements for insurance set forth in the group policy.

Elimination Period   Specified number of days at the beginning of each period of disability during which no disability income benefits are paid.

Enrollment Card   Document signed by an eligible person as notice of desire to participate in an employer group insurance plan. For a contributory plan, this card also authorizes an employer to deduct contributions from an employee's pay. If group life and accidental death and dismemberment coverage are involved, the card usually includes the beneficiary's name and relationship.

Evidence of Insurability   Any statement or proof of a person's physical condition and/or other factual information affecting acceptability for insurance. Required in group insurance only in specific situations: when an eligible person fails to enroll during the open enrollment period; for reinstatement after having previously withdrawn from the plan when receiving an overall maximum benefit; or when applying for excess amounts of group life or disability insurance.

Exclusions (Exceptions)   Specified conditions or circumstances, listed in the policy, for which the policy will not provide benefits.

Exclusive Provider Organizations (EPO)   Form of managed care in which participants are reimbursed for care received only from affiliated providers.

Experience   Relationship, usually expressed as a percent or ratio, of claims to premium for a stated period.

Experience Rating   Process of determining the premium rate for a group risk based wholly or partially on that risk's experience.

Experience Refund   Amount of premium returned by an insurer to a group policyholder when the financial experience of a particular group (or the experience refund class to which the group belongs) has been more favorable than the premiums collected from the group anticipated.

F

Family Expense Policy   A policy that insures both the policyholder and his or her immediate dependents (usually spouse and children).

Flat Schedule   A type of schedule in group insurance under which everyone is insured for the same benefits regardless of salary, position, or other circumstances.

Franchise Insurance   Individual insurance contracts issued to members of a specific group (such as employees of a common employer or members of an association) under a group-like arrangement in which the employer or the association collects and remits premiums.

Fraternal Insurance   Cooperative insurance provided by social organizations for their members. The social group may pay premiums into a fund and withdraw monies to pay claims upon the death of one of its members.

G

Geographic Divisions of the United States

Northeast
New England: Connecticut, Maine, Massachusetts, New Hampshire, Rhode Island, Vermont
Middle Atlantic: New Jersey, New York, Pennsylvania
Midwest
East North Central: Illinois, Indiana, Michigan, Ohio, Wisconsin
West North Central: Iowa, Kansas, Minnesota, Missouri, Nebraska, North Dakota, South Dakota

South

South Atlantic: Delaware, District of Columbia, Florida, Georgia, Maryland, North Carolina, South Carolina, Virginia, West Virginia

East South Central: Alabama, Kentucky, Mississippi, Tennessee

West South Central: Arkansas, Louisiana, Oklahoma, Texas

West

Mountain: Arizona, Colorado, Idaho, Montana, Nevada, New Mexico, Utah, Wyoming

Pacific: Alaska, California, Hawaii, Oregon, Washington

Grace Period   Specified time (usually 31 days) following the premium due date during which insurance remains in force and a policyholder may pay the premium without penalty.

Group Contract (Policy)   Contract of life or health insurance made with an employer or other entity, called the policyholder, that covers a group of persons as a single unit.

Guaranteed Renewable Contract   Contract under which an insured has the right, commonly up to a certain age, to continue the policy in force by the timely payment of premiums. However, the insurer reserves the right to change premium rates by policy class.

H

Health Insurance   Coverage that provides for the payments of benefits as a result of sickness or injury. Includes insurance for losses from accident, medical expense, disability, or accidental death and dismemberment.

Health Maintenance Organization (HMO)   Organization that provides for a wide range of comprehensive health care services for a specified group at a fixed periodic prepayment.

Hospice   Care provided to terminally ill patients and their families that emphasizes emotional needs and coping with pain and death rather than cure.

Hospital Indemnity Insurance   Form of health insurance that provides a stipulated daily, weekly, or monthly payment to an insured during hospital confinement, without regard to the actual expense of the confinement.

Hospital Medical Insurance   Coverage that provides benefits for the cost of any or all of the numerous health care services normally covered under various health care plans.

I

Incontestable Clause A provision in a policy that the insurer may not contest the validity of an insurance contract after it has been in force for two (sometimes three) years.

Incurred Claims Incurred claims equal the claims paid during the policy year plus the claim reserves as of the end of the policy year, minus the corresponding reserves as of the beginning of the policy year. The difference between the year end and beginning of the year claim reserves is called the increase in reserves and may be added directly to the paid claims to produce the incurred claims.

Indemnity Benefits paid in a predetermined amount in the event of a covered loss.

Individual Insurance Policies that provide protection to the policyholder and/or his or her family. Sometimes called Personal Insurance as distinct from Group and Blanket insurance.

Injury Independent of All Other Means An injury resulting from an accident, provided that the accident was not caused by an illness.

Insurable Risk The conditions that make a risk insurable are (a) the peril insured against must produce a definite loss not under the control of the insured, (b) there must be a large number of homogeneous exposures subject to the same perils, (c) the loss must be calculable and the cost of insuring it must be economically feasible, (d) the peril must be unlikely to affect all insureds simultaneously, and (e) the loss produced by a risk must be definite and have a potential to be financially serious.

Insurance Plan of risk management that, for a price, offers the insured an opportunity to share the costs of possible economic loss through an entity called an insurer.

Insurance Company Any corporation primarily engaged in the business of furnishing insurance protection to the public.

Insuring Clause Stipulation in an insurance policy that states the type of loss the policy covers and the parties to the insurance contract.

Integration The combining of two or more benefit plans to prevent duplication of benefit payments.

K

Key-Person Insurance   Insurance designed to protect a business firm against the loss of business income resulting from the disability or death of an employee in a significant position.

L

Lapse   Termination of coverage provided in an insurance contract because of the nonpayment of a premium within the time period.

Legal Reserve   The minimum reserve that a company must keep to meet future claims and obligations as they are calculated under the state insurance code.

Level Premium   Rating structure in which the premium level remains the same throughout the life of the policy.

Lifetime Disability Benefit   Disability income provision payable for an insured's lifetime as long as the insured is totally disabled.

Limited Policy   Policy that covers only specified accidents or sicknesses.

Long-Term Care   Continuum of maintenance, custodial, and health services for the chronically ill or disabled. Such services may be provided on an inpatient (rehabilitation facility, nursing home, mental hospital) or outpatient basis, or at home.

Long-Term Disability Income Insurance (LTD)   Benefits plan that helps replace earned income lost through inability to work because of disability caused by an accident or illness.

M

Major Medical Expense Insurance   Form of health insurance that provides benefits for most types of medical expense up to a high maximum benefit. Such contracts may contain internal limits and usually are subject to deductibles and co-insurance.

Managed Care   Systems that integrate the financing and delivery of appropriate health care services to covered individuals by means of arrangements with selected providers to furnish a comprehensive set of health-care services to members; explicit criteria for the selection of health-care providers; formal programs for ongoing quality assurance and utilization review; and significant financial incentives for members to use providers and procedures associated with the plan.

Manual Premium Rate Premium charge for a group's coverage developed from the insurer's standard rate tables; it is the cost usually quoted in an insurer's rate or underwriting manual.

Medicaid Government insurance program for persons of all ages whose income and resources are insufficient to pay for health care; Medicaid is state-administered and financed by both the states and the federal government (through the Social Security Administration).

Medicare Government insurance program that provides hospital benefits (Medicare Part A) and medical benefits (Medicare Part B) to persons age 65 and older, and to some other eligibles. (Medicare covers short-term acute medical conditions rather than long-term, chronic conditions that require custodial care.) Medicare is administered by the Social Security Administration.

MedSup (also Medigap) Private insurance products that can be purchased to supplement Medicare.

Minimum Group The fewest number of employees permitted under a state law to constitute a group for insurance purposes; the purpose of minimum group is to maintain a distinction between individual and group insurance.

Minimum Premium Plan Combination approach to funding an insurance plan aimed primarily at premium tax savings. The employer self-funds a fixed percentage (e.g., 90 percent) of the estimated monthly claims, and the insurer covers the remainder.

Miscellaneous Expense Expenses connected with hospital insurance; hospital charges other than room and board, such as x-rays, drugs, laboratory fees, and other ancillary charges.

Morbidity Frequency and severity of sicknesses and accidents in a well-defined class or classes of persons.

Multiple Employer Trust (MET) A legal trust established by a plan sponsor that brings together a number of small, unrelated employers for the purpose of providing group medical care coverage on an insured or self-funded basis.

N

National Association of Insurance Commissioners (NAIC) National organization of state officials charged with regulating insurance. It has no official power but wields tremendous influence. The association was formed to provide national uniformity in insurance regulations.

Noncancellable Policy Contract that the insured can maintain in force by the timely payment of the set premium until at least age 50 or, in the case of a policy issued after age 44, for at least five years from its date of issue. The insurer may not unilaterally change any contract provision of the in-force policy, including premium rates.

Noncontributory Plan   Group insurance plan under which the employer does not require employees to share in its cost.

Nondisabling Injury   Any injury that may require medical care but does not result in the loss of working time or income.

Nonoccupational Policy   Policy that provides coverage only for non-job-related accidents or sicknesses not covered under any workers' compensation law.

Nonparticipating Policy   Policy that does not provide for the payment of a dividend.

Nonprofit Insurers   Corporations organized under special state laws to provide medical benefits on a not-for-profit basis (for example, Blue Cross/Blue Shield and Dental Service Corporations).

O

Occupational Hazards   Dangers inherent in the insured's occupation, which expose him or her to greater than normal physical danger by its very nature.

Optional Renewable Policy   Health insurance contract that the insurer has the right to terminate at any policy anniversary, or, in some cases, at any premium date.

Overhead Expense Insurance   Form of health insurance for business owners designed to help offset continuing business expenses during an insured's total disability.

P

Partial Disability   Inability to perform one or more functions of one's regular job.

Participating Policy   Policy under which the policyholder is eligible to receive dividends.

Physician's Expense Insurance   Coverage that provides benefits toward the cost of such services as doctor's fees—for surgical care in the hospital, at home, or in a physician's office, and x-rays or laboratory tests performed outside of a hospital. (Also called Regular Medical Expense Insurance.)

Point-of-Service Plan (POS)   Health care delivery method offered as an option of an employer's indemnity program. Under such a program, employees coordinate their health care needs through a primary care physician.

Policy   Legal document or contract issued by the insurer to the insured that contains all the conditions and terms of insurance.

Policy Term   That period for which an insurance policy provides coverage.

Precertification   Utilization management program that requires the individual or the provider to notify the insurer prior to a hospitalization or surgical procedure. The notification allows the insurer to authorize payment, as well as to recommend alternate courses of action.

Preexisting Condition   Any physical and/or mental condition or conditions of an insured that exist prior to the effective date of coverage.

Preferred Provider Organization (PPO)   Mode of health care delivery through which a sponsoring group negotiates price discounts with providers in exchange for more patients. The sponsor may be an insurer, employer, or third-party administrator.

Premium   Periodic payment required to keep a policy in force.

Prepaid Group Practice Plan   A plan under which specified health services are rendered by participating physicians to an enrolled group of persons, with a fixed periodic payment made in advance by (or on behalf of) each person or family. If a health insurance carrier is involved, a contract to pay in advance for the full range of health services to which the insured is entitled under the terms of the health insurance contract. An HMO is an example of a prepaid group practice plan.

Principal Sum   Amount payable in a lump sum in the event of accidental death and, in some cases, accidental dismemberment.

Professional Standards Review Organization (PSRO)   Organization responsible for determining whether care and services provided were medically necessary and meet professional standards regarding eligibility for reimbursement under the Medicare and Medicaid programs.

Proration   Modification of policy benefits because of a change in the insured's occupation or the existence of other insurance.

Prospective Payment   Payment of a lump-sum benefit to an institution for care of an insured based on a predetermined amount correlated with diagnoses.

Q

Qualified Impairment Insurance A form of substandard or special class insurance, which restricts benefits for the insured person's particular condition.

R

Reasonable and Customary Charge (R&C) Amounts charged by health care providers that are consistent with charges from similar providers for identical or similar services in a given locale.

Recurring Claim Provision A provision in some health insurance policies that specifies a length of time during which the recurrence of a condition is considered to be a continuation of a previous period of disability or hospital confinement.

Rehabilitation Process and goal of restoring disabled insureds to maximum physical, mental, and vocational independence and productivity (commensurate with their limitations). Rehabilitation is achieved by identifying and developing residual capabilities, job modification, or retraining. A "rehabiliation provision" appears in some long-term disability policies; this provides for continuation of benefits or other financial assistance during the rehabilitation period.

Reinstatement Resumption of coverage under a policy that had lapsed.

Reinsurance Acceptance by one insurer (the reinsurer) of all or part of the risk of loss underwritten by another insurer (the ceding insurer).

Renewal Continuance of coverage under a policy beyond its original term by the insurer's acceptance of the premium for a new policy term.

Residual Disability Benefits A provision in an insurance policy that provides benefits in proportion to a reduction of earnings as a result of disability, as opposed to the inability to work fulltime.

Rider A document that modifies or amends an insurance contract.

Risk The probable amount of loss foreseen by an insurer in issuing a contract. The term sometimes also applies to the person insured or to the hazard insured against.

S

Self-Administration Maintenance of all records and assumption of responsibility, by a group policyholder, for insureds covered under its insurance plan, including preparing the premium statement for each payment date and submitting it with a check to the insurer. The insurance company, in most instances, has the contractual prerogative to audit the policyholder's records.

Self-Insurance   A program for providing group insurance with benefits financed entirely through the internal means of the policyholder, in place of purchasing coverage from commercial carriers.

Senior Citizen Policies   Contracts insuring persons 65 years of age or older; in most cases, these policies supplement the coverage afforded by the government under the Medicare program.

Short-Term Disability Income Insurance   Form of health insurance that provides benefits only for loss resulting from illness or disease and excludes loss resulting from accident or injury.

Social Security Freeze   A long-term disability policy provision that establishes that the offset from benefits paid by Social Security will not be changed regardless of subsequent changes in the Social Security law.

Special Risk Insurance   Coverage for risks or hazards of a special or unusual nature.

Specified Disease Insurance   Insurance providing an unallocated benefit, subject to a maximum amount, for expenses incurred in connection with the treatment of specified diseases, such as cancer, poliomyelitis, encephalitis, and spinal meningitis. These policies are designed to supplement major medical policies.

Standard Insurance   Insurance written on the basis of regular morbidity underwriting assumptions used by an insurance company and issued at normal rates.

Standard Provisions   Policy provisions setting forth certain rights and obligations of insureds and insurers under health insurance policies. Originally introduced in 1912, these provisions were replaced by the Uniform Policy Provisions Law (UPPL).

Standard Risk   Person who, according to an insurer's underwriting standards, is entitled to purchase insurance without paying an extra premium or special restrictions.

State (Compulsory) Disability Plan   Plan of short-term income replacement insurance required by some states to cover eligible persons employed within that state.

State Insurance Department   An administrative agency that implements state insurance laws and supervises (within the scope of these laws) the activities of insurers operating within the state.

Stop-Loss Insurance Protection purchased by self-funded buyers against the risk of large losses or severe adverse claim experience.

Substandard Insurance Insurance issued with an extra premium or special restriction to persons who do not qualify for insurance at standard rates.

Substandard Risk Persons who cannot meet the normal health requirements of a standard health insurance policy.

Surgical Expense Insurance Health insurance policies that provide benefits toward the physician's or surgeon's operating fees. Benefits may consist of scheduled amounts for each surgical procedure.

Surgical Schedule List of maximum amounts payable by an insurance policy for various types of surgery, with the amount based on the severity of the operation.

T

Third-Party Administration (Administrator) (TPA) Method by which an outside person or firm, not a party to a contract, maintains all records regarding the persons covered under the insurance plan. Entity also may pay claims using the draft book system.

Time Limit A specified number of days in which a notice of claim or proof of a loss must be filed.

Total Disability Generally, a disability that prevents insureds from performing all occupational duties. The exact definition varies among policies.

Travel Accident Policies Limited contracts covering accidents that occur only while an insured person is traveling on business for an employer, away from the usual place of business, and on named conveyances.

U

Unallocated Benefits Benefits for which reimbursement is provided up to a maximum amount but without specific limits on the extent of benefit for each service rendered.

Underwriter The term generally applies to (a) a company that receives the premiums and accepts responsibility for the fulfillment of the policy contract, (b) the company employee who decides whether or not the company should assume a particular risk, or (c) the agent who sells the policy.

Underwriting Process by which an insurer determines whether or not and on what basis it will accept an application for insurance.

Unearned Premium   That portion of a premium already received by the insurer for which the protection of the policy has not yet been provided.

Uninsurables   High-risk persons who do not have health care coverage through private insurance and who fall outside the parameters of risks covered as a result of standard health underwriting practices.

W

Waiting Period   The amount of time a person must wait from the date of entry into an eligible class (or from application for coverage) to the date the insurance becomes effective. While similar to elimination periods, waiting periods are often paid retroactively.

Waiver (Exclusion Endorsement)   An agreement, attached to the policy and accepted by the insured, to eliminate a specified preexisting physical condition or specified hazard from coverage under the policy.

Waiver of Premium   A policy provision that, under certain conditions, a person's insurance will be kept in full force by the insurer without further payment of premiums. It is used most often in the event of permanent and total disability.

Workers' Compensation   Liability insurance requiring certain employers to pay benefits and furnish medical care to employees for on-the-job injuries, and to pay benefits to dependents of employees killed by occupational accidents.

Written Premiums   The entire amount in premiums due in a year for all policies issued by an insurance company.

INDEX